WEST EUROPEAN POLITICS

Volume 21 Number 2

April 1998

D1609947

A FRANK CASS JOURNAL

WEST EUROPEAN POLITICS

Editors: **Gordon Smith,** London School of Economics and Political Science
Vincent Wright, Nuffield College, Oxford
Reviews Editor: **Mark Donovan,** University of Wales, Cardiff

Editorial Board

Malcolm Anderson, University of Edinburgh
Stefano Bartolini, European University Institute
Suzanne Berger, MIT, Cambridge, MA
Klaus von Beyme, University of Heidelberg
Sabino Cassese, University of Rome
Hans Daalder, The Hague
Lord Dahrendorf, House of Lords
Victor Perez-Diaz, Complutense University, Madrid
Jack Hayward, St Antony's College, Oxford
Arnold J. Heidenheimer, Washington University
Jan-Erik Lane, University of Geneva
Yves Mény, EUI, Florence
Peter Mair, University of Leiden
Peter Merkl, University of California, Santa Barbara
Geoffrey Pridham, Centre for Mediterranean Studies, University of Bristol
F. F. Ridley, University of Liverpool
Kurt Sontheimer, University of Munich
Sidney Tarrow, Cornell University

Articles appearing in this journal are abstracted and indexed in *Social Science Index, Social Science Abstracts, Political Science Abstracts, International Political Science Abstracts, ABC Pol Sci, Sociological Abstracts* and *British Humanities Index* among others.

Manuscripts, editorial communications, books for review and advertisement enquiries should be directed to The Administrative Editor, *West European Politics*, at the address given below.

Annual subscription: (Vol.21 1998)	Institutions	£170.00/$245.00 postage included
	Individuals	£40.00/$65.00 postage included
	Single issue and back issue prices available from the publisher.	

West European Politics is a refereed journal. Authors should consult the Notes for Contributors at the back of the journal before submitting their final draft. The editors cannot accept responsibility for any damage to or loss of manuscripts. Statements of fact or opinion appearing in *West European Politics* are solely those of the authors and do not imply endorsement by the editors or publisher.

Published in January, April, July and October

© Frank Cass & Co. Ltd., 1998

900 Eastern Avenue, Ilford, Essex IG2 7HH, UK
Tel: + 44 (0)181 599 8866; Fax: +44 (0)181 599 0984; E-mail: info@frankcass.com
Website: http://www.frankcass.com

All rights reserved. No part of this publication may be reproduced, stored in a retrieval system, or transmitted in any form, or by any means, electronic, mechanical, photocopying, recording, or otherwise, without the prior permission of Frank Cass & Co. Limited.

Printed in Great Britain by Antony Rowe Ltd., Chippenham, Wilts.

Contents

For details of past and future contents of this and our other journals please visit our website at *http://www.frankcass.com/jnls*

Book Reviews

About the Contributors

Ingrid van Biezen is a doctoral candidate in the Department of Political Science, University of Leiden. Her research involves a comparative analysis of party organisations in Southern and Eastern Europe.

Dieter Fuchs is a Senior Fellow at the Berlin Science Centre (WZB) and a member of the Faculty of Political Science at the Free University of Berlin. His main research interests lie in the analysis of democratic systems and political support. On this topic he has recently edited, together with Hans-Dieter Klingemann, *Citizens and the State* (1995).

Oddbjørn Knutsen is a Professor of Political Science at the University of Oslo. His main research interests concern values and value change, cleavages and political parties in Western Europe. He has published widely in academic journals, including *Acta Sociologica*, *Comparative Political Studies* and the *European Journal of Political Research.*

Christoph Kunkel is a PhD candidate in the Department of Government at Cornell University. His dissertation research deals with the privatisation and restructuring of airlines and telecommunications in OECD countries.

Christos Paraskevopoulos is a PhD candidate at the London School of Economics. His research interests focus on the role of social capital and institutional learning in European regional policy. His publications include: *Social Capital and Learning Institutional Networks: Making Sense of Subsidiarity in European Regional Policy* (1997), in *TOPOS* Review of Urban and Regional Studies (in Greek).

Jonas Pontusson is an Associate Professor of Government and Director of the Institute for European Studies at Cornell University. His publications include *The Limits of Social Democracy: Investment Politics in Sweden* (1992) and, as co-editor, *Bargaining for Change: Union Politics and Intra-Class Conflict in Western Europe and North America* (1992) and *Unions, Employers and Central Banks: Wage Bargaining and Macro-economic Regimes in an Integrating Europe* (forthcoming). His current research focuses on the interface of social-policy regimes and labour markets.

Robert Rohrschneider is an Associate Professor of Political Science at Indiana University, Bloomington, USA. His research interests focus on public opinion, political parties and the electoral process. He is in the process of completing a monograph on the effect of regime experience on eastern and western Germans' democratic visions. Results from this project have appeared in journals such as the *American Political Science Review* and the *Journal of Politics*.

Henning Tewes is a PhD student at the Institute for German Studies at the University of Birmingham. He has published 'The Emergence of a Civilian Power: Germany and Central Europe', in *German Politics* 6/2 (Aug. 1997) and 'Das Zivilmachtkonzept in der Theorie der Internationalen Beziehungen', in *Zeitschrift für Internationale Beziehungen* 4/2 (1997), forthcoming.

José I. Torreblanca is a Fellow at the Juan March Institute in Madrid. Currently he is the European Union Scholar-in-Residence at the George Washington University in Washington DC where he is teaching a course on EU's eastern enlargement. He has published (with Philippe Schmitter) on the subject of EU institutional reform (Robert Schuman Centre, Policy Paper 97/1). His PhD on EU relations with eastern Europe will be published this year by Ashgate.

Corporatism versus Social Democracy: Divergent Fortunes of the Austrian and Swedish Labour Movements

CHRISTOPH KUNKEL and JONAS PONTUSSON

In Austria, the social democrats suffered major electoral losses in the 1980s and the first half of the 1990s, and these losses translated primarily into gains for right-wing populism. In Sweden, by contrast, the social democrats have pretty much held their own in recent elections (except for 1991) and protest voting has assumed leftist as well as rightist forms. Commonly regarded as prototypical instances of 'corporatism', the two countries have also diverged with respect to union density, which fell precipitously in Austria while it rose in Sweden from 1970 to 1990. This dual divergence suggests that strong unions remain an important electoral asset for social-democratic parties. The divergent trajectories of trade-union membership are in turn related to differences between Austrian and Swedish corporatism.

This article addresses two related but distinct questions. The first question concerns the electoral fortunes of social-democratic parties and the ideological hegemony of social democracy in an era of internationalisation and liberalisation of advanced capitalist political economies. Comparing Austria and Sweden, we ask, why is it that the SPÖ (*Sozialdemokratische Partei Österreichs*) has experienced a succession of severe electoral setbacks while its Swedish sister party, the SAP (*Socialdemokratiska arbetarpartiet*), has pretty much held its own over the last 15–20 years? And why is it that in Austria social-democratic electoral losses have been primarily translated into gains for a populist protest party of the radical right, while in Sweden social-democratic losses primarily have been translated into gains for other left parties? The second question concerns the fortunes of trade unions, traditional supporters and allies of social-democratic parties: why is it that union density fell precipitously in Austria in the 1970s and 1980s, while it rose in Sweden?

The broad brush-stroke pictures of Austria and Sweden provided by the corporatism literature suggest that these political economies are very much

West European Politics, Vol.21, No.2 (April 1998), pp.1–31
PUBLISHED BY FRANK CASS, LONDON

alike. At first sight, then, comparing these two countries would seem to represent an almost ideal 'most similar systems' design, making it possible to identify the causes of decline in the social-democratic parties and trade unions with a great deal of precision.[1] However, a more detailed look at these cases yields many striking contrasts, which can plausibly be invoked as explanations of the divergent outcomes that concern us here. The goals of this article are essentially heuristic to identify puzzles and to suggest arguments or hypotheses. More rigorous causal analysis would require a more closely-matched pair of country cases or an altogether different research design.

It is not the case that Austria and Sweden have 'corporatism' in common while they differ in other respects, for some of the most interesting differences between Austria and Sweden concern the extent and character of corporatist arrangements. Sweden's claim to rank at the top of the corporatist league hinges on the highly centralised system of economy-wide wage bargaining that came into being in the 1950s. For our present purposes, the voluntary basis of Swedish labour market organisations and wage bargaining or, conversely, the limited extent of direct state intervention deserve to be emphasised. Also, the role of tripartite commissions and administrative boards in the realm of public policy has sometimes been exaggerated. The well-known story of the introduction of the ATP pension system, passed by a one-vote parliamentary majority in 1959, illustrates the continued role of class mobilisation and partisan conflict during the heyday of post-war consensus in Sweden.[2]

Austria was always more corporatist than Sweden or, more to the point, the post-war Austrian variety of corporatism approximated to the original meaning of the term 'corporatism' more closely than its Swedish counterpart. By comparison with Sweden, four features of Austrian corporatism stand out.[3] First, three of its four organisational pillars, the chambers of Labour, Business, and Agriculture, are based on mandatory membership, the only voluntary pillar being the union movement. Second, the Austrian case is distinguished by a more complete interpenetration of parties and interest groups as illustrated, on the one hand, by the existence of party factions within all the major interest groups and, on the other hand, by the large number of interest-group officials who serve as MPs. Third, the Austrian *proporz* system, whereby the main political families (*Lagers*) are represented in public administration and the management of nationalised industry, has no equivalent in the Swedish case. And, finally, the Austrian tradition of coalition government deserves to be mentioned here. At the federal level, the SPÖ and its main rival, the Christian-democratic ÖVP (*Österreichische Volkspartei*), have governed jointly for 31 of the 52 years since the end of the Second World War and, even when a single party has held all cabinet posts, the federal structure of the Austrian state has entailed significant power-sharing.

Austria and Sweden can also be contrasted in terms of the trajectories of corporatism since the late 1970s. Whether or not a general decline of corporatism has occurred is a matter of debate among students of advanced capitalist political economies, but everyone agrees that Sweden is a case of corporatist decline, and that employers have been the key instigators of corporatist decline in the Swedish case.[4] Since the early 1980s, Sweden's export-oriented engineering employers have successfully pushed for more decentralised forms of wage bargaining and, in the early 1990s, the employers' association simply withdrew its representatives from tripartite boards of state agencies. In Austria, too, corporatist arrangements – in particular, mandatory membership in the *Kammer* system – have recently been called into question. However, this challenge has come from new political parties rather than employers, and has yet to be transformed into any major institutional changes.[5] Broadly speaking, then, Austria might be characterised as a case of corporatist stability and social-democratic decline and Sweden as a case of social-democratic stability and corporatist decline. This twofold divergence serves to make the relationship between 'corporatism' and 'social democracy' problematic and calls into question the common practice of conflating the two concepts.[6]

In what follows, we do not propose a single explanation of the divergent fortunes of the Austrian and Swedish labour movements, rather, we set out an explanatory framework that draws on the analytical concerns of comparative political economy and emphasises the legacies of past policy choices as well as cross-national differences in the organisation of trade unions and union–party relations. Two basic themes connect the various strands of our discussion. First, we argue that strong unions remain an important electoral asset for social-democratic parties. Second, we argue that the Austrian variety of corporatism has reinforced the dominant position of male industrial workers within the union movement, and constrained the ability of Austrian unions to mobilise new categories of wage earners. Prior to the development of these arguments, we first elaborate further on the outcomes to be explained and engage in a critique of alternative analytical perspectives.

DIVERGENT OUTCOMES: ELECTORAL SUPPORT AND UNION DENSITY

For both countries, Table 1 shows the share of popular vote polled by social-democratic parties and the entire Left in each national election since 1970. The Left's total vote includes votes cast for Greens and communist or post-communist parties as well as for social-democratic parties.[7] In Austria, the

TABLE 1
ELECTORAL SUPPORT FOR SOCIAL DEMOCRACY AND OTHER LEFT-WING PARTIES, 1970–95

	Sweden		Austria	
	SAP	Total	SPÖ	Total*
1970	45.3	50.1	48.4	49.4
1971			50.0	51.4
1973	43.6	48.9		
1975			50.4	51.6
1976	42.7	47.4		
1979	43.2	47.8	51.0	53.0
1982	45.6	52.9		
1983			47.6	51.6
1985	44.7	50.1		
1986			43.1	48.6
1988	43.2	53.5		
1990			42.8	49.6
1991	37.7	45.6		
1994	45.3	56.2	34.9	42.2
1995			38.1	42.9

*Total = Social Democrats + Communists + Greens

Sources: Mikael Gilljam and Sören Holmberg, *Väljarnas val* (Stockholm: Fritzes 1995) p.16. Fritz Plasser, Peter Ulram and Günther Ogris (eds.) *Wahlkampf und Wählerentscheidung* (Vienna: Signum 1996) Appendix, Table A1, pp.344–5.

Communist Party was thoroughly marginalised during the Cold War, and the difference between the SPÖ's vote share and that of the entire Left was very small until the Greens made their appearance as an electoral contender in 1983. In Sweden, by contrast, the Communist Party survived the Cold War, and renamed itself the Left Party-Communists as part of an opening to the 'New Left' in the 1960s. In 1990, the party dropped the reference to 'communism' altogether, so that it is now known simply as the Left Party. Name changes notwithstanding, the party has cleared the four per cent threshold of parliamentary representation in every post-war election but one (1968), and accounts for the lion's share of the difference between the SAP's share of the vote and that of the entire Left until 1988, when the Greens cleared the threshold of four per cent for the first time.

As Table 1 shows, the SPÖ did much better than the SAP at the polls in the 1970s. Exceeding 50 per cent in three consecutive elections, the SPÖ's vote share was larger than that of the entire Swedish left from 1971 through to the end of the decade. This impressive string of electoral victories provided the basis for majoritarian social-democratic government from 1971 to 1983. However, the election setback of 1983 forced the SPÖ to return to the tradition of coalition government. In the first instance, the SPÖ formed a coalition government with the liberal FPÖ (*Freiheitliche Partei Österreichs*), but the FPÖ proved to be an unstable coalition partner. By 1986, the right wing of the FPÖ, headed by the charismatic Jörg Haider, had taken over the party, triggering a government crisis and new elections. As the SPÖ again suffered heavy losses, it could only remain in power by forming a grand coalition government with the ÖVP.

The 1983 election proved to be the first of four consecutive setbacks for the SPÖ, and three of these setbacks were quite severe. Remarkably, the SPÖ's share of the vote fell from 51 per cent in 1979 to 34.9 per cent in 1994. While the Greens gained support in every election over this period, their gains were sufficient to offset social-democratic losses in only one election (1990) and, consequently, the Left's total share of the vote declined significantly as well. Polling 38.1 per cent of the vote, the SPÖ staged something of a recovery in the extraordinary election of 1995, but the Left's total share increased by less than one percentage point. As noted by numerous post-election commentaries, the fear that the election might yield an ÖVP–FPÖ coalition government seems to have led some left-leaning voters with green sympathies to cast their votes for the SPÖ in 1995.[8]

By historical standards, the 1970s were a difficult decade for the Swedish social democrats. Following a brief stint of majoritarian government (1968–70), the SAP governed on a minority basis from 1970 to 1976, seeking to strike issue-specific deals with one of the parties of the centre (the Centre Party and the Liberals) and, in absence of such deals, relying on the Left Party's unwillingness to join the bourgeois parties against the government. Relatively minor electoral losses for both SAP and the Left Party in 1976 led to a reversal of government and opposition, and the bourgeois parties again prevailed by a narrow margin in 1979. Gains scored by both the SAP and the Left Party enabled the social democrats to return to power in 1982 – again relying on shifting legislative alliances to govern – and two subsequent elections in the 1980s confirmed Sweden's return to a situation of electoral dominance by the Left.

The election of 1991 represents a sharp departure from the Swedish pattern of electoral stability. While the SAP and the Left Party both suffered major losses, the Greens fell below the four-per-cent threshold in this election. On the bourgeois side, the Conservatives regained the momentum they had enjoyed in the early 1980s while the Centre Party and the Liberals continued to lose support, but the big winners were two bourgeois parties that had not previously been represented in parliament: the Christian Democrats and the populist New Democracy Party. As in the 1970s, the bourgeois parties took over the reins of government just as the economy faltered and this, along with New Democracy's failure to sustain its appeal among potential protest voters, set the stage for yet another comeback for the Left in 1994. Including the Greens, the Swedish Left polled a larger share of the vote in 1994 than in any previous election since 1945; and the figure for the SAP and the Left Party alone (51.4 per cent) represents their third-best combined post-war score (following 1968 at 53.1 per cent and 1948 at 52.4 per cent).

Going beyond the evidence in Table 1, it should be noted that support for the SAP in public-opinion polls plummeted in 1995–96, and the SAP polled only 28 per cent of the vote in Sweden's first European Parliament (EP) elections in the autumn of 1995, less than what the SPÖ polled in Austria's first EP elections in the following spring (29 per cent). In retrospect, the social-democratic victory of 1994 may prove to have been an aberration and the defeat of 1991 a crucial turning point – the beginning of an erosion of electoral support of proportions quite similar to that experienced by the SPÖ from 1979 to 1994. On the other hand, popular support for the SAP improved during 1997 and, in view of the current economic recovery as well as recent electoral victories for the Left in Italy, Britain and France, this trend may continue through the election campaign of 1998. Be that as it may, the crucial point is that the SAP's loss of popular support in 1995–96 was transformed into remarkable gains for the Left Party and the Greens, and that a majority of voters continues to express support for one of the left-wing parties. This situation stands in sharp contrast to that of Austria, where social-democratic losses have primarily been converted into right-wing populist gains.[9]

As indicated at the outset, we are concerned not only with the electoral fortunes of social-democratic parties, but also with the mobilisational capacity and political influence of trade unions, traditional supporters and allies of the social-democratic parties. Union density represents a commonly used quantitative measure of union power, and on this score the Austrian and Swedish cases diverge even more sharply than they do with respect to electoral support for the left. As shown in Table 2, the labour movements of these two countries entered the 1970s at roughly similar levels of unionisation, but from 1970 to 1992, Austria's rate of union density fell from 62 per cent to 43 per cent while Sweden's rate increased from 68 per cent to 91 per cent.[10] In proportion to prior levels, the Austrian figures represent the second-largest union density decline of any European OECD country over this period (France being in first place).

Union members have traditionally been and remain more likely to vote for the Left than non-union members in both Austria and Sweden. Hence explaining the divergence of union density trends should take us some way towards an explanation of the divergence of electoral fortunes in the 1980s and 1990s. But the divergence of union density also represents an important outcome in and of itself, with important implications for the politics of social democracy.

TABLE 2
NET RATES OF UNION DENSITY (EMPLOYED UNION MEMBERS AS PER CENT OF EMPLOYED LABOUR FORCE), 1970–93

Year	Sweden (%)	Austria (%)
1970	68	62
1975	74	58
1980	80	56
1985	84	51
1990	84	46
1992/93	91	43

Source: Jelle Visser, 'Unionisation Trends Revisited', (Centre for Research of European Societies and Industrial Relations, Amsterdam 1996).

ALTERNATIVE PERSPECTIVES

For Austrian political scientists, the problem of explaining the electoral decline of the SPÖ has largely been subsumed under the problem of explaining increased voter volatility and diminishing support for *both* of the major parties. The 'decline of the *Lager* mentality' sums up the basic theme of this literature, which shows that voters have become more individualistic and issue-oriented, and that party leaders, election campaigns, and mass media have become increasingly influential.[11] From the comparative perspective adopted here, this way of thinking about the decline of social democracy is obviously problematic, for the variables invoked to explain the SPÖ's electoral difficulties are by no means unique to the Austrian case. Similar developments have been observed by Swedish students of electoral behaviour, yet they have not meant comparable electoral losses for the SAP.

This article seeks to illustrate how the concerns of comparative political economy might be linked to the analysis of electoral outcomes. Relative to the mainstream of comparative political economy, we correct for the tendency to neglect electoral politics and, relative to the political economy tradition that does address electoral outcomes, we go beyond its almost exclusive preoccupation with the implications of macro-economic performance. As shown in Table 3, Austria consistently averaged higher rates of real GDP growth and lower rates of inflation than Sweden from 1970 through to the first half of the 1990s. From 1976 to 1991, the Austrian rate of unemployment was higher than the Swedish, but the Austrians were much more successful than the Swedes in keeping the lid on mass unemployment in the first half of the 1990s. Had the Austrian and Swedish social democrats held government power throughout this period (1970–95), their divergent electoral fortunes would constitute strong evidence against (retrospective) economic voting, but, of course, the Swedish social democrats were in opposition from 1976 to 1982 and again from 1991 to 1994, and this makes matters more complicated.

TABLE 3
MACRO-ECONOMIC PERFORMANCE, 1970–93

	Sweden			Austria		
	1974–79	1980–89	1990–94	1974–79	1980–89	1990–93
Unemployment	1.9	2.5	5.2	1.7	3.3	3.6
Inflation (CPI)	9.8	7.9	6.7	6.3	3.8	3.6
Real GDP growth	1.8	2.0	–0.2	2.9	2.0	2.5

Source: OECD Historical Statistics (electronic database).

Restricting the comparison of macro-economic performance to periods of social-democratic government, the difference in unemployment rates in the 1980s constitutes the only hook on which one might hang a straightforward macro-economic explanation of divergent electoral fortunes. It seems far-fetched to think that a one-percentage-point unemployment differential, albeit one that persisted for about a decade, could have such large electoral consequences. On the other hand, the timing of business cycles and elections clearly constitutes a crucial component of the electoral success of the Swedish social democrats. Macro-economic performance deteriorated markedly during periods of bourgeois government – in each case, the 'misery index' (unemployment plus inflation) jumped while the growth of real GDP plummeted (see Table 3) – and this, in turn, served to boost electoral support for the SAP. In a sense, the Swedish social democrats have been extraordinarily lucky, twice losing power just as the economy entered a deep recession. Indeed, there may be more than simply luck at work here: in the mid-1970s, the policies pursued by the social democrats in effect postponed the impact of the international recession until 1976, and social-democratic policy choices in the 1980s were at least in part responsible for the Swedish employment crisis of the early 1990s.[12] The puzzle is why (or how) the SAP managed to avoid being blamed for economic difficulties, and why the SPÖ has received so little credit for Austria's stable and rather strong macro-economic performance.

Economic voting models are limited by their focus on 'swing voters' at the centre of the political spectrum, and by their conception of these voters

TABLE 4
EMPLOYMENT STRUCTURE (AS PERCENTAGE OF TOTAL EMPLOYMENT)
1968 AND 1990

	Sweden			Austria		
	1968	1990	Change	1968	1990	Change
Agriculture	9.1	3.3	–5.8	16.0	7.9	–8.1
Industry	41.1	29.1	–12.0	40.9	36.8	–4.1
Private services	31.4	35.8	+4.4	30.3	34.7	+4.4
Govt. services	18.4	31.7	+13.3	12.8	20.6	+7.8

Source: OECD Historical Statistics (electronic database).

as individuals without strong ideological commitments or distributive interests, responding to the movement of macro-economic indicators much like market actors respond to price changes. Quite obviously, such models leave unanswered questions about the size of the swing electorate and, for multi-party systems, the direction of its swings in response to poor economic performance – to the Left or to the Right of the government of the day? As we seek to understand variations in the centre of political gravity across countries and over time, we need to pay more attention to the core constituencies of different parties.

Until quite recently, the core constituency of both the SPÖ and the SAP was unquestionably the industrial working class. Could it be that the divergence of their electoral fortunes, and perhaps the divergence of union density as well, is attributable to a more rapid shift of employment out of industry into services, that is, a greater shrinkage of the industrial working class in Austria than in Sweden? Table 4 shows that the opposite is in fact the case: with industry accounting for just about the same proportion of total employment in both countries in 1968, Sweden underwent much more rapid deindustrialisation than Austria over the next two decades. At the same time, Table 4 points to the size of the public-service sector as a major difference between our two cases. Already in 1968, the public sector was a more important source of employment in Sweden than in Austria and, while its share of total employment grew in both countries in the 1970s and the 1980s, this growth was stronger in Sweden.[13] As we shall see, public-sector employees have become an increasingly important constituency for unions and social-democratic parties in both countries.

In a recent book on European social democracy, and an article devoted exclusively to a comparison of the SPÖ and the SAP, Herbert Kitschelt argues that the expansion of education and 'people-processing' occupations in the service sector, especially public services, since the 1960s has given rise to a new cleavage axis in Western European politics, and that the challenge facing social democratic parties is to reposition themselves so as to appeal to voters with 'left–libertarian' values.[14] For Kitschelt, the behaviour of other parties may constrain the ability of social democratic parties to realign themselves, but strategic innovation and electoral success is first and foremost a function of party organisation and internal party politics. Kitschelt's discussion of the organisational conditions for strategic flexibility is subtle and complex; what matters for our present purposes is his claim that union influence over party organisation and decision making represents an obstacle to the kind of programmatic realignment that is necessary to achieve electoral success.

Writing between the Swedish elections of 1991 and 1994, Kitschelt conceives both Austria and Sweden as cases of 'social democracy in crisis'. His comparison of these cases does not turn on differences in union influence, and makes no mention of divergent union-density trends. Thus Kitschelt misses the dual divergence of electoral fortunes and trends in union density noted above. As Kitschelt's thesis of union-induced strategic rigidity is first and foremost an argument about union influence within the party (*vis-à-vis* party leaders and non-union constituencies), it is not necessarily contradicted by this dual divergence. However, to invoke Kitschelt's thesis as an explanation of the electoral outcomes that we seek to explain, one would have to argue that union influence over the social-democratic parties has been significantly greater in Austria than in Sweden, which is not by any means self-evident. The closest Kitschelt himself comes to making this claim is his assertion that 'the party-union linkage has been *closer* in Austria than in Sweden'.[15]

INSTITUTIONAL DIFFERENCES BETWEEN AUSTRIA AND SWEDEN

To go beyond the preliminary discussion of the previous section, it is necessary to look more closely at the organisation of unions, party–union relations and other institutional features that distinguish the Austrian and Swedish cases from each other. Against the background provided in the following pages, subsequent sections will more directly address electoral outcomes and trends in union density.[16]

Union Organisation

As in the case of West Germany, the post-war reconstruction of the Austrian trade-union movement was based on the twin principles of political unity and industrial unionism. The first principle meant that social democrats, communists and Christian Democratic union activists would be part of the same unions, and that these unions would not be formally affiliated to any party. The establishment of a separate union for privately employed white-collar employees (*Privatangestellte*) compromised the principle of industrial unionism – workers organised on the basis of their employer (sectors) rather than the jobs they perform – but the upshot was still a remarkably coherent structure. Today, there are but 14 national unions in Austria, all affiliated to the ÖGB (*Österreichischer Gewerkschaftsbund*): four public-sector unions, which organise blue-collar and white-collar employees alike, nine blue-collar unions for the private sector, organised on an industrial basis, and one white-collar union for the entire private sector.

In Sweden, by contrast, no unions organise both blue-collar and white-collar employees, and the blue-collar unions affiliated to the LO (*Landsorganisationen*) have always had official ties to the SAP. In effect, there is not one, but two union movements in Sweden: a social-democratic blue-collar union movement, and a politically neutral (unitary) white-collar union movement. The white-collar union movement is in turn divided into two separate confederations, the TCO (*Tjänstemännens Centralorganisation*) and the SACO-SR (*Sveriges Akademikers Centralorganisation-Statstjänstemännens Riksförbund*). While the TCO, like the LO, is organised on the basis of industrial unionism, and seeks to represent all white-collar employees, membership in the SACO-SR is largely restricted to people with academic or professional degrees, and its affiliates are organised on the basis of professions.[17]

Union-Party Relations

In Austria, the principle of political neutrality has been coupled with formalised politicisation of internal union affairs. Factions affiliated with the two major parties, the SPÖ and the ÖVP, run candidate slates in works council elections, and the results of these elections provide the basis for allocation of union offices among the factions. The Socialist Trade-Union Faction (*Fraktion Sozialistischer Gewerkschafter*, henceforth FSG) usually receives 65–70 per cent of the votes in works council elections, while the Christian Trade-Union Faction and various independent groups receive 15–20 per cent each.[18] By similar means, but with somewhat smaller margins, the FSG also dominates the Chamber of Labour (*Arbeiterkammer*), based on compulsory membership for all wage earners. With official representation on the executive committee of the SPÖ, the FSG is the direct link between the three pillars of the Austrian labour movement.

Until the SAP officially abolished collective affiliation in the late 1980s, it was the common practice of the branches of LO unions to affiliate to the district party of their locality, with individual union members being provided the opportunity to opt out of collective affiliation. Roughly 75 per cent of SAP members were affiliated through their unions when this practice ended. In contrast to the British Labour Party, collective affiliation was a local matter, and did not involve 'bloc votes' at party congresses. Rather, local union leaders cast proxy votes for collectively affiliated members in pre-congress deliberations at the district party level, and this remains possible under the new rules adopted by the SAP congress of 1987 – the difference being that the influence of local union leaders now depends on their ability to get their membership to join the SAP individually.[19] At the national level, the only formal tie between the LO and the SAP is the *ex-officio* appointment of the LO president as a member of the party's executive committee.

While the SAP has no formal ties to white-collar unions, it began to promote social-democratic activism within the TCO unions in the 1950s and, by the 1970s, the TCO leadership began to acquire a distinctively social-democratic profile.[20] More or less formalised consultations, personal contacts and people holding official positions in both wings of the labour movement are, of course, crucial features of LO-SAP and ÖGB-SPÖ relations as well. Whereas dual office-holding rarely occurs at the national level in Sweden, this has been and remains common practice in Austria. High-ranking officials of labour associations (unions and *Arbeiterkammer*) accounted for 45–48 per cent of all SPÖ MPs in the 1970s, a figure which had only fallen to 38 per cent by 1991. Small wonder, then, that 'the FSG and the SPÖ traditionally had identical or similar positions on most issues'.[21]

It is difficult to compare the SPÖ-ÖGB pair and the SAP-LO pair in terms of the balance of power between party and unions. As Kitschelt points out, the separation of party and union functions is more pronounced in the Swedish case. However, this does not mean that the LO has stayed out of politics. Quite the contrary, the LO appears to have been more assertive in the political arena than the ÖGB. It is well-known that some of the most innovative and distinctive features of the Swedish Model, such as active labour-market policy, were conceived by people inside the LO, and that the LO provided the clout that ensured that these policies would prevail against the resistance of some party leaders. The autonomous political role of the LO reached its apogee in the 1970s, with the LO initiating major reforms on its own: first, co-determination, and then wage-earner funds.[22] The failure of the latter initiative clearly weakened the LO's influence within the SAP, but the LO and its affiliated unions have continued to play a very active role in the political debate – in the 1990s, as critics of the policy priorities of bourgeois and social-democratic governments alike.

According to Wolfgang Müller, conflicts between the union and party wings of the Austrian labour movement have become more common since the late 1980s.[23] By comparison with Sweden, this represents a belated development and, overall, the posture of the ÖGB appears to have been more defensive than that of the LO. Why, then, has the ÖGB been politically more docile than the LO? Our tentative answer to this question is twofold. On the one hand, the need to accommodate the Christian Trade-Union Faction and other non-socialist forces within the ÖGB, institutionalised by the system of proportional representation, has served as a constraint on socialist trade-union activists and leaders. On the other hand, the conditions of coalition government have strengthened the moderates within the SPÖ leadership, reducing the scope for successful trade-union initiatives.

Electoral Competition

The divergent fortunes of the Austrian and Swedish social democracy cannot be explained entirely by looking at the social-democratic parties and their union allies. As Kitschelt has rightly emphasised, the nature of the competition confronting these parties in the electoral arena must also be taken into account. Leaving aside the recent rise of radical-right populism in Austria, there are two important differences between Austria and Sweden on this score, to which we have already alluded.

First, there is a party to the Left of social democrats in Sweden, but not in Austria, and this is a party with a tradition of appealing to blue-collar workers. The reasons why this is so need not concern us here. Suffice it to say that the SAP has always had to worry about losing left-leaning as well as right-leaning supporters, and that this has strengthened the influence of leftist forces within the party. Also, the Left Party has become a vehicle of protest voting in the last decade or so. Had such a party existed in Austria, the rise of the FPÖ would perhaps have been less meteoric, and the SPÖ's room for strategic manoeuvring greater.[24]

The second difference concerns the nature of the competition to the Right. Divisions among the bourgeois parties have often been invoked as one of the main reasons for the historic dominance of social democracy in Sweden, and Scandinavia more generally.[25] Coalitions with the Agrarian (now Centre) Party enabled the SAP to consolidate control of the government in the 1930s and to stay in government despite electoral setbacks in the 1950s. On many issues, the social democrats have been able to play the three bourgeois parties off against one another. Indeed, during the 1960s and the 1970s, the Centre Party and the Liberals often sought to project themselves as more progressive than the SAP on issues such as co-determination, gender equality and the environment. By contrast, the SPÖ essentially confronted a single competitor during most of the post-war era – a party (the ÖVP) with broad popular appeal, strong connections to the

Catholic Church, and well-organised core constituencies. Even at the peak of its electoral dominance in the 1970s, the SPÖ was a party competing for hegemony rather than a hegemonic party.

Post-War Political Economies

Sweden exemplifies Esping-Andersen's conception of a social-democratic welfare state, characterised by universalism, decommodification and an emphasis on directly provided services over transfer payments.[26] To characterise Austria, in the 1980s or 1990s, as a conservative welfare state is surely somewhat misleading, but with respect to most of the features that come into play in Esping-Andersen's analysis, the Austrian welfare state diverges from the social democratic model in a conservative direction. First, transfer payments (social insurance) constitute a significantly larger component of total welfare benefits provided by the state in Austria than Sweden. This is indicated by the fact that while social security as a percentage of GDP was roughly the same in 1990 (just below 20 per cent), total government spending as a percentage of GDP was much higher in Sweden (60.8 per cent) than in Austria (49.4 per cent) and also by the greater relative importance of public-sector employment in Sweden (Table 4). Second, occupational distinctions remain important features of social insurance in Austria. Third, the major social insurance schemes (pensions, sick pay and unemployment) provide lower rates of average earnings replacement than in Sweden. Finally, the financing of social insurance relies more heavily on individual contributions, relative to payroll taxes and general tax revenues.[27]

It is a commonplace argument that universalism shores up political support for the welfare state by providing the middle class with material stakes in its maintenance. Construed as an explanation of the divergent electoral fortunes of the SPÖ and the SAP, this line of argument would lead us to expect that the SPÖ has primarily lost support among white-collar strata. As we shall see, this is not the case. Still, welfare-state universalism may be an important ideological variable at work here.[28] And, again, public-sector employment provides an important linkage between patterns of post-war welfare-state development and electoral outcomes in the 1980s and 1990s.

The role of public-sector employment expansion as a mechanism to bring women into the labour force in Sweden deserves to be noted here. From 1968 to 1990, labour force participation among Swedish women aged 15–64 increased from 56.6 per cent to 81.1 per cent, while the labour force participation rate for Austrian women only increased from 49.8 per cent to 55.4 per cent. In 1985, women constituted an enormous 67.1 per cent of the public-sector labour force in Sweden, as compared to 36.9 per cent in

Austria.[29] Mostly due to the differences in female labour-force participation, Sweden also outpaced Austria in terms of total labour-force participation in the 1970s and 1980s (83.2 per cent as compared to 67.7 per cent in 1990). While both countries avoided mass unemployment, Swedish employment policy was clearly more ambitious than its Austrian counterpart. It is also noteworthy that Austria is at the very bottom, and Sweden at the top, when OECD countries are ranked by the share of GDP devoted to active labour-market policy.[30]

The differences between the size of the public sector in Austria and Sweden diminish if nationalised industry is included. In 1983–84, state-owned enterprises accounted for 18 per cent of industrial employment in Austria, and 9.5 per cent in Sweden. As commonly noted, nationalised industry has been an important tool of employment policy and a bastion of union strength in Austria.[31] This distinctive feature of Austria's post-war political economy may be linked to the decline of social democracy in at least two ways. First, in the 1980s, participation in the management of nationalised industry involved the union movement, as well as social-democratic officials, in a series of scandals relating to patronage, misappropriation of funds, and illegal arms deals with foreign countries. Second, the importance of the nationalised sector to the union movement would appear to have reinforced the dominance of skilled, male workers and their interests, and perhaps constrained the ability of the ÖGB to extend and rejuvenate its membership base.

Related to this last point, it is well-known that Sweden has the most egalitarian wage structure of any OECD country, but it is commonly overlooked that Austria has the largest inter-sectoral wage differentials and the largest gap between average male and female earnings of any rich European country.[32] Initiated by the LO, solidaristic wage policy emerged as a central feature of the Swedish model in 1960s, and became official policy of the TCO unions as well in the 1970s. By contrast, the ÖGB never committed itself strongly and consistently to wage solidarity and, in practice, its approach to wage bargaining has been guided by the idea that in order to preserve employment wages must be allowed to vary according to corporate profitability.[33] Now, the determinants of wage-distributive outcomes are complex, and union policy is certainly only part of the story. For our present purposes, it is the implications of the politics of wage distribution for the mobilisational capacity of unions and the electoral fortunes of social-democratic parties that matter.

ELECTORAL PERFORMANCE DISAGGREGATED

Perhaps the most obvious way to adjudicate among contending explanations of the electoral decline of Austrian social democracy is to ask, who abandoned the SPÖ in the 1980s and early 1990s? Contrary to what a macro-economic account of electoral performance would lead us to expect, the SPÖ's electoral losses in this period were indeed concentrated in particular segments of the electorate, but it is not the case that the SPÖ primarily lost support among middle-class voters tired of paying high taxes.

For both Austria and Sweden, Table 5 traces the social democrats' share of the votes cast by various socio-economic and demographic categories of voters over a number of recent elections (1979–94 for Sweden and 1986–95 for Austria).[34] Relating the social democrats' share of the votes cast by a particular category of voters to their share of the total vote, it is possible to identify the constituencies where they have the greatest support as well as the constituencies where they are weak. Also, relative gains and losses can be identified by relating the change in vote share for a particular voter category to the change in the total vote over the time period in question. The following analysis compares the SPÖ and the SAP on both counts, but, of course, the question of change over time is of primary importance for our present purposes.

Looking at the mid-1980s figures, there are strong similarities between the SAP and the SPÖ in terms of their bases of support. Most notably, both parties enjoyed a huge electoral edge among blue-collar voters and union members. The SAP's share of the blue-collar vote was a huge 20 points higher than its share of the total vote, and its share of the union vote was 10 points higher than its share of the total vote.[35] The corresponding figures for the SPÖ were +14 and +19. On the other hand, both parties did very poorly among students and the self-employed, and also underpeformed among white-collar voters. The SAP's share of the white-collar vote fell short of its share of the total vote by ten points. On this score, the SPÖ did significantly better (–3), and this is all the more impressive because the Austrian figures on white-collar voters do not include civil servants (*Beamte*) and, as shown in Table 5, civil servants (+6) were more inclined to vote for the SPÖ than any socio-economic category other than blue-collar workers. This distinctive feature of the Austrian case is perhaps related to the politicisation of administrative appointments. In general, however, the SPÖ did as well among private-sector employees as it did among public-sector employees, which is also true for the SAP.

Both parties enjoyed an edge among retired voters, matched by poor performance among young voters. This pattern is more pronounced for the SPÖ, whose share of the retired vote exceeded its share of the total vote by six points, and whose share of the under-30 vote fell four points short (SAP: +2 and -3). Finally, Table 5 shows that both parties enjoyed a slight edge among women in the mid-1980s. At least in the Austrian case, this gender

TABLE 5
THE SOCIAL-DEMOCRATIC SHARE OF VOTES CAST BY VARIOUS SOCIO-ECONOMIC AND DEMOGRAPHIC CATEGORIES, 1979–95

	SAP				SPÖ		
	1979	1985	1994	Change (1979/94)	1986	1995	Change (1986/95)
Total Vote	43	45	45	+2	43	38	–5
Blue-collar	66	64	63	–3	57	41	–16
White-collar[1]	33	35	41	+8	40/49	32/48	–8/–1
Self-employed[2]	13	14	17	+4	14	18	+4
Retired[3]	47	47	50	+3	49	45	–4
Students	25	26	29	+4	18	25	+7
Housewives					36	38	+2
Men	43	41	47	+4	42	35	–7
Women	45	46	44	–1	43	40	–3
Male wage earners		41			41	34	–7
Female wage earners		45			46	35	–11
Private-sector empl.	46	43	43	–3	51	36	–15
Public-sector empl.	43	43	51	+8	51	44	–7
Union members[4]	55	55	57	+2	62	55	–7
Under age 30	42	42	39	–3	39	30	–9

Notes:
1. For Austria: first figure refers to Angestellte, second figure refers to Beamte.
2. Includes farmers for Sweden, but not for Austria.
3. For Sweden 'retired' refers to voters above the age of 60, for austria 'retired' refers to pensioners.
4. Swedish figures include LO and TCO members, but not SACO members.

Sources: Sören Holmberg, *Svenska väljare* (Stockholm: Publica 1981). Sören Holmberg and Mikael Gilljam, *väljare och val i Sverige* (Stockholm: Bonniers 1987). Mikael Gilljam and Sören Holmberg, *Väljarnas val* (Stockholm: Fritzes 1995). Fritz Plasser and Peter Ulram, 'Wandel der Politischen Konfliktdynamik', in Wolfgang Müller; Fritz Plasser and Peter Ulram (eds.) *Wählerverhalten und Parteienwettbewerb* (Vienna: Signum 1995) pp.471–503. Fritz Plasser, Peter Ulram and Gilig Seeber, '(Dis-)Kontinuitäten und neue Spannungslinien im Wählerverhalten', in Fritz Plasser, Peter Ulram and Günther Ogris (eds.) *Wahlkampf und Wählerentscheidung* (Vienna: Signum 1996) pp.155–210.

gap would appear to be entirely attributable to stronger-than-average support among working women. While the SPÖ's share of the female wage-earner vote exceeded its share of the total vote by three points, its share of the housewife vote was seven points lower than its share of the total vote.[36]

Turning now to an analysis of relative gains and losses, the Swedish experience can be summarised as follows. From 1979 to 1995, the SAP suffered considerable losses among blue-collar workers, and especially among blue-collar workers in the private sector. While its share of the total vote increased by two points, its share of the blue-collar vote and the private-sector vote declined by three points, which, in our terminology, equals a relative loss of 5 ('–5'). The SAP suffered roughly similar losses among young voters, and also lost some support among women. For all other categories of voters, the Swedish social democrats either held their own or made disproportionate gains. Their gains among white-collar voters and public-sector employees (+6 for both categories) are particularly noteworthy.

The SPÖ suffered a severe haemorrhage of blue-collar support from 1986 to 1995. Altogether, the party's share of the blue-collar vote fell by 16 percentage points. Relative to the change in its share of the total vote, this represents a loss of 11 points (as compared to 5 points for the SAP). As in the case of the SAP, the SPÖ's losses among blue-collar workers appear to have been concentrated in the private sector, but the SPÖ, in marked contrast to the SAP, also suffered relative losses among white-collar workers (–3) and public-sector employees (–2). The large relative loss of support among female wage earners (–6) is noteworthy as well, but, again, the SPÖ also lost greater-than-average support among male wage earners (–2). Indeed, the SPÖ suffered relative losses among *all* categories of wage earners except civil servants. Its relative gains occurred among students, the self-employed, housewives, civil servants and retired people, all of whom, except the self-employed, might perhaps be characterised as 'welfare state claimants'.

The evidence in Table 5 suggests that the SPÖ faced a steeper trade-off between white-collar and blue-collar support than the SAP: that is, gaining a certain amount of support (or minimizing losses) among white-collar voters entailed a larger loss of blue-collar support than it did for the SAP.[37] This is rather puzzling given that blue-collar and white-collar employees belong to the same unions or, at least, the same union confederation in Austria – a situation that one might expect to be more favourable to the formation of a wage-earner political identity than the Swedish one. Evidently, rates of unionisation matter more than union structure in this context.

Table 6 tracks the differences in the vote share between men and women, between private-sector and public-sector employees, and between blue-collar and white-collar employees for social democratic parties and the entire Left in Austria and Sweden over the period 1985–95. The first panel shows that women have tended to be more left-leaning than men in both countries, but this gender gap diminished in Sweden in the 1990s. For the SAP alone, the gender gap actually reversed itself in 1994. Also, the first

TABLE 6
VOTE DIFFERENTIALS (PERCENTAGE POINTS), 1985–95

	1985	1986	1988	1990	1991	1994	1995
A. Male/Female							
SAP	–5		–3		0	+3	
Total Swedish Left	–4		–4		–3	–1	
SPÖ		–1		–5		–2	–5
Total Austrian Left		–2		–6		–5	–6
B. Private/Public							
SAP	0		+4		–7	–8	
Total Swedish Left	–6		–4		–13	–15	
SPÖ		0		+5		+1	–8
Total Austrian Left		–1		+1		–6	–7
C. Blue/White Collar							
SAP	29	27		22	22		
Total Swedish Left	26	26		19	24		
SPÖ		17		14		18	9
Total Austrian Left		14		9		10	5

Sources: Sören Holmberg, *Svenska väljare* (Stockholm: Publica 1981). Sören Holmberg and Mikael Gilljam, *Väljare och val i Sverige* (Stockholm: Bonniers 1987). Mikael Gilljam and Sören Holmberg, *Väljarna inför 90-talet* (Stockholm: Norstedts 1993). Mikael Gilljam and Sören Holmberg, *Väljarnas val* (Stockholm: Fritzes 1995). Fritz Plasser and Peter Ulram, 'Wandel der Politischen Konfliktdynamik', in Wolfgang Müller; Fritz Plasser and Peter Ulram (eds.), *Wählerverhalten und Parteienwettbewerb* (Vienna: Signum 1995) pp.471–503. Fritz Plasser, Peter Ulram and Gilig Seeber, '(Dis-)Kontinuitäten und neue Spannungslinien im Wählerverhalten', in Fritz Plasser, Peter Ulram and Günther Ogris (eds.) *Wahlkampf und Wählerentscheidung* (Vienna: Signum 1996) pp.155–210.

panel of Table 6 shows that the Greens attracted many left-leaning Austrian women in 1994, and that these voters swung back to the SPÖ in 1995.

In the second panel, we observe that in Sweden public-sector employees have been more inclined than private-sector employees to vote for the Left in every election since 1985, but until 1991, this gap manifested itself primarily through above-average public-sector support for leftist parties other than the SAP. In 1991 and 1994, however, the private-public vote differential became more evenly distributed between the SAP and the other leftist parties. In relative terms, Austrian public-sector employees became more left-wing in the 1990s. In the first instance, this shift benefited the Greens, but public-sector employees swung sharply towards the SPÖ in 1995. As a whole, the Swedish Left continues to enjoy a much larger edge than the Austrian Left among public-sector employees.

Finally, the third panel of Table 6 shows that while the SAP's reliance on blue-collar support declined significantly from 1985 to 1994, the blue-collar/white-collar differential in support for the left as a whole remained essentially constant in Sweden over this period. Apparently, other leftist parties, most obviously the Left Party, have been able to mobilise many disaffected working-class voters. In Austria, by contrast, total voting for the left has been in close parallel with the SPÖ in terms of the decline of the blue-collar/white-collar differential.

This analysis suggests that the contrast in electoral performance between the SAP and the SPÖ has two quite distinct components. On the one hand, the SPÖ has lost support among male blue-collar workers in the private sector to the FPÖ. Many of these workers are likely to be unskilled and relatively poorly paid; certainly, they are likely to perceive themselves as economically insecure. The SAP has also lost support within this constituency, but its losses have been smaller, and protest voting among blue-collar workers has assumed more leftist forms in Sweden than in Austria.[38] On the other hand, the SPÖ has been less successful than the SAP in mobilizing or sustaining its support among women working in public or private services. Working women appear to have abandoned the SPÖ primarily in favour of the Greens and the Liberal Forum.

TRENDS IN UNION DENSITY

As we have seen, the SPÖ and the SAP have both enjoyed a significant electoral edge among union members, and this edge has not changed very much since the late 1970s. It would appear that the divergence of their electoral fortunes does not have to do with the ability of union allies to deliver the votes of their members. By the same token, it would appear that a great deal of this divergence can be explained in terms of divergent trends in union density, that is, by the fact that union members today constitute a significantly smaller percentage of the Austrian electorate than they did in the 1970s, while the opposite is true for Sweden. It is time to tackle the question of what accounts for the divergent trends in union density.

It should first be noted that changes in aggregate rates of union density may be due to changes in the composition of the labour force as well as changes in density rates within particular categories of the labour force. Everything else being equal, the rate of union density will decline if the share of total employment of sectors with above-average union density declines. Tables 7 and 8 disaggregate union density by sectors of employment and by gender. The disaggregation by sectors does not go very far, but so far as it goes, Table 7 indicates that a decline in union density has occurred across all sectors of the Austrian economy, and that the rise of union density in Sweden is, similarly, a pervasive rather than sector-specific phenomenon. Holding within-sector rates of union density constant at 1970 levels, employment

TABLE 7
UNION DENSITY BY TYPE OF ECONOMIC ACTIVITY

	Sweden		Austria	
	1970	1988	1970	1988
Manufacturing	84	100	68	53
Finance/business services	70	72	37	28
Social & personal services	59	87	54	44
Construction	91	100	58	46
Wholesale/retail/tourism	38	49	29	22
Transportation/communication	83	89	97	88

TABLE 8
UNION DENSITY BY PRIVATE/PUBLIC SECTOR (%)

	Sweden		Austria	
	Private	Public	Private	Public
1970			55	78
1975			51	73
1980	80	81	49	68
1985	82	88	44	61
1989			41	57

TABLE 9
UNION DENSITY BY GENDER (%)

	Sweden		Austria	
	Men	Women	Men	Women
1970	77	54	73	45
1975	79	68		
1980	81	79	63	40
1985	83	86	57	37
1989	82	88		

Source: OECD, 'trends in Trade Union Membership', *Employment Outlook* (July 1991) pp.97–134.

shifts among the six sectors identified in Table 7 predict a 3.1 percentage-point decline in aggregate union density in Austria from 1970 to 1988. As aggregate union density actually declined by 14.1 percentage points, we might say that intersectoral employment shifts account for only about one-fifth of the total decline in union density. For Sweden, intersectoral employment shifts predict an aggregate decline in density of 2.1 percentage points, but aggregate union density increased by 17.6 points.[39]

As Table 8 indicates, a significant gap in union density between private and public-sector employees did not open up in Sweden until the 1980s. With union density rates about the same for private and public-sector employees, the expansion of public-sector employment does not explain Sweden's increased union density in the 1970s. In Austria, by contrast, the public sector (not including nationalised industry) was already much more unionised than the private sector in 1970, and the gap remained constant as union density declined in both sectors in the 1970s and 1980s. In this case, the expansion of public-sector employment – less rapid than in Sweden, but still significant (see Table 4) – counteracted the decline in union density within sectors.

What might explain the divergence of union density rates within sectors? The first point to be made is that Austrian unions bargain over wages and employment conditions with the *Wirtschaftskammer*, to which all employers must belong by law. As a result, virtually all employees are covered by collective bargaining agreements, whether or not they themselves are union members. The inherent problem that this poses for the unions has been exacerbated since the early 1980s because the *Arbeiterkammer*, in response to the erosion of its legitimacy, began to provide a variety of individual, such as legal advice and group insurance, which the unions have traditionally relied upon as selective membership incentives.[40]

Following a similar logic, the differences between the Austrian and Swedish systems of unemployment insurance might be invoked to explain the divergent trends in union density. Whereas the Austrian system is financed and administered by the state, the Swedish is a Ghent-type system in which the state subsidises union-administered unemployment funds. It is possible to belong to one of these funds without joining the union that runs it, but the Swedish system encourages employees to join unions.[41] The fact that the Swedish rate of union density, which was stagnant in the second half of the 1980s, increased again during the employment crisis of the early 1990s (see Table 2) lends credibility to the argument about the significance of unemployment insurance.

To attribute the decline of union density within the industrial sector in Austria to privatisation clearly will not do, for privatisation did not assume significant proportions until the second half of the 1980s.[42] As suggested earlier, it is more plausible to argue that the importance of the nationalised sector for the internal politics of the ÖGB has constrained its ability to extend its membership base, and especially to recruit low-wage employees in private services. The persistence of a huge gap between male and female rates of union density in Austria is most noteworthy here, particularly in view of the contrast to Sweden, where the female rate has exceeded the male rate since the early 1980s (Table 9). When we add differences in rates of female labour-force participation, the following picture emerges: in 1970, women constituted 28 per cent of total union membership in Austria, and 32 per cent in Sweden; by 1994, the Austrian figure was 32 per cent and the Swedish figure 48 per cent.[43]

The fact that Swedish working women are far more likely to work in the public sector than their Austrian counterparts clearly constitutes an important reason behind cross-national differences in the relative propensity of male and female wage earners to join unions. Also, there can be no doubt that women have been the principal beneficiaries of solidaristic wage bargaining in Sweden, and it is plausible to suppose that this has drawn female wage earners towards the unions, especially in the absence of any formal provisions for the extension of union contracts to non-union employees.

POLICY CHOICES AND POLITICS

One final question remains to be discussed. Simply put, might the divergent fortunes of the Austrian and Swedish labour movements be attributed to strategic choices made by their leaders? In government, did the Swedish social democrats pursue policies that served to sustain or broaden their electoral support while the Austrian social democrats did not? Space does not permit a detailed comparison of economic and social-policy decisions in Austria and Sweden. The basic point is that in terms of the substance of policy change, the stories to be told about these two countries are strikingly similar. In Austria and Sweden alike, social-democratic governments retreated from selective industrial policy and introduced market-oriented structural reforms in the 1980s. In both cases, structural reforms included various measures to liberalise financial markets, and tax reforms that sharply reduced marginal income tax rates while curtailing deductions and other loopholes. On the benefits side of the welfare state, neither country saw any major cutbacks in the 1980s. As a percentage of GDP or total employment, the growth of the public sector levelled off in the course of this decade, but in absolute (real) terms, public spending and employment continued to increase. The need for fiscal austerity became paramount in the early 1990s, however, and governments in both countries began to cut welfare entitlements and to rationalise and restructure the public sector. In the Swedish case, this reorientation took on radical proportions under the bourgeois government of 1991–94, but it had been initiated by the social democrats in 1990–91, and continued under the social-democratic government of 1994.

In both cases, the decision to apply for membership of the European Union (EU) represents a crucial component of the politics of political and economic reform. Fritz Plasser and Peter Ulram suggest that some of the shift of working-class voters from the SPÖ to the FPÖ has been motivated by opposition to EU membership.[44] There can be little doubt that the Swedish social democrats' embrace of the EU has also hurt them among some working-class constituencies, but, again, such losses have led to increased support for other parties of the Left. The divergence between the SAP's and the SPÖ's fortunes predates the emergence of EU membership as a major political issue and, since the two parties made the same decisions on EU membership, the issue would seem to have limited explanatory relevance. By and large, this assessment holds for tax reform and welfare-state cutbacks as well. With respect to the welfare state, it is clearly not the case that the SPÖ has moved more forcefully in a neo-liberal direction, thereby alienating traditional working-class supporters to a greater extent than the SAP.

Staying with the focus on economic management and distribution, this leaves two major policy divergences between Austria and Sweden. The first concerns exchange rates and monetary policy. While the Austrian government pegged its currency to the D-Mark in the mid-1970s, and thus abandoned control over interest rates, the Swedish social democrats opted for a large devaluation in 1982, and pursued a more accommodating macro-economic policy stance through the 1980s. Since Austrian policies yielded better macro-economic performance, however, this policy divergence hardly explains the divergence of electoral outcomes.

The second point of policy divergence concerns the fact that privatisation has been a much more important feature of domestic reform in Austria than in Sweden. This is not so much a question of policy choices in the 1980s, but rather a reflection of the greater prominence of state-owned industry in Austria. In any case, the relevance of this variable for the outcomes we are trying to explain is dubious. As noted earlier, privatisation did not assume significant proportions until the late 1980s in Austria, and therefore could only explain a small part of the unions' membership losses. While privatisation has undoubtedly had an adverse impact on the economic circumstances of some traditional SPÖ constituencies, it is by no means clear that these are the working-class constituencies that have abandoned the SPÖ. Specifically, the privatisation of state-owned industry does not seem very relevant to SPÖ losses among working women. And public opinion in general appears to have been out ahead of the SPÖ on the privatisation issue.

We do not wish to argue, as a general proposition, that policy choices are of not consequence for the fortunes of social-democratic labour movements. The point is rather that the policy choices that matter for the comparison of Austrian and Swedish social democracy are not so much recent decisions concerning economic liberalisation and welfare-state retrenchment, but rather earlier decisions concerning the size of the public (service) sector, female labour-force participation and wage solidarity. The approach to these issues that Swedish social democrats adopted in the 1960s and 1970s created political and social circumstances favorable to their continued mobilisation of electoral support in the 1980s and 1990s – one of these circumstances being sustained union membership growth. The question of why the Austrian social democrats did not adopt the same approach lies beyond the scope of this article, but it should be clear that any attempt to address this question would have to confront the ideological and cultural legacy of Catholicism, at least as far as the role of women is concerned.

With respect to the 1980s and 1990s, one might well argue that the preceding discussion focuses too narrowly on the substance of new policy initiatives. The framing of policy choices may matter more than their substance. In Sweden, the social democrats' embrace of market-oriented reforms, fiscal austerity and the EU occurred in the context of a sustained campaign by employers to restructure Sweden's political economy, and the ascendancy of neo-liberal ideas within the non-socialist bloc. This enabled the social democrats to project themselves as committed to reforming the economy and the state while preserving the basic values of the Swedish model or, in other words, preventing the radical dismantling of the welfare state suggested by the Conservatives' call for a 'system shift'. In comparison with the Swedish case, the Austrian business community remained content and politically quiescent through the 1980s, and the ÖVP did not seek to project itself as an advocate of radical change until very recently. As a result, the Austrian social democrats were perhaps less able to project a distinctive approach to market-oriented reforms, and to deflect the blame for growing economic insecurity and inequality. The more neo-liberal and confrontational posture adopted by the ÖVP clearly helped the SPÖ in the 1995 election.

CONCLUSION

As noted at the outset, the Austrian and Swedish cases are too different from each other to allow us to establish a parsimonious explanation for the divergent fortunes of social-democratic parties and labour movements. At the same time, the comparison of these cases generates many conceptual distinctions and causal arguments that are relevant to the questions which were raised at the outset. Focusing on the question of explaining electoral performance, we have identified several conditions pertaining to employment structure and labour-market dynamics that might be invoked to explain the contrast between the decline of Austrian social democracy and the stability of Swedish social democracy. As these conditions are closely related to one another, they should perhaps be conceived not as discrete independent variables, but rather as the constitutive elements of what might be called a 'causal syndrome'. A second set of conditions, similarly related to one another, that might be invoked to explain the divergent fortunes of Austrian and Swedish social democracy pertain to the structure and dynamics of competition in the political arena.

Starting with conditions of political competition, three main points emerge from the preceding discussion. First, the existence of a party to the left of social democracy, with strong working-class roots, has traditionally forced the Swedish SAP to worry about appeasing its left-leaning constituencies and has served as a vehicle of protest voting, pre-empting the abandonment of social democracy for right-wing populism that we have observed in Austria. Second, the aggressive advocacy of neo-liberal ideas by Swedish employers and the non-socialist parties in the 1980s and 1990s provided a foil for the SAP, enabling the party to project itself as representing a distinctive (socially responsible) approach to economic 'modernisation'. By comparison, Austrian politics would seem to be distinguished by the absence of clearly delineated policy alternatives. Third, the timing of business cycles and alterations in government have been extremely fortuitous for the Swedish social democrats. Governing continuously since 1971, the Austrian social democrats have been unable to shift the blame for economic stagnation, insecurity and growing inequality to other political forces.

The labour-market conditions which we have shown to be relevant are essentially the following: (1) the public sector accounts for a much larger proportion of total employment in Sweden than in Austria; (2) by the 1980s, union density is much higher in Sweden than in Austria; (3) wage solidarity has been a core feature of union ideology in Sweden but not in Austria, and Swedish wage differentials, especially gender differentials, are more compressed than Austrian wage differentials; and (4) female labour-force participation is much higher and working women are more likely to belong to unions in Sweden than in Austria. Again, the expanding public sector was the principal source of new job opportunities for Swedish women in the 1960s and 1970s, and women account for about two-thirds of public-sector employees in Sweden. In both countries, public-sector employees are more likely to belong to unions than private-sector employees, especially people working in private services, and both public-sector employment and union membership correlate strongly with voting for the Left. (Over the period studied here, these correlations have not changed that much.)

In Sweden, public-sector unions have been particularly solidaristic in their approach to wage bargaining, and public-sector employers (often social-democratic government officials) have been more willing to accommodate solidaristic wage demands than their private-sector counterparts.[45] With civil servants (*Beamte*) accounting for a larger share of public-sector employment, the dynamics of public-sector wage bargaining have been different in Austria, but even here pay differentials for men and women in the same jobs are much smaller in the public sector than the private sector. In general, the larger size of the public sector takes us some way towards explaining why wage differentials are more compressed in Sweden than in Austria, and wage solidarity might in turn be invoked to explain the success of Swedish unions in organising women – and poorly paid men as well, of course.

To reiterate, it is not the case that the SPÖ's appeal to women is weaker than its appeal to men – in fact, the opposite is true in the 1990s. In comparison with the SAP, what is distinctive about the SPÖ is that its appeal to housewives and retired women is much stronger than its appeal to working women (see Table 5). This is, of course, closely related to the fact that the SPÖ does much better among older people, and that its electorate has aged more than the SAP electorate over the last 15–20 years.

The question of why unionised wage earners are more likely than non-unionised wage earners to support social-democratic parties lies beyond the scope of this article, but our analysis clearly suggests that strong unions remain an important electoral asset for social-democratic parties. This brings us back to Kitschelt's contention that unions constitute an obstacle to strategic innovation and electoral success for these parties. In terms of union strength or influence in society at large, there can be no doubt that the Swedish labour movement is stronger than its Austrian counterpart. In terms of union influence within the party, the comparison of the two cases is less clear-cut, but it would be difficult to argue that the SPÖ has been significantly more union-dominated than the SAP in the post-war period.

This said, our analysis is entirely consistent with a modified version of Kitschelt's thesis. Drawing on the logic of Mancur Olson's argument about 'encompassment',[46] one might argue that union influence over party decisions constitutes an obstacle to strategic innovation and electoral success to the extent that unions represent the particularistic interests, perhaps privileges, of certain segments of the labour force (and the electorate). Furthermore, the two dimensions of union influence that we have distinguished are not entirely separate, for unions that represent only a small segment of the labour force are unlikely to have a strong voice in party politics. Thus the problem of union-induced strategic rigidity should be most pronounced when traditionally strong unions undergo rapid membership losses. The Austrian case would seem to exemplify this situation; further comparative research would enable us to determine whether the argument applies more generally.

The preceding discussion does not provide a definitive explanation of the decline in union membership in Austria, but it suggests, contrary to the conventional view, that corporatism (at least a certain type of corporatism) may curtail the inclination and/or ability of unions to mobilise new categories of wage earners. As noted above, the Austrian *Kammer* system reduces the incentives for wage earners to belong to unions. Also, our analysis suggests that corporatist arrangements have preserved the dominance of privileged worker groups – in particular, skilled men working in nationalised industry – within the labour movement, and thus rendered Austrian unions less responsive than their Swedish counterparts to other wage-earner interests.

NOTES

The authors wish to express their thanks to Ruth Berins Collier, Chris Howell, Wolfgang Müller, Sidney Tarrow and Graham Wilson for their comments on an earlier draft of this article.

1. Cf. Adam Przeworski and Henry Teune, *The Logic of Comparative Social Inquiry* (NY: Wiley 1970) Ch.2.
2. Cf. Jonas Pontusson, *The Limits of Social Democracy Investment Politics in Sweden* (Ithaca, NY: Cornell UP 1992).
3. For recent contributions to the literature on Austrian corporatism, see Günter Bischof and Anton Pelinka (eds.), *Austro-Corporatism* (London: Transaction 1996); and Mark Crepaz, 'An Institutional Dinosaur: Austrian Corporatism in the Post-industrial Age', *West European Politics* 18/4 (Oct. 1995) pp.64–88.
4. Peter Lange, Michael Wallerstein and Miriam Golden, 'The End of Corporatism?', in Sanford Jacoby (ed.) *The Workers of Nations* (NY: OUP 1995) pp.76–100; Victor Pestoff, 'Towards a New Swedish Model of Collective Bargaining and Politics', in Franz Traxler and Colin Crouch (eds.) *Organised Industrial Relations in Europe* (Aldershot: Avebury 1995) pp.151–82; Jonas Pontusson and Peter Swenson, 'Labour Markets, Production Strategies and Wage-bargaining Institutions', *Comparative Political Studies* 29/2 (April 1996) pp.223–50; and Torben Iversen, 'Power, Flexibility and the Breakdown of Centralised Wage Bargaining', *Comparative Politics* 28 (July 1992) pp.399–436.
5. Helmut Peter, 'Die Zukunft des Kammerstaates', *Österreichisches Jahrbuch für Poltik 1994* (Vienna: Verlag für Geschichte und Politik 1995) pp.609–22; Emmerich Talos, 'Corporatism', in Volkmar Lauber (ed.) *Contemporary Austrian Politics* (Boulder, CO: Westview Press 1996) pp.103–23; and Franz Traxler, 'From Demand-side to Supply-side Corporatism?', in Traxler and Crouch (note 4) pp.271–86.
6. E.g., David Cameron, 'Social Democracy, Corporatism, Labour Quiescence, and the Representation of Economic Interest in Advanced Capitalist Society', in John Goldthorpe (ed.) *Order and Conflict in Contemporary Capitalism* (Oxford: Clarendon Press 1984) pp.143–78; and Geoffrey Garrett, *Partisan Politics in the Global Economy* (Cambridge: CUP forthcoming). The alternative perspective presented here resonates with some of the arguments advanced by Göran Therborn, 'Lessons from "Corporatist" Theorisations', in Jukka Pekkarinen, Matti Pohjola and Bob Rowthorn (eds.) *Social Corporatism* (Oxford: Clarendon Press 1992) pp.24–43.
7. As some readers might find this identification of Green parties with the Left problematic, it should be noted that the Swedish Greens have consistently avoided aligning themselves with the bourgeois (non-socialist) parties and have entered into parliamentary deals with the SAP,

and that most Austrian voters perceive the Greens as being to the left of the SPÖ. On the latter point, see Fritz Plasser, Peter Ulram and Gilig Seeber, '(Dis)Kontinuitäten und neue Spannungslinien im Wählerverhalten', in Plasser, Ulram and Günther Ogris (eds.) *Wahlkampf und Wählerentscheidung* (Vienna: Signum 1996) pp.155–210.

8. For example, Melanie Sully, 'The 1995 Austrian election', *West European Politics* 19/3 (July 1996) pp.633–40.
9. The FPÖ's share of the popular vote increased from 5.0 per cent in 1983 to 22.5 per cent in 1994, and then fell back slightly in 1995 (21.9 per cent). With 26.7 per cent of the vote, the FPÖ came within two percentage points of the SPÖ in the EP election of 1996.
10. The figures in Table 1 refer to 'net union density', that is, unemployed and retired union members have been subtracted from total union membership. Gross union density in Austria fell from 63.6 per cent in 1970 to 57.5 per cent in 1989 according to Traxler, 'Austria', in Anthony Ferner and Richard Hyman (eds.) *Industrial Relations in the New Europe* (Oxford: Blackwell 1992) p.285.
11. Cf. Fritz Plasser, Peter Ulram and Alfred Grausgruber, 'The Decline of "Lager Mentality"and the New Model of Electoral Competition in Austria', *West European Politics* 15/1 (Jan. 1992) pp.16–44, as well as various contributions to Plasser, Ulram and Ogris (note 7) and Wolfgang Müller Fritz Plasser and Peter Ulram (eds.) *Wählerverhalten und Parteienwettbewerb* (Vienna: Signum 1995).
12. Pontusson, 'At the End of the Third Road: Swedish Social Democracy in Crisis', *Politics and Society* 20/3 (Sept. 1992) pp.305–32.
13. As measured by the OECD, the 'public sector' refers to public administration and services: the government employment figures in Table 4 do *not* include employees of nationalised industry.
14. H. Kitschelt, *The Transformation of European Social Democracy* (NY: CUP 1994), and 'Austrian and Swedish Social Democrats in Crisis', *Comparative Political Studies* 27/1 (April 1994) pp.3–39. For a more comprehensive critique, see Pontusson's review of *The Transformation of European Social Democracy*, in ibid. 28/3 (Oct. 1995) pp.469–83.
15. Kitschelt, 'Austrian and Swedish Social Democrats' (note 14) p.24; emphasis added.
16. For a broad-ranging comparison of Austrian and Swedish industrial relations, which touches on many of the points developed in this section, see Traxler, 'European Transformation and Institution-building in East and West', in David Good and Randall Kindley (eds) *Internationalisation and Institution-building* (Boulder, CO: Westview Press, forthcoming).
17. In 1994, the 21 unions affiliated with the LO accounted for 56.8 per cent of total union membership, and the 20 unions affiliated with the TCO accounted for 33.3 per cent. Statistiska centralbyrån, *Statistisk årsbok för Sverige* (1996) p.194.
18. Traxler, 'Austria' (note 10) p.281.
19. The new rules were introduced to pre-empt legislation that would abolish collective affiliation It should be noted that in the case of the SPÖ as well, recent organisational changes have weakened the influence of the unions; for an introductory discussion, see Kitschelt, 'Austrian and Swedish Social Democrats' (note 14).
20. Torsten Svensson, *Socialdemokratins dominans* (Uppsala: Acta Universitatis Upsaliensis 1994).
21. Wolfgang Müller, 'Political Parties', in Lauber (note 5) p.78; figures from Ferdinand Karlhofer, 'The Present and Future State of Social Partnership', in Bischof and Pelinka (note 3) p.140.
22. Pontusson (note 2).
23. Müller (note 21) p.78.
24. This conjecture may seem counter-intuitive from the point of view of spatial voting theory (why would competition from the Left pre-empt losses to the Right?) The premise here is that protest voters do not chose parties based on a Left–Right continuum.
25. Francis Castles, *The Social Democratic Image of Society* (London: RKP 1978); Gösta Esping-Andersen, *Politics Against Markets* (Princeton UP 1985); and Pontusson, 'Swedish Social Democracy and British Labour', *Occasional Papers*, Western Societies Program, Cornell University, 1988.
26. G. Esping-Andersen, *The Three Worlds of Welfare Capitalism* (Princeton UP 1990).

27. See also G. Esping-Andersen and Walter Korpi, 'Social Policy as Class Politics in Post-War Capitalism', in John Goldthorpe (ed.) *Order and Conflict in Contemporary Capitalism* (Oxford: Clarendon Press 1984) pp.179–208.
28. See Stefan Svallfors, *Välfärdsstatens moraliska ekonomi* (Umeå: Boréa 1996) for a comprehensive analysis of Swedish public opinion, showing that core welfare programs enjoy deep and widespread support.
29. Swedish figure from Esping-Andersen, *Three Worlds* (note 26) p.202; Austrian figure based on Öesterreichisches Statistisches Zentralamt, *Mikrozensus*. All figures on labour force participation have been taken from OECD, 'Historical Statistics' (electronic database).
30. Thomas Janoski, 'Direct State Intervention in the Labour Market', in Thomas Janoski and Alexander Hicks (eds.) *The Comparative Political Economy of the Welfare State* (NY: CUP 1994) p.35. More broadly on employment policy, see Fritz Scharpf, *Crisis and Choice in European Social Democracy* (Ithaca, NY: Cornell UP 1991).
31. Scharpf, ibid. Cf. also Peter Katzenstein *Corporatism and Change* (Ithaca, NY: Cornell UP 1984) and Paulette Kurzer, *Business and banking* (Ibid. 1993). The preceding figures on the size of nationalised industry were taken from Delia Meth-Cohn and Wolfgang Müller, 'Looking Reality in the Eye: The Politics of Privatisation in Austria', in Vincent Wright (ed.) *Privatisation in Western Europe* (London: Pinter 1994) p.161, and Pontusson, 'The Triumph of Pragmatism: Nationalisation and Privatisation in Sweden', *West European Politics* 11/4 (Oct. 1988) p.131.
32. Bob Rowthorn, 'Corporatism and Labour Market Performance', in Pekkarinen (note 6) pp.82–131.
33. Alois Guger, 'Lohnpolitik und Sozialpartnerschaft', in Emmerich Talos (ed.) *Sozialpartnerschaft* (Vienna: Verlag für Gesellschaftskritik, 1993) pp.227–41; see also Pontusson, 'Wage Distribution and Labour Market Institutions in Sweden, Austria and other OECD Countries', Working Paper, Institute for European Studies, Cornell University, 1996.
34. Trying hard, we were unable to locate this kind of data for Austrian elections prior to 1986.
35. The Swedish figures on the SAP's share of the union vote include votes cast by LO and TCO members, but not SACO-SR members (many of whom would be classified as *Beamte* in Austria). In 1985, the SAP polled 67 per cent of the LO vote (more than the SPÖ's share of the ÖGB vote) and 38 per cent of the TCO vote. Sören Holmberg and Mikael Gilljam, *Väljare och val i Sverige* (Stockholm: Bonniers 1987) p.188.
36. Perhaps because there are so few housewives in Sweden, the election surveys do not report their votes separately. It is important to keep in mind that Table 5 does not take into account the relative size of these different constituencies: needless to say, an edge among blue-collar workers is much more valuable than an edge among, say, students.
37. Cf. Adam Przeworski and John Sprague, *Paper Stones* (U. of Chicago Press 1986).
38. The potential for rightist protest voting among Swedish blue-collar workers is indicated by the success of New Democracy in 1991, which accounts for that year's sharp drop in the blue-collar/white-collar differential in total voting for the Left (see Table 6). For quantitative evidence on the FPÖ's appeal among male blue-collar workers see Mark Crepaz and Hans-Georg Betz, 'Postindustrial Cleavages and Electoral Change in an Advanced Capitalist Democracy: The Austrian Case', Department of Political Science, University of Georgia (n.d.).
39. Admittedly very rough, these calculations are based on the OECD's *Labour Force Statistics*.
40. Franz Traxler *et al.*, 'Labour Market Regulation and Employment in Austria', Department of Sociology, University of Vienna (n.d.). On collective-bargaining coverage, as distinct from union density, see also OECD, 'Collective Bargaining', *Employment Outlook* (July 1994) pp.167–94.
41. Bo Rothstein, 'Labour-market Institutions and Working Class Strength', in Sven Steinmo, Kathleen Thelen and Frank Longstreth (eds.) *Structuring Politics* (NY: CUP 1992) pp.33–56.
42. Meth-Cohn and Müller (note 31).
43. OECD, 'Trends in Trade Union Membership', *Employment Outlook* (July 1991) p.116; ÖGB *Tätigkeitsbericht 1995* (Vienna: Verlag des ÖGB 1996) p.157; and Statistiska Centralbyrån, *Statistisk årsbok för Sverige* (1996) p.194.

44. Plasser and Ulram, 'Wandel der politischen Konfliktdynamik', in Müller *et al.* (note 11) pp.471–503.
45. Pontusson, 'Wage Distribution' (note 2).
46. Mancur Olson, *The Rise and Decline of Nations* (New Haven, CT: Yale UP 1982).

Building Party Organisations and the Relevance of Past Models: The Communist and Socialist Parties in Spain and Portugal

INGRID VAN BIEZEN

This article explores the development of the party organisations of the communist and socialist parties in contemporary Spain and Portugal. An attempt is made to answer the question of whether these parties resemble the western European mass party model of organisation, which is characterised by the representation and integration of a particular segment of society within the organisational structure. From the contrasting western and southern European paths towards democracy, a hypothesis is generated contending that the limited opportunities and the lack of necessity diminish the likelihood for southern European working-class parties to build mass organisations. The empirical findings, analysing the nature and size of individual membership, as well as the nature of the linkages between parties and trade unions, reveal that, with the possible exception of the Portuguese communists, the classic mass party is not reproduced in southern Europe. At the same time, however, the model of the party as a membership organisation apparently has not lost its legitimacy.

THE PATH TOWARDS DEMOCRACY

The classic typology of political regimes elaborated by Robert Dahl in 1971 not only provides a tool for the classification of political systems, but also allows us to depict the process of transformation from a non-democratic system into a democracy.[1] It is this particular process, or path towards democracy, that can be very influential in determining the type of parties that will emerge in the new democratic system. According to the typology, two basic dimensions underlying a political system can be distinguished. On the one hand, regimes vary according to the degree of public contestation or political competition, that is, the extent to which institutions are openly available and fully guaranteed to those members of the political system who wish to contest the conduct of government. On the other hand, regimes

West European Politics, Vol.21, No.2 (April 1998), pp.32–62
PUBLISHED BY FRANK CASS, LONDON

differ regarding their inclusiveness or degree of participation. This dimension refers to the proportion of the population entitled to participate on a more or less equal basis in controlling and contesting the conduct of the government, namely those who are entitled to participate in the system of public contestation.

In order for a political system to be qualified as a democracy, a minimal requirement is that both the dimensions of political competition and participation are fully maximised. Thus, a democracy is a political system with a maximum freedom to organise and to compete, in which the right of participation is granted to all (adult) citizens. Democracy is then located at the upper-right corner in Figure 1, which presents Dahl's typology of political regimes based upon these two dimensions.[2] The opposite of a democratic regime is a closed hegemony, which denotes a regime that imposes the most severe restrictions on the expression, organisation and representation of political preferences, and on the opportunities available to the opponents of the incumbent government. In these systems, individuals are prohibited from expressing public opposition to the policies and ideology of the ruling leaders, as well as to the major social, economic and political structures as a whole. Organised dissent and opposition are prohibited in any form.[3] Moving from this type of regime towards a larger degree of participation, we encounter the inclusive hegemonies at the other extreme of the dimension. These regimes provide extensive opportunities for participation, but without acknowledging opportunities for public contestation. The opposite of such a system, a competitive oligarchy, is located in the upper-left corner. These are regimes that provide extensive opportunities for public contestation, but only to a very small proportion of society.

FIGURE 1
TYPOLOGY OF POLITICAL REGIMES

Political Competition	Low		High
High	Competitive Oligarchies		Democracies
Low	Closed Hegemonies		Inclusive Hegemonies
	Low	*Participation*	High

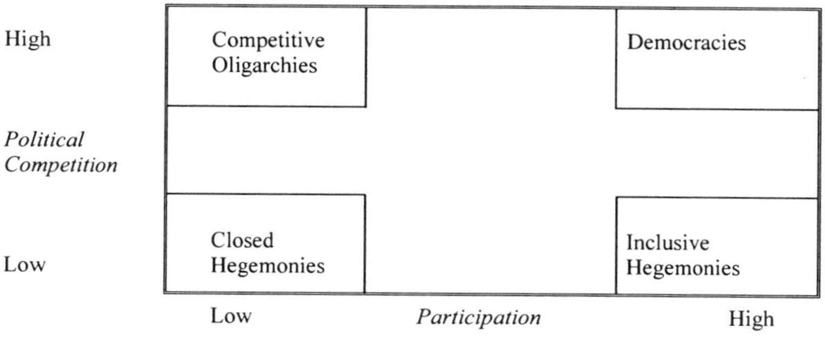

Source: Dahl (note 1).

The typology reveals that basically three different paths towards democracy can be distinguished. If liberalisation precedes inclusiveness, a closed hegemony is transformed into a competitive oligarchy by increasing the possibilities for public contestation, and this regime can subsequently develop towards a democracy by increasing the level of participation. If inclusiveness precedes liberalisation, on the other hand, a closed hegemony first becomes inclusive, and is then transformed into a democracy by increasing the opportunities for public contestation. Finally, regimes can pursue a 'shortcut' from a closed hegemony to democracy, through a simultaneous expansion of suffrage and rights of public contestation.[4]

The three paths can thus be distinguished according to the particular sequence in which political competition and participation are expanded. The relevance of this sequence for the emergence of particular types of party organisation is demonstrated in the next sections of this article, which contrast the processes towards democratisation of late nineteenth and early twentieth-century western Europe with the southern European path of the 1970s. This will offer an illuminating example of how the former is connected to the existence of cadre parties and led to the rise of mass parties, while the latter will prove to leave few opportunities and provide few incentives for a similar development of classic mass parties.

THE WESTERN EUROPEAN EXPERIENCE

By the end of the nineteenth century, only four western European countries had introduced universal male suffrage.[5] Thus, most countries were characterised by a very low level of inclusiveness, whereas at the same time, the degree of public contestation had already reached a relatively high level. During the first half of the twentieth century, all countries established male universal suffrage, which produced a substantial increase in the degree of inclusiveness. The final step towards democracy followed the Second World War, when the restrictions on suffrage for women were abolished, except in Switzerland, where the suffrage for national elections was restricted to adult men until 1971. Hence, the western European regimes of the late nineteenth and the early twentieth century can be classified as competitive oligarchies, characterised by a relatively high degree of political competition and a low level of inclusiveness, which transformed themselves into democratic systems by increasing the level of participation, that is, by introducing universal suffrage. The democratisation process thus involved, most of all, the enlargement of the degree of participation or inclusiveness in already competitive political systems.

How, then, does this path towards democracy relate to the particular type of party that existed or emerged in western Europe? The most important observation to be made here is that liberalisation preceded inclusiveness. In the competitive oligarchies a constitutional system with an elected parliament was already in existence before the right of participation was extended to the population at large. This system was supported by an allegiant middle class and led by an experienced political élite. The restrictive suffrage excluded a large group of society from the political system and thus it was a small élite closely connected to the powerful élites of civil society that dominated politics in this era. Since these political élites were in a position to make direct demands on the state, there was no need for intermediaries between civil society and the state. In order to be elected, these élites heavily relied on local status and connections. As a consequence, in this type of political system there was little need for highly-structured political organisations. The liberal and conservative parties, which are usually among the oldest parties in each system, in this period can be characterised as cadre parties.[6] As Katz and Mair suggest, these parties were basically committees of those who constituted the leadership in both the state and civil society.[7]

Thus, in terms of the cleavage structure, the political system mirrored the class cleavage almost perfectly, in that it included the 'owners' and excluded 'workers', and also women, from participating. As a product of nineteenth-century industrialisation, a working class of a considerable size had emerged before the members of this class were granted the right to vote. The sharp separation of the subordinate working classes from the middle classes and the aristocracy, nourished their awareness of the need for the representation of their own distinct interests. As the urban and rural working classes increased in numbers, they began to develop political consciousness and demands and increasingly felt the necessity of organising not only industrially but also politically, which led to the emergence of working-class parties. It can be argued that European class-conscious socialism was partly fostered by the long delay in universal suffrage and that the institutional arrangement, which excluded the working classes from the political system provided the basis for the organisation of socialist working-class parties.[8]

These parties were usually created externally, that is, outside the legislature.[9] In the case of internally created parties, the leaders held public office first and established relationships with local electoral committees and followers afterwards. Conversely, working-class parties – and, in some countries, also religious parties – were movements outside parliament before they were parties competing for power. Because of the need felt to mobilise an underprivileged class which, in most countries, until then had been denied a role in the political system, organisation was achieved before they engaged in electoral competition. For its success, the working-class party had to depend on large numbers of supporters. Individually, the workers were too weak. Michels puts it as follows:

> It is easy to understand [...] that organization has become a vital principle of the working class, for in default of it their success is a *priori* impossible. [...] It is only by combination to form a structural aggregate that the proletarians can acquire the faculty of political resistance and attain to a social dignity. The importance and influence of the working class are directly proportional to its numerical strength. [...] For the representation of that numerical strength organization and coordination are indispensable. The principle of organization is an absolutely essential condition for the political struggle of the masses.[10]

In order to challenge the existing economic and political order effectively and to gain access to the existing structures the working-class parties had to rely on a large number of supporters. Moreover, members were needed for financial reasons. Unlike parties representing the entrepreneurial classes, working-class parties could not count on large contributions from wealthy individuals. Membership dues are, therefore, the most important financial resource for a working-class party. Since these dues cannot be high, large numbers of members are needed in order to generate significant financial resources. The creation of a mass-based party, therefore, was an organisational necessity.[11] Furthermore, the concurrence of economic and political demands has made a significant contribution to a 'natural affinity' between working-class parties and trade unions, because of their common roots as the 'Siamese twins' of the labour movement.[12] In most countries an 'interlocking' cross-linkage between socialist parties and unions existed, that is, as Bartolini points out, one 'characterised by a profound interpenetration of corporate and electoral organisations, reinforcing each other on the basis of leadership and membership overlap and interchange, support-base coincidence, and a wide arena of common collective activities'.[13]

When the ruling political élites of the upper and middle classes faced this serious crisis, generated by the class conflict, and potentially endangering the persistence of parliamentary democracy, the problem was how to gain the allegiance of the working class without alienating the other social strata. In most western European countries the traditional élites reacted to this crisis by accommodating the emergent demands. The ruling political élites succeeded in acquiring the support of the alienated working class for the already operating parliamentary system by peacefully offering them participation in political life.[14] The political leaders representing the working class were allowed to build their organisational networks drawing support from the working classes, and, thus, in most countries viable working class parties were formed before the right to vote was acquired for all workers. Moreover, the political leaders representing the working classes were permitted to participate in political decisions and in some cases even to enter coalition governments. The political élites in parliament, then consisting of both the upper and middle classes, on the one hand, and the working class, on the other, subsequently agreed upon the extension of suffrage, after which the parties started to encapsulate large parts of the suddenly available electorate. The working classes thus played a decisive role in the final push for democracy in western Europe, although their success depended on the collaboration of other classes.[15]

Hence, the emergence of working-class mass parties in late nineteenth and early twentieth-century Europe is to a large extent due to the particular circumstances on the eve of the breakthrough to democratisation and mass mobilisation. To a large extent, it has been the institutional arrangement, that is the institutionalised division of political rights of participation, including a certain economically privileged sector and at the same time excluding economically underprivileged ones, which can be held accountable for the existence of cadre parties and the subsequent emergence of mass parties. That is, the sequence of developments, in which liberalisation precedes inclusiveness, allowed for the development of a parliamentary system with parties of the cadre type and the subsequent emergence of working-class mass parties. In virtually all countries, universal suffrage was introduced only after the creation of mass parties with a national party organisation had been accomplished.

THE SOUTHERN EUROPEAN PATH

Following the same logic, the nature of the political regimes before democratisation in southern Europe needs to be established in order to assess the impact of the path towards democracy on the type of parties that emerge. Spain and Portugal were authoritarian regimes, which denied the legitimacy of opposition movements contesting the policy or ideology of the regime, whereas in the early western European systems with a high degree of public contestation the validity of organised dissent was recognised and opposition was institutionalised. In southern Europe, the monopolistic position held by the ruling party impeded the existence and voluntary creation of competing political organisations. Franco's aversion to political parties and political pluralism, which he believed would lead to conflict and disintegration and would threaten the national unity, caused him to ban all political organisations other than the *Movimiento*.[16] A large majority of the seats in parliament were occupied by ex-officio members of the Falange and appointees designated personally by Franco. In municipal elections, some of the seats were allocated by 'inorganic' vote, to which only the heads of families and married women were entitled.[17]

As in Spain, the authoritarian regime in Portugal did not achieve the institutionalisation of permanent mediating structures between citizenry and government or the establishment of an organic-corporatist state.[18] In Salazar's *Estado Novo* there was not much room for the organisation of political opposition to the predominant *União Nacional*. Furthermore, the regime showed little interest in mass mobilisation. Although elections were held regularly, illiterates were excluded from participation, as were women until 1968. Moreover, due to the government manipulation of the registration process, the number of electorate actually registered was considerably smaller than the population potentially eligible to vote, amounting to only seven or eight per cent of the population.[19]

Because of the limited possibilities to organise dissent in order to 'contest the conduct of government' and the equally limited level of inclusion of citizens within the political system, the authoritarian regimes of Portugal and Spain can be classified as closed hegemonies. While in western Europe the path towards democracy departed from a competitive oligarchy and primarily entailed the extension of participation in an already reasonably developed system of public contestation, the process of democratisation in southern Europe essentially involved the sudden and virtually simultaneous enlargement of both political competition and participation. This particular path, as is argued in the following section, reduces both the need and the opportunities for southern European working-class parties to create a party organisation resembling the classic mass party.

DISINCENTIVES FOR THE EMERGENCE OF MASS PARTIES

Limited Opportunities

The political parties that originated after the outset of the transition, that is, after the military coup in Portugal and the death of Franco in Spain, emerged in a very volatile institutional environment. Unlike in western Europe, a party system was absent when the southern European working-class parties appeared. This is not to say that there were no parties whatsoever, but it refers to the absence of an institutionalised configuration of patterned interactions between political parties, through which the emerging demands could be channelled. A host of political parties and associations rapidly emerged or, in the case of the parties that had survived the decades of authoritarianism underground, resuscitated their organisation. All actors involved competed to capture a permanent position in the political vacuum left behind by the collapse of the regimes. In

Portugal, this process was accompanied by a high level of political turmoil and mass upheaval, whereas in Spain the transition was managed effectively 'from above' through what has become known as a *ruptura pactada* or *reforma pactada*: a gradual and negotiated change of the regime.

What is important to note is that the future shape of the institutional framework itself was the principal focus of all the parties involved. Even though neither in Portugal nor in Spain was it clear from the beginning that the country was heading towards a liberal democracy resembling the western European model, it was obvious that the status quo could not be maintained. The principal concern of all parties was, therefore, the nature of the successor regime. That the different actors involved often had diametrically opposed preferences – such as the democratic parties in Portugal which tried to impose a counterweight against the too radical aspirations of the communist forces, or the neo-Franquist *Alianza Popular* in Spain, which initially firmly opposed the dismantling of the old regime or a democratic opening up of the system – is less relevant in this regard. What all parties shared was a preoccupation with the future shape of the institutions, and the uncertainty about the outcome enhanced the pressures on institutional changes from all parties.

Even after the first elections were held, the new democratic institutional architecture was far from completed. Parties now engaged in debates and negotiations over the writing of the new constitution, the powers to be granted to parliament and president, the reform of the judiciary, the submission of the military to civilian control, and the question of regional autonomy. In addition to these political-institutional matters, they had to deal with questions of economic and agricultural reform, the construction of a welfare state, as well as the demands imposed by the international environment. Given the magnitude and the extent of the parties' duties, we may expect that the organisation of government and parliament, if not democracy as a whole, as well as the formation of public policy, will have occupied relatively much of the parties time and energy. Time and energy concentrated on the activities of parties in parliament and government is likely to have been spent at the expense of attention towards the building and structuring of the party organisation on the ground. This is true for both government and opposition parties. Panebianco argues that for parties in opposition 'strengthening their organisation, making it able to mobilize the party's supporters efficiently and continuously, is usually the only practicable way to overcome the disadvantages in the competition with governmental parties.'[20] But this observation seems to hold true primarily once the party system has acquired a certain degree of stability and the new democratic system has become more or less institutionalised. In newly emerging democratic polities, on the other hand, the boundaries between government and opposition parties may not always be sufficiently crystallised, or institution building and policy formation may be based on a mutual involvement of both government and opposition parties, making the analytic distinction on the basis of governmental status less relevant for the consequences on the type of party organisation.

In addition to the focus on the governing function and institution building, the state of the party organisations at the time of the transition plus the short time-span available for organisational development may have a strong impact on the type of party organisation. A lot of parties were newly created formations, founded only shortly before or during the transition. These parties usually consisted of a group of prominent élites at the national level and lacked a solid organisational infrastructure.[21] Similarly, the organisational structure of the parties that could count on a history dating back to the pre-authoritarian period – namely the Spanish Socialist Workers' Party (PSOE) and the communist parties in both countries, the PCE in Spain and the PCP in Portugal – was in a very weak condition. The decades of having to work in secret during the authoritarian regimes had seriously hindered their organisational development, simply because dissident political organisation was not tolerated and, most of the time, these parties were pointedly harassed. Unlike the western European working-class parties, whose extra-parliamentary mobilisation efforts were left relatively undisturbed, their southern European counterparts were forced to operate as underground movements. The different organisational units were often loosely connected to each other, while the party leadership in exile increasingly lost touch with the organisation at home. While the working-class parties in western Europe gradually passed what Rokkan referred to as the thresholds of legitimation, incorporation, representation and, eventually, executive power,[22] in southern Europe they did not overcome the first hurdle until after the fall of the authoritarian regime. Where in most western European countries working-class mobilisation had preceded the creation of a national party organisation, the parties in Portugal and Spain followed a reverse process. Moreover, by the time they finally were able to initiate serious efforts to mobilise members and supporters, there were other things at stake, such as the shaping of the new institutions, which may have had a higher priority.

This leads to the next consideration, which is the time-span between passing the thresholds of legitimation and incorporation on the one hand, and representation and executive power on the other. Recalling the western European experience, working-class parties emerged in an institutional environment in which the right to demonstrate and participate provided them with the opportunity to mobilise and construct an extra-parliamentary mass organisation prior to acknowledging their right to representation and executive power. Only after surmounting the latter two thresholds was their party organisation expanded with an additional element: the party in public office. That is, the party in parliament first, and later the party in government. In general, the party in public office acted as an agent of the earlier created extra-parliamentary party or the party on the ground.[23]

In southern Europe, the period in which these thresholds were overcome was much shorter. In fact, it could be argued that all four were surmounted more or less simultaneously. In Spain, for example, the PSOE was legalised only four months before the 1977 elections, whereas for the PCE the interval between legalisation and elections was only six weeks. It would then take another five years before the PSOE acquired executive power, but the PCP and the PS in Portugal already participated in the provisional governments installed after the revolution.[24] Hence, they almost immediately exceeded the last hurdle, which in western Europe usually had been the final step after a protracted process of organisational development.[25] Thus, before an articulated extra-parliamentary organisation had been developed, southern European working-class parties acquired parliamentary representation and, as in the case of Portugal, government responsibility, forcing them to divide their attention between extra-parliamentary and intra-parliamentary affairs. Because of the significance of the latter, and especially the importance of shaping the new institutional framework, it is likely that this will have diminished a concern for the extra-parliamentary party, and particularly the party organisation on the ground. In addition to the relevance of the party in public office as such, I would argue that it is perhaps equally important to notice the particular moment in the parties' organisational development when the party in public office acquires importance, that is, before, or concurrent with, the opportunities for a substantial development of the extra-parliamentary party, as this may enhance the parties' orientation towards the state and reduce the incentives to connect the party organisation to society.

In addition, the short interval between the beginning of the transition and the first elections not only provided parties with relatively little time for approaching members and expanding the extra-parliamentary party organisation, it also compelled parties to make a strategic choice in the electoral arena. Given the virtual absence or relatively weakness of the party organisation, largely as a result of the oppression of the authoritarian regimes, southern European communist and socialist parties had never been able to mobilise and integrate or even encapsulate major components of the society. With the sudden expansion of the level of participation almost immediately after the collapse of the authoritarian regimes, millions of newly enfranchised voters entered the electoral arena. Parties needed to capture their votes, but unlike the western European mass parties, they lacked the stable constituencies with durable political identities which had allowed these parties to narrow down the electoral market and ultimately resulted in the freezing of the cleavages and the stabilisation of the party systems in western Europe. Because of the absence of stable party identities and party alignments in Spain and Portugal, in combination with the absence of a stable and solid constituency, an expansive electoral strategy may seem to have been the most effective way in an open electoral market to approach the new and highly available electorate in order to maximise the number of parliamentary seats. Rather than defending the interests of a specific *classe gardée*, parties will be encouraged to attract as many voters as possible, thereby crossing the boundaries of social or economic divisions in society. Voters are probably the first objective, while members and party structures may come later.[26]

Lack of Necessity

As argued above, the need to organise working-class mass parties in western Europe largely stems from the institutionalised exclusion of the workers from participation in the political system. Large numbers of members and supporters were indispensable in order to be able to challenge the existing order. It could be contended that the closed nature of the authoritarian regimes in Spain and Portugal provided the excluded sector of society with a similar basis to organise and need to mobilise in order to overthrow the regime. However, if that were to be the case, and if the parties opposing the political regime indeed felt a similar need to mobilise a large number of supporters, aspirations for a mass organisation could not materialise because of the hegemonic character of the regime, which ensured that dissenting elements were effectively thwarted. After the demise of the authoritarian regimes, when the level of political competition was expanded and thus the factors obstructing organisational development had become largely irrelevant, large numbers of party members were no longer an organisational prerequisite for challenging the political order, simply because of the subsequent expansion of the participation, that is, the abolition of political exclusion. With the evaporation of the political dimension, the basis for the organisation of working-class parties had been reduced to merely an economic one, in which the socio-economic stratification which had persisted under the authoritarian regimes provided a social underpinning for parties representing and defending the interests of the working class. But, given the disappearance of political inequalities and the increase of public contestation, which allowed parties to penetrate the parliamentary arena almost immediately, the parties may have found it as opportune to operate from within rather than outside parliament in order to achieve their objectives. They may even have considered the seizure of a large number of seats, in order to strengthen their influence in the decision-making process or to enhance the likelihood of government responsibility, a more appropriate strategy in this respect.

Another incentive for the early western European working-class parties to attract as many members as possible was provided by finances. The parties in the new democracies of Spain and Portugal, however, do not need the financial contributions of affiliated citizens for their organisational survival. In both countries, parties have been quite generous to themselves in introducing large amounts of state subventions. Both the parliamentary group and the party central office receive annual subsidies from the state in order to cover regular organisational expenditures and an additional amount is granted to the parties for the expenditures during election years.[27]

Although this amount of money is not always sufficient to cover all the expenses and a lot of parties are seriously in debt, an analysis of the parties' budgets reveals that membership dues contribute only a very small proportion of the total income. For some parties, state subsidies contribute almost 95 per cent of their income, indicating a virtually complete dependence on the state. Moreover, the fact that the state subsidies are granted in accordance with the electoral results of the parties makes them highly reliant on favourable electoral outcomes. An unfortunate electoral result can bring the party to the verge of bankruptcy, as happened to the PCE after the 1982 elections, when the party fell back from 23 to only 4 seats. Since voters are financially more valuable than members, an indirect consequence of the large amounts of state subsidies is that they may shift the balance towards electoral rather than membership mobilisation.

Evidently, it can be argued that party membership not only entails costs but also benefits.[28] For example, a large membership equips the party with a substantial source of human resources necessary to fulfil the function of political recruitment. A high level of membership may also be valuable because members are the most loyal party voters. Or a large membership may be regarded as proof that the party has significant roots in society, thus serving as a source of legitimacy. On the other hand, members may be a nuisance because they tend to support vote-losing policies. That is, they may be motivated by ideological concerns, even at the expense of electoral defeat.[29] They may also waste organisational resources which could have been used to approach the undecided voters. In general, although parties will need to develop at least some structures on the ground, if only to recruit candidates for national and local public office,[30] in the new southern European democracies there seem to be few incentives for large- scale membership mobilisation.

It can also be expected that parties and trade unions in new democracies act more autonomously of one another than their western European counterparts. The absence of concurrent political and economic demands has made the establishment of strong links between parties and trade unions less necessary. Although connections with organised interests may encourage the stabilisation of a party's constituency and may be regarded as a source of legitimacy, they also constitute a restraint, in that close relationships may require too narrow commitments and put a constraint on electorally expansionist strategies, and may also be conducive to intra-party conflicts. Moreover, the trade unions themselves may be wary of too close linkages, and prefer to approach the parties in parliament or government directly, thus maintaining a more autonomous relationship with the parties.

In sum, there seem to be few opportunities and little necessity to develop a mass type of party organisation for the socialist and communist parties in southern Europe. The fact that the democratisation process departed from a closed hegemony, characterised by a low level of political competition, implies that the opportunities for organisation building had been severely curtailed as a result of the oppressive nature of the pre-democratic regime. Consequently, parties entered the post-authoritarian era with an insignificant or underdeveloped organisational structure, which was probably even weaker in the case of newly created parties. The simultaneous expansion of both public contestation and participation left parties with very little time to prepare for the first elections, in which they faced a relatively unaligned electorate. This, in addition to the significance of the parties' duties in reshaping the institutional environment and the quick access to representation and executive power, will restrict the opportunities for southern European working-class parties to mobilise the citizenry and build a strong party organisation on the ground. Given the absence of the need to build a political organisation representing an excluded and underprivileged segment of society, the creation of a mass party can hardly be considered an organisational necessity in the new southern European democracies. Furthermore, large numbers of members were not needed for financial reasons, and, more generally, the benefits traditionally associated with a sizeable party membership may not have outweighed the costs of the establishment of a large membership organisation, or the short term benefits of a more electoralist linkage.

For all these reasons, and in contrast to the early western European experience, it is unlikely that the size or structure of developing party organisations in southern Europe will have a lot in common with the classic mass party.[31] In the following sections, therefore, it is intended to review the empirical evidence to see whether features of the mass party have actually been reproduced in these countries, or whether, for the reasons outlined above, these parties have persisted as parliamentary rather than societal organisations.

THE PRACTICE OF ORGANISATIONAL DEVELOPMENT

This section analyses the constitutions and other internal party documents of the communist and socialist parties in Spain and Portugal: the PCP, the PCE, the PSOE and the PS.[32] Special emphasis will be upon the nature and size of individual membership, namely those who individually join the party, and on organised interest groups: the external organisations which are either affiliated 'en bloc' to a party or which are not officially affiliated but nevertheless maintain close contacts with a particular party.[33] This analysis of the official position of the party with regard to individual and corporate membership probes into the question of the development of the party as a membership organisation, which is one of the crucial characteristics of a mass-type of organisation.

Individual Membership

In order to assess the nature of individual membership, party attitudes towards membership as well as the position of individual members within the party organisation, emanating from official party documents, will be examined. From the party constitutions, a clear division between the PCP, the PCE and the PSOE, on the one hand, and the PS, on the other, emerges. Both communist parties demand a very strong commitment from their members. It is their duty to participate actively within and outside the party organisation. Members have to attend party meetings on a regular basis, defend and promulgate the policy and ideology of the party by maintaining close links with the population in general and the working class in particular, they have to recruit new members for the party and contribute actively to the distribution of the party's output. Moreover, not only do they have to accept the programme and constitution of the party – which is a common requirement for most parties – but they also have to be acquainted with the party's ideological orientation and have to increase their level of political and ideological knowledge through a constant study of the party's ideological principles and its political activities. Since the revision of the constitution at the PCE's 13th Congress in 1991, the demands with regard to the members' duties, especially those concerning the ideological commitment, are reduced somewhat. An active participatory posture is, however, still required.

Although the PSOE does not demand an equally strong ideological commitment from its members, the constitution of this party, too, requires an active participation in the activities and meetings organised by the party, as well as 'the realisation of their political, social and trade-union duties'. For the members of the PS, in contrast, participation is a right rather than a duty. Only at the party's second congress in 1977, the new constitution introduced the party members' duty to participate at least once a month in the meetings of the local branch to which they belong. Very soon, however, participation ceased to be a duty and became a right, thereby reducing the required active involvement of its members in party activities.

Thus, from the constitutions, which are an indication of the official position of the party, it can be concluded that the PS is the only one of the four parties considered here, that does not demand an active involvement of its members. The other three emphasise the importance of a participatory linkage with their membership, which is an important characteristic of a mass-type of organisation. More remarkably, from the resolutions of the national congresses, it becomes clear that they all four claim to be a mass party. This seems to deviate from the hypothesis, which led us to expect that parties would not need or want to develop an organisation with well entrenched members on the ground. Apparently, the lack of need does not diminish the desire to develop a mass-party organisation.

However, not all parties continue to propagate this aspiration. The resolutions reveal that the PSOE moderates its radical rhetoric first after its extraordinary congress of 1979, when the Marxist ideology was abolished, and even more after entering government in 1982, after which it gradually ceases to be a class-based mass party. For the PS, the mass-party aspirations seem to be even more ephemeral, since such proclamations appear only in the resolutions of 1979. In this respect, the two socialist parties seem to confirm the initial expectations. For the PSOE, its historical organisational model initially may have pushed the party to continue its original model of organisation building. Once in government, the priority of intra-parliamentary affairs acquires an additional relevance and the care for the organised party on the ground diminishes accordingly. Like the PSOE, the PS was also a party of government. Moreover, since it was a newly created party that did not emerge out of the conflict of labour and capital it was, unlike the PSOE, not hindered by constraints imposed by an organisational or ideological heritage. Thus, it is not surprising that the PS closely approaches the hypothesis, in that it never made a serious effort to construct a mass party and does not wish to create an actively organised membership. Moreover, both socialist parties occupy an important position in the respective party systems as they are located close to the centre. This enhances the opportunities for expansive electoral strategies, reaching out to non-working-class segments situated close to the centre of the political spectrum. However, all this is not to say that membership as such has become less relevant. A closer look at the levels of individual affiliation (see Table 1) and the parties' attitudes towards developments in this area will further clarify this.[34]

Due to its virtual monopoly as opposition movement under Franco, the

PCE in comparison with the other parties already possessed a substantial number of party members at the outset of the transition. It is estimated that at that time, the party could count on some 15,000 members. The organisational strategy followed by the PCE after the transition emphasised the further mobilisation of the masses and the expansion of membership. The increase in party membership was indeed impressive. By late 1977 the PCE had more than 200,000 members.[35] The party clearly followed a strategy of mass mobilisation and aspired to construct a party in accordance with the characteristics of a mass party. However, the party seems to have reached its peak already by the end of 1977, after which membership figures started to decline rapidly. Especially during the early 1980s, when the PCE suffered from heavy internal disputes, the loss of members was dramatic. Between 1981 and 1983 almost half of the members abandoned the party. The declining trend appeared to be irreversible, although it continued thereafter at a lower rate. In 1995 party affiliation had fallen to less than 35,000.[36]

The PCP also followed an effective strategy of membership mobilisation, but unlike its Spanish counterpart, its success was not limited to the period immediately after the fall of the authoritarian regime. Between 1974 and 1976, membership increased rapidly from almost 15,000 to 115,000, and continued to grow to a level of over 200,000 in 1983. Until 1988 the level of affiliation remained pretty stable, after which it dropped to about 163,000 in 1992 and further decreased to approximately 140,000 in 1996.[37] Despite this decline, the membership organisation of the PCP continues to be the largest of all Portuguese parties.

In its early post-authoritarian existence, the PSOE also strongly advocated efforts to build a mass organisation. The increase in membership from about 4,000 to over 50,000 on the eve of the elections in 1977 can be regarded as a step in this direction. Only one year later the party had nearly doubled its membership, now totalling almost 100,000 members. Over the years, the affiliation to the PSOE continued to increase, with only one small dip between 1979 and 1981. During its first years in government, the PSOE membership received a new impetus, with an increase of almost 33,000 in one year. But the last two years of the first socialist legislature were less successful in this respect, when membership grew by only 7,000 between 1984 and 1986. Until the fourth legislature, membership increased fairly constantly by an average of 25,000 to 30,000 per year. After 1993, the growth rate diminished somewhat, but there is no sign of stagnation or decline. The figures for the PS are more difficult to interpret, but it can be concluded that in its early years the party performed somewhat better in terms of membership registration. After a decline, the number of members seems to have stabilised at about 70,000 in the 1990s.

TABLE 1
PARTY MEMBERSHIP

	PCP	PS	PCE	PSOE
1974	14,593	35,971		
1975	100,000	81,654	15,000	4,000
1976	115,000	91,562		9,141
1977				51,552
1978	142,000	96,563	201,740	99,500
1979	164,713			101,082
1980	187,018			
1981			160,000	97,356
1982				112,591
1983	200,753	130,181	84,652	145,471
1984		139,000		153,076
1985			70,000	
1986		46,655		160,000
1987				
1988	199,275		49,000	213,015
1989		62,117		
1990				262,900
1991		69,351	44,775	
1992	163,506	70,000		325,424
1993				
1994				350,173
1995			34,704	362,662
1996	140,000			365,090

Note: The figures for the PS in 1983 and 1984 are uncertain. The 1996 figure for the PSOE corresponds to May 1996.

Sources: Gunther (note 58); Gunther *et al.* (note 21), José Ramón Montero, 'Partidos y Participación Política: Algunas Notas sobre la Afiliación Política en la Etapa Inicial de la Transición Española', *Revista de Estudios Políticos* 23 (1981); Leonardo Morlino, 'Political Parties and Democratic Consolidation in Southern Europe', in Richard Gunther, P. Nikiforos Diamandouros, and Hans-Jürgen Puhle (eds.) *The Politics of Democratic Consolidation: Southern Europe in Comparative Perspective* (Baltimore, MD: Johns Hopkins UP 1995); José Félix Tezanos, 'Continuidad y Cambio en el Socialismo Español: El PSOE durante la Transición Democrática', in idem, Ramón Cotarelo and Andres de Blas (eds.) *La Transición Democrática Española* (Madrid: Sistema 1989); and official party data.

How do the parties evaluate their own levels of affiliation? The party resolutions indicate a serious concern about the number of affiliated citizens or the need to further increase affiliation, regardless of whether a party has experienced growth or decline. The PCE has the most reasons to worry, since, first of all its aspirations to a mass rank-and-file have never materialised. Second, it has seen its level of membership decline very rapidly, to represent a very insignificant proportion of the electorate: from 0.9 at its affiliational peak in 1978 to only 0.1 in 1995. Table 2 presents the figures on partisan mobilisation; membership is calculated as a percentage of the electorate (M/E) and as a percentage of the number of votes for the party (M/V). The figures on member-to-voter ratio show that the PCE never had a large basis of loyal supporters. Between 1978 and 1983, about every tenth voter was also a member of the party, which decreased to one in 65 in 1995. This weak partisan mobilisation constitutes a continuing source of concern for the party.

TABLE 2
PARTISAN MOBILISATION (%)

	PCP		PS		PCE		PSOE	
	M/E	M/V	M/E	M/V	M/E	M/V	M/E	M/V
1975	1.6	14.0	1.3	3.8				
1976	1.8	14.6	1.4	4.8				
1977							0.2	1.0
1978	2.2	18.1	1.5	5.1	0.9	11.8	0.4	1.9
1979	2.4	14.6					0.4	1.9
1980	2.7	18.5						
1981					0.6	8.3	0.4	1.8
1982							0.4	1.1
1983	2.7	19.5	1.7	6.3	0.3	10.0	0.5	1.4
1984			1.9	6.7			0.6	1.5
1985					0.7	8.3		
1986			0.6	3.9			0.6	1.8
1987								
1988	2.5	28.9			0.2	5.2	0.7	2.4
1989			0.8	4.9				
1990							1.0	3.2
1991			0.8	4.2	0.2	2.4		
1992	1.9	32.4	0.8	4.2			1.1	4.0
1993								
1994							1.1	3.8
1995					0.1	1.5	1.2	4.0
1996	1.6	27.8					1.1	3.9

Note: The percentages for the years in which no national elections were held are based on the size of the electorate or the number of votes in the previous election year. For the PCP, the number of votes are those cast on the electoral coalitions (*Aliança Povo Unido* – APU and *Coligação Democrática Unitária* – CDU) in which the party participated as the most important part of the coalition since the 1979 legislative elections. For the PCE, from 1986 onwards, the number of votes are those cast on *Izquierda Unida* (IU).

Sources: For the election results in Spain: *Ministerio de Justicia e Interior*; for Portugal: *Comissão Nacional de Eleições* and *Assembleia da República*. For the data on party membership: see Table 1.

Despite the continuing growth, the development of its membership does not seem altogether satisfactory for the PSOE either. In 1979, the federal executive commission observed that '[t]he political events that our country is experiencing occur more rapidly than our efforts to provide the PSOE with an infrastructure that permits the consolidation of the public projection of the party in harmony with its own infrastructure'.[38] At this time, not even two per cent of the voters for the party were also members. The low level of membership continues to be one of the major organisational problems of the party, and, consequently, 'corrective measures' to overcome this deficiency have a high priority. It is clear that the PSOE aspires to a strong implantation in society for which an expansion of the organisation is absolutely necessary. In 1994, the party observed that the level of affiliation still did not correspond to the political role that the PSOE played in the Spanish society. Partisan mobilisation is still very low, only one out of 25 voters is a member of the party. Therefore, a permanent increase in membership remains one of the party's primary objectives.

Like the Spanish Socialist Party, the Portuguese PS has a much larger electoral constituency in comparison with its membership adhesion. In 1986, this induced the party to initiate a large campaign to improve organisational implantation and to expand its membership.[39] However, even though the PS preserves the model of the party as a membership organisation, the traditional mode of integration is no longer considered appropriate:

> [T]he model that has served as a matrix for the traditional organisation of democratic-socialist, social-democratic and labour parties, has been put aside by modern society (which is open, atomised and communicational), by the increasing complexity of the political debate and by the alteration in the conditions and modes of political participation. In a modern political party, the essential function is no longer recruitment, mobilisation or integration, but the collection and production of information and its communication.[40]

The PCP on the other hand, is quite successful in terms of partisan mobilisation. Although its membership as a percentage of the electorate is rather low, the organisational encapsulation of voters reveals that the PCP has established a relatively large core of loyal party supporters. In 1996, almost every third voter for the PCP was also a member of the party. Still, as for all four parties, the need to increase the recruitment of new militants never diminishes.

In general, it can be concluded that increasing the level of membership is one of the parties' principal objectives. However, one important difference between the PCP, on the one hand, and the other three parties on the other, deserves special attention. The PCP seems to be more concerned with the creation of an active cadre of militants, rather than with increasing the level of affiliation as such: 'a party member who continues to consider his affiliation to the party as a formal act, which is not linked to an activity, to a contribution to the general actions of the party, has evidently not assimilated the fundamental element of our party constitution and our political practice'.[41] For the PCP, participation in other parties is a facade and merely consists of the meaningless periodical exercise of the delegation of power by means of voting. In contrast, the Portuguese communists are primarily concerned with the establishment of a participatory linkage through the encadrement of their rank-and-file, and the enhancement of the level of participation of their members within the party as well as on the shopfloor.

In part, this can be explained by the marginal position of the PCP in the Portuguese party system, largely due to its persisting adherence to an orthodox Marxist-Leninist ideology.[42] The PS, the PSOE and, to a lesser extent, the PCE, on the other hand, seem to appreciate having a large membership in general. This indicates that it is not the model of the party as a membership organisation that has lost its validity, but rather the model of the party that consists of a bottom-up structure wherein members are integrated and organised into local branches. A clear example of the persisting relevance attributed to party members, while at the same time contrasting most visibly with the mass organisational characteristics of the PCP, is provided by the PS. At its 10th Congress in 1992, the party increased the level of direct participation of its members by allowing them to directly elect the secretary-general. Similar to many other western European parties, the party ceded more decision-making powers to its members whereby 'the process of intra-party democratisation is being extended to the members as individuals rather than to what might be called the *organised* party on the ground'.[43]

The following section deals with the relationship between parties and organised interest groups and examines whether the nature of the linkages corresponds to the expected autonomy, and how the relationship relates to the developments of individual membership described above.

Organised Interests

An analysis of the party constitutions reveals that the PSOE was the only party with a formalised link to a trade union, the General Workers' Union (*Unión General de Trabajadores* – UGT): party members were obliged by the constitution to affiliate to the UGT. That is as far as the formal linkage went. There were no other provisions concerning the relationship between party and trade union, such as, for example, the rights the UGT enjoyed with regard to participation within the party organisation or representation on the party's executive committees. The constitutions of the other parties make no explicit reference whatsoever to affiliated trade unions.

However, from this absence of formalised linkages between political parties and trade unions it cannot directly be inferred that close linkages do not exist. It is important to underline that they actually do exist in political practice.[44] Traditionally, the PSOE had been closely related to the UGT, which was founded by the party in 1888. The Spanish Communist Party, the PCE, had found an ally in the Workers' Commissions (*Comisiones Obreras* – CCOO), which co-operated closely with it as an underground resistance movement under Franco. Its Portuguese counterpart, the PCP, was closely connected to the General Confederation of Portuguese Workers (*Confederação Geral dos Trabalhadores Portugueses* – CGTP) ever since their joint mobilisation efforts during the Revolution. The deviant case, that is different from the other parties, but closest to confirming the hypothesis, seems to be the Portuguese PS, which was the only political party without an affiliated trade union at the time of the transition. When this party founded the Portuguese General Workers' Union (*União Geral dos Trabalhadores* – UGT) in 1978, it did so in co-operation with the Social Democratic Party (PSD), primarily to impose a counterweight to the monopolistic position of the communist-led CGTP.

An evaluation of the party resolutions reveals that the PS is the only one of the four parties that does not seem to be concerned with maintaining a close relationship with a 'fraternal' trade union. This is consistent with the expected autonomy of parties and trade unions. It also further confirms the absence of a mass-like structure, in which 'indirect' organisation of corporate associations – such as trade unions and youth organisations – generally play an important role. The only time that the PS seems to have been involved officially and participated actively in the organisational affairs of the UGT was at the time of the foundation of the trade union and in the early years of its existence. The UGT seems to occupy a relatively autonomous position *vis-à-vis* the PS, mainly because the trade union is not linked to a single party, but to both the PS and the PSD. An indication is the composition of the UGT's executive committee, in which the members are more or less equally divided between both parties.[45] This dual loyalty sometimes generates internal conflicts within the UGT, especially since the collapse of the 'central bloc' government in 1985, a coalition in which both the PS and the PSD participated, after which the PSD formed a government without the PS. At the same time, it has encouraged the UGT to adopt a moderate position and has prevented it from a close identification with the class struggle.[46]

At the other extreme, the PCP and the CGTP virtually embody the mass-party ideal of a solidaristic and organic linkage between party and trade union. Without explicitly referring to the CGTP, the party constitutions state that, in defense of the interests of the masses, the members of the PCP have to engage in trade-union activities. The PCP acts in defence of the working class, and strives to strengthen the trade union, which is an indispensible actor in the class struggle. The interests of the working class can only be defended by a strong and unitary trade-union movement, that is, the CGTP, which the party considers to be the only true trade-union representative of the Portuguese workers. According to the PCP, the demands for trade-union pluralism and the creation of the UGT impose a threat to the unity of the working class, which cannot but harm its interests. Consequently, these 'divisionist' strategies invoke indignation within the communist ranks: 'Frankly, we don't understand why the workers should have to split up into trade unions according to different political alternatives, once they all confront the same problems deriving from the same patrons, regardless of their political opinion or religious belief.'[47]

The tone used about the need for unity of the trade unions, and the hostile attitude towards the UGT, have not diminished over the years. The fact that the CGTP, with the public consent of the PCP, decided to enter the tripartite Permanent Council for Social Concertation (*Conselho Permanente de Concertação Social* – CPCS) in 1987 should, therefore, be regarded as a tactical manoeuvre enforced by the negative prospects of the absolute parliamentary majority of the PSD government, which compelled the confederation to institutional co-operation with the UGT, rather than to an acceptance of the divisionism within the labour movement. Consistent with its Marxist-Leninist ideology, the PCP is continuing the class struggle to bring about a radical change in economic and political structures. Hence, the objectives of a tight linkage with the working class, the encouragement of party members to join the trade union, active efforts to support and strengthen the CGTP, and the unity and strong organic cohesion of the labour movement remain high on the PCP's organisational agenda.

Whereas the position of both Portuguese parties on the relationship between party and trade union has remained fairly unaltered over the years, in both Spanish parties a clear shift is detectable. This first became apparent in the PSOE. Initially, the relation between party and union was of a solidaristic nature, not so much because of the mutual interests, but because of mutual commitment and an exclusive dedication.[48] Party and trade union maintained an organic and dialectic relationship as two arms of the labour movement striving to accomplish the same goals: '[t]he socialist struggle is not merely electoral. [...] It is evident that without the UGT the PSOE would be condemned to being an electoralist party without a working class basis'.[49] The PSOE clearly depicted itself as a working-class party, for which the mobilisation of the workers and their integration into the party and the trade union was a fundamental objective. Therefore, it offered active support for the trade union[50] and encouraged its members to fulfil their party obligation of joining the UGT.[51] Similar to the Portuguese PCP, the PSOE and the UGT strove for a hegemonic position of the trade union in the labour movement, and both party and trade union rejected the notion of united action with the communist CCOO.

From 1985 onwards, however, the relationship between the PSOE and the UGT deteriorated. Nevertheless, the party has continued to emphasise the need to strengthen the position of the union and to carry on co-operating with the UGT:

> [W]e should not forget that the workers' movement, organised in class trade unions, should be the principal strategic ally for the socialist project. Hence, the necessity for the party to strengthen the consolidation of the UGT as the principal trade-union force of the country, and to maintain close relationships of co-operation between the two organisations, which have converging interests and shared principles.[52]

However, a careful attempt towards a more independent position can be detected. The party has begun to recognise the diversity of electoral support which is coming from broader sectors in society than merely the working class. Therefore, the resolutions declare, it should be acknowledged that the party basically is an instrument of the social majority that supports the PSOE's project of change. Although the 'socialist project' is the *raison d'être* of the PSOE, the UGT and the socialist youth movement, it also encompasses other organisations to which the party should listen and with which it should associate, 'without committing the error of considering our project an exclusive prerogative of socialists'.[53]

After the resignation of the UGT's secretary-general, Redondo, as a socialist MP in 1987 and the ensuing general strike in December 1988, it has become clear that the relationship has been seriously damaged. For the first time, the UGT did not openly support the PSOE, first in the European elections in 1989, and later in the national legislative elections that year. The PSOE has deprecated the critical position of the UGT towards its government policies: 'the trade unions [...] cannot supplant the sovereign will, represented in parliament, with a dynamic of permanent social mobilisation'.[54] The message is clear, democracies may need trade unions, but their actions should be confined to their exclusive sphere of competence. The party refused to bend to political pressure from outside the margin of elections and the national legislature.[55]

Gradually the PSOE has shifted hesitantly at first, but later more decisively, towards expanding the relationship with other sectors in society and towards relationships with various social movements. The new party constitution approved in 1990 abolished the obligatory affiliation to the UGT. Party members are now encouraged to engage in activities within a social movement. Where this involves a trade union, it should preferably be the UGT. The PSOE itself is increasingly an open and heterogenous party, corresponding to its broad electoral constituency. Its connections with society are through a network of different organisations and associations, and it continuously needs to amplify and diversify its contacts with social sectors supporting the party. Trade unions are considered to be merely one type within the large variety of interest organisations and social movements that share progressive values, and with whom dialogue needs to be maintained. The resolutions adopted at the congress in 1994 state that '[t]he democratic party of participation should be a party model of broad affiliation, with a territorial and sectoral implantation, whose political action is directed and projected towards a more plural and complex array of groups and collectives than merely those which have been the traditional supporters of democratic socialism'.[56] The traditional mode of integration of a particular segment of society that characterised the party organisation in its early years has been replaced by a more open model of direct linkages with a variety of interest groups, indicating the increased 'catch-all' nature of the party.[57]

The PCE has from the outset maintained a somewhat distant position *vis-à-vis* the CCOO, not so much because of a lower ideological commitment, but mainly for strategic reasons. With regard to its electoral constituency, the CCOO has always been much more heterogeneous than the UGT. Whereas the large majority of UGT members voted for the PSOE in the legislative elections, the CCOO had a considerable number of members not voting for the PCE.[58] In order to avoid the alienation of the non-communist CCOO voters and to prevent them for voting for the UGT in the workers' councils elections, party and union had to be careful about promoting too close a public allegiance. Yet, in practice, the PCE and the CCOO were closely connected. The Spanish communists too, considered a strong trade union a necessary ally in the class struggle, and they openly declared their 'fraternal' support for the CCOO.

The party made attempts to increase trade-union membership among its party members, and the low levels of actual involvement in the CCOO constituted a major concern. At the élite level, the degree of personnel interpenetration remained high until 1991. As in the PSOE, the national and provincial executive committees resembled 'interlocking directorates' because of the large personnel interpenetration.[59] In 1988 the number of CCOO executives in the party's central committee increased from 10 to 17 out a total of 40, but, three years later at the PCE's 13th Congress, the federal committee no longer included members of the CCOO executive. According to Gillespie, this was the result of an example set by the trade union's secretary-general, Gutiérrez, 'who ruled himself out of the contest in the belief that greater autonomy from the PCE was essential to his union's future development, especially if it is to draw still closer to the UGT'.[60]

Since the PCE joined the electoral coalition *Izquierda Unida* (IU) in 1986, it had gradually begun to open up its organisation and diminish its traditional class-based ideology. However, even after the constitution of IU as unified political movement, the PCE was reluctant to give up its separate identity and the party continues to exist concurrently with IU. It still aspires to be a mass party, although nowadays with a larger emphasis on linkages with a variety of social movements. In 1988 the then secretary-general of the PCE ended several years of rivalry with the UGT, reaching an agreement on a programme of joint action directed towards the government's policies.[61] Nevertheless, at the PCE's 14th Congress in 1995, Anguita, the party's secretary-general, still sought to preserve the dominant position of the communists within the ranks of the CCOO. This aroused the indignation and anger of Gutiérrez, who firmly defended the independence of the trade union. The tension culminated in the highly divided 6th Congress of the confederation in 1996. Eventually, the *oficialistas* of the secretary-general, promulgating a total autonomy of the CCOO with respect to political parties, defeated those who opted for a close alliance with other progressive social and political actors. With this decision, it is the trade union that has taken the initiative for a complete detachment from the party, compelling the PCE to abandon the historical linkage in favour of more direct relationships with interest groups in general.

CONCLUSION

The empirical findings reveal that, with the exception of the Portuguese Communist Party, neither of the southern European parties included in this analysis can be considered a classic mass party. Regarding the PCP, it not only claims to be a mass party but has also followed a corresponding organisational strategy of mobilisation and integration of the working class as an active organisation on the ground. The figures on partisan mobilisation show that it has been quite successful in this attempt. Similarly, the relationship with the CGTP corresponds to the traditional organisational model of the early working-class parties, in that the PCP considers the electoral and the corporate organisations as two inseparable arms of a single and unitary labour force. Presumably, the need to create a mass organisation is felt stronger in the PCP, which is one of the few parties remaining in Europe that continues to struggle for a radical transformation of the economic and political status quo.

With regard to the other parties, the conclusions are twofold. On the one hand, it seems that the initial expectations have been confirmed and that none of the three has developed as a classic mass party. The absence or loosening of the demands for active involvement of the party members and a similar detachment from the trade union organisations seems to validate the hypothesis. Indeed, it appears that the southern European path towards democracy, through a parallel aperture of political competition and participation, discourages the orientation towards the extra-parliamentary party and in particular the organisation on the ground. This is illustrated by the low levels of partisan mobilisation, on the one hand, and the increasing approval of direct links between party and citizens or social movements, on the other, rather than the channelling of these demands through the party organisation. Enhanced by the relevance of institution building and the ascendancy to public office in an early stage of party formation, it is clear that parties are more orientated towards the activities of the party in parliament and government.

The most telling example in this regard is the PS, which adopts an outspoken posture in defence of a direct 'communicational' linkage with society, thereby rejecting the traditional model of integration. A similar development can be detected in the PSOE, although to a somewhat lesser extent. Perhaps constrained by its ideological and organisational heritage, which traditionally connected the party to the working class and the socialist trade union, the process of disentangling the historical linkage proved to be a more laborious process. Even the PCE has not escaped from the erosion of the original organisational model. The fact that it is lagging a bit behind on the PSOE, in that it still aspires to be a mass party and is reluctant to accept the autonomisation of the trade union, could be partly accounted for by its relatively marginal position in the Spanish party system, facilitating the adherence to a past model.

On the other hand, the empirical findings reveal that the lack of necessity apparently does not diminish the aspirations to a mass organisation, at least as far as the building of a mass membership is concerned. Even though the objectives of creating a mass party vanished relatively quickly, all parties still cling to the Western model of the party as a membership organisation. Even the Portuguese socialists wish to preserve this particular image of the party. Although it might be argued that parties simply need to recruit members in order to fill the candidacies in public office, it appears that membership may also have an intrinsic value. In other words, even in new democracies, an electoral legitimacy derived from the mandate of the voters can not supplant the legitimacy derived from a large membership. In this sense, the southern European left-wing parties maintain a participatory conception of democracy, and in this sense also, despite their relatively recent arrival on the stage and despite expectations, they do not differ so markedly from their older counterparts in the established democracies.

NOTES

This research was sponsored by the Foundation for Law and Public Administration (Reob), which is part of the Netherlands Organisation for Scientific Research (NWO). An earlier version of this article was presented at the ECPR Joint Sessions of Workshops in Bern, 1997, and was subsequently awarded the Rudolf Wildenmann Prize. In addition to the participants of this workshop, I would like to thank Petr Kopecký, Peter Mair and Cas Mudde for their valuable comments on an earlier draft of this article.

1. Robert A. Dahl, *Polyarchy: Participation and Opposition* (New Haven, CT: Yale UP 1971) p.4. Following Dahl, the terms political competition and public contestation are used interchangeably. Equally, the degree of participation of a political system is used as synonymous for its degree of inclusiveness.
2. Democracy may involve more than merely these two dimensions and, therefore, Dahl prefers to use the term 'polyarchy' rather than 'democracy', to maintain the distinction between democracy as an ideal system and the 'real-world' systems that are closest to the upper-right corner in Figure 1. Since this analysis does not deal with ideal systems, the term democracy will be used for those regimes which Dahl calls polyarchies, namely regimes that are relatively democratised. Or, in other words, regimes that have been substantially popularised and liberalised, that is, highly inclusive and extensively open to public competition. See: ibid. pp.8–9.
3. Robert A. Dahl (ed.) *Regimes and Oppositions* (New Haven, CT: Yale UP 1973) p.3.
4. Dahl (note 1) p.34.
5. See Stein Rokkan, *Citizens, Elections, Parties: Approaches to the Comparative Study of the Processes of Development* (Oslo: Universitetsforlaget 1970) pp.84–5.
6. See Maurice Duverger, *Political Parties: Their Organization and Activities in the Modern State* (London: Methuen 1954).
7. See Richard S. Katz and Peter Mair, 'Changing Models of Party Organization and Party Democracy: the Emergence of the Cartel Party', *Party Politics* 1/1 (1995) pp.5–28.
8. In the United States, the sequence of these two events was reversed. Before a proletariat of a significant size came into existence, workers already had acquired the right of political participation. Since they did not find themselves outside the political system, workers were never alienated from the political system as a result of being excluded from it. The relatively weak class consciousness of American workers, in combination with a strong system of patronage, explains to a large extent why a European-style working-class mass party never developed in the United States. See Robert A. Dahl (ed.) *Political Oppositions in Western Democracies* (New Haven, CT: Yale UP 1966) pp.363–4; Leon Epstein, *Political Parties in Western Democracies* (New Brunswick, NJ: Transaction Books 1980) pp.104–11.
9. Duverger (note 6) p.xxx; see also: Joseph LaPalombara and Myron Weiner, 'The Origin and Development of Political Parties' in ibid. (eds.) *Political Parties and Political Development* (NJ: Princeton UP 1966) p.10.
10. Robert Michels, *Political Parties: A Sociological Study of the Oligarchical Tendencies of Modern Democracy* (NY: Free Press 1962/1911) pp.61–2.
11. Epstein (note 8) p.130.
12. Stephen Padgett and William E. Paterson, *A History of Social Democracy in Postwar Europe* (London and NY: Longman 1991) p.177.
13. Stefano Bartolini, 'Electoral, Partisan, and Corporate Socialism: Organizational Consolidation and Membership Mobilisation in Early Socialist Movement',

Estudio/Working Paper 83 (Madrid, Instituto Juan March de Estudios e Investigaciones 1996) p.8.

14. Dahl (note 8) p.361.
15. Dietrich Rueschemeyer, Evelyne Huber Stephens and John D. Stephens, *Capitalist Development and Democracy* (Cambridge: Polity Press 1992) pp.97–8.
16. Juan J. Linz, 'Opposition in and under an Authoritarian Regime: The Case of Spain', in Dahl (note 3) pp.171–2.
17. Furthermore, national plebiscites were held occasionally, as for example in the case of the law of succession in 1947. Apparently, a large majority of the citizens was entitled to participate in these events. See Stanley G. Payne, *The Franco Regime, 1936–1975* (Madison: U. of Wisconsin Press 1987).
18. Walter C. Opello Jr, *Portugal's Political Development: A Comparative Approach* (Boulder, CO: Westview Press 1985) pp.53–6.
19. Philippe C. Schmitter, 'The Impact and Meaning of 'Non-Competitive, Non-Free and Insignificant Elections in Authoritarian Portugal, 1933–1974' in Guy Hermet, Richard Rose and Alain Rouquié (eds.) *Elections without Choice* (London: Macmillan 1978) pp.146–7.
20. Angelo Panebianco, *Political Parties: Organization and Power* (Cambridge: CUP 1988) p.69.
21. About the parties incorporated in coalition of the Spanish UCD (*Unión del Centro Democrático*), for example, a UCD official stated that '[t]hey could not by any stretch of imagination be called national parties. In most provinces, "branches" of these political parties consisted of little more than personal contacts with national leaders. There was virtually no core of militants within these parties.' Quoted in Richard Gunther, Giacomo Sani and Goldie Shabad, *Spain after Franco: The Making of a Competitive Party System* (Berkeley: U. of California Press 1986) p.96.
22. The first threshold acknowledges the right of criticism, petition and demonstration against the regime, the second the formal rights of participation, the third concerns the right to representation in the legislature, and the fourth the right to government participation. Rokkan (note 5) p.79.
23. Katz and Mair (note 7) p.12.
24. Tom Gallagher, *Portugal: A Twentieth-Century Interpretation* (Manchester UP 1983) pp.196–7.
25. In 1913, for example, the Dutch Social Democratic Party (SDAP) was heavily divided internally over the question whether or not to accept the cabinet portfolios the party had been offered. Ultimately, the decision of the party congress was negative, because it considered the party not prepared enough to accept government responsibility. P.J. Oud, *Staatkundige Vormgeving in Nederland, 1840–1940* (Assen: Van Gorcum 1990) pp.210–11. It is difficult to conceive of parties in the new southern European democracies being disquieted by the proficiency of their party organisation before accepting government responsibility.
26. Paul Heywood, 'The Emergence of New Party Systems and Transitions to Democracy: Spain in Comparative Perspective', in Geoffrey Pridham and Paul G. Lewis (eds.) *Stabilising Fragile Democracies: Comparing New Party Systems in Southern and Eastern Europe* (London and NY: Routledge 1996) p.148.
27. The provisions regarding party financing in Spain can be found in Pilar del Castillo, *La Financiación de Partidos y Candidatos en las Democracias Occidentales* (Madrid: Centro de Investigaciones Sociológicas 1985), especially part II, and Pilar del Castillo, 'Financing of Spanish Political Parties', in Herbert E. Alexander (ed.) *Comparative Political Finance in the 1980s* (Cambridge: CUP 1989) pp.172–99. For the regulations in Portugal, see: José Manuel Meirim, *O Financiamento dos Partidos Políticos e das Campanhas Eleitorais* (Lisbon: Aequitas/Editorial Notícias 1994).
28. Susan E. Scarrow, 'The "Paradox of Enrolment": Assessing the Costs and Benefits of Party Membership,' *European Journal of Political Research* 25/1 (1994) pp.41–60. For an alternative view, see Richard S. Katz, 'Party as Linkage: a Vestigial Function?', *European Journal of Political Research* 18/2 (1990) pp.143–61.
29. Stefano Bartolini, 'The Membership of Mass Parties: The Social Democratic Experience, 1889–1978', in Hans Daalder and Peter Mair (eds.) *Western European Party Systems:*

Continuity and Change (London: Sage 1983) pp.177–220.

30. For a similar argument applied to the new parties in post-communist democracies, see Petr Kopecký, 'Developing Party Organizations in East-Central Europe: What Type of Party is Likely to Emerge?', *Party Politics* 1/4 (1995) p.520.
31. In addition to this, it could be argued that the changed nature of communication between parties and society provides a further disincentive for the development of mass parties. In contrast with the classic mass party, which had to rely on party controlled press organs to reach out to its constituency, the parties in the new democracies emerged in an era in which the existing network of mass communication allows them to present themselves directly at the electorate through newspapers, radio and television. Parties can communicate directly with society, rather than having to integrate citizens within the party organisation first.
32. The principal sources for this analysis include, for the PCP: *IX Congresso do PCP* (Lisbon: Edições Avante! 1979); *X Congresso do PCP: Resolução Política* (Ibid. 1983); *XII Congresso do PCP* (Ibid. 1988); *XIV Congresso do PCP* (Ibid. 1992); *Renovar e Reforçar a Organização e a Intervenção do Partido no Seio dos Trabalhadores*, Conferência Nacional (Ibid. 1994); *Resolução Política* 1996. For the PS: *Declaração de Princípios/Programa e Estatutos do Partido Socialista* 1974; *Estatutos do Partido Socialista* 1977, 1981, 1983, 1986, 1988 and 1992; *A Questão Sindical: Análise, Projecto, Táctica*, Secretariado Nacional, 1977; *Relatório do Secretário-General* 1979, 1981, 1983 and 1992. *Reformar com Coragem*, Moção de Jorge Sampaio ao X Congresso do Partido Socialista, 1992. For the PCE: *Noveno Congreso del Partido Comunista de España: Informes, Debates, Actas y Documentos* (Madrid: Ediciones PCE 1978); *Estatutos del Partido Comunista de España*, 1981, 1983, 1985, 1991 and 1995; *Resoluciones al X Congreso*, 1981; *Resoluciones al XI Congreso*, 1983; *Resoluciones al XII Congreso*, 1988. For the PSOE: *Resoluciones del 27 Congreso*, 1976; *Resoluciones del 28 Congreso*, 1979. *Resoluciones del 29 Congreso*, 1981; *Resoluciones del 30 Congreso*, 1984; *Resoluciones del 32 Congreso*, 1990; *Memoria de Gestión de los Organos Federales al 33 Congreso*, 1994. Other primary sources are referred to elsewhere in the text.
33. Distinction derived from Richard S. Katz and Peter Mair, 'Three Faces of Party Organization: Adaptation and Change', European Policy Research Unit Working Papers, University of Manchester 1990; See also Richard S. Katz and Peter Mair (eds.) *Party Organizations: A Data Handbook on Party Organizations in Western Democracies, 1960–1990* (London: Sage 1992).
34. It is important to emphasise that the membership figures for all parties should be interpreted with care, because all parties exhibit a tendency to inflate their membership figures. Moreover, both primary and secondary sources frequently provide contradictory figures, and not every party distinguishes at all times between card-carrying members and those who actually pay their dues.
35. Eusebio Mujal-León, 'Decline and Fall of Spanish Communism', *Problems of Communism* 35/2 (1986) p.7.
36. In 1986, the PCE joined other left-wing parties in the electoral coalition of *Izquierda Unida* (IU), which was transformed into a unified movement in 1992. In 1994, IU claimed to have a membership of 52,711 (see *Documentos IV Asamblea: Informe Balance, Actas*, 1994). However, since the constituent elements of the coalition were not dissolved, citizens can be affiliated to either the PCE or to IU, or to both parties simultaneously. Thus, there is a certain overlap between the membership of IU and the PCE, although it is not known to what extent, since neither of the two parties maintains records including data on the level of mutual registration.
37. The party itself primarily attributes the decline between 1988 and 1992 to the concretisation of the orientations of its 12th Congress in 1988, which envisaged a closer correspondence between the registered number and the really effective number of members. At that particular congress a new article was added to the statutes, which states that members who have ceased to participate in the partisan activities and have not renewed their membership card twice consecutively, will lose their membership of the party. Whether or not this has been the actual cause of the reduction in membership, it is in itself an interesting indication of the level of active involvement the PCP demands from its members.

38. *Memoria de Gestión de la Comisión Ejecutiva Federal al 28 Congreso* 1979, p.162.
39. See *Plano de Acções Imediatas da Organização*, Secretariado Nacional para a Organização, 1986.
40. *Relatório do Secretário-General*, IX Congresso 1990, p.14.
41. *VIII Congresso do PCP* (Lisbon: Edições Avante! 1976) p.48.
42. In 1990, the PCP held an extraordinary congress to discuss the collapse of communism in eastern Europe and the consequences for the identity of the party. It was concluded that: '[t]he PCP firmly rejects the opinions according to which, both because of the events in the socialist countries and because of a supposed democratic evolution of capitalism, the objective conditions for the existence of communist parties should have disappeared. [...] It firmly rejects the opinions according to which the PCP should abandon its revolutionary objectives and [...] turn into a party approximating social democratic principles and orientations.' See *XIII Congresso (Extraordinário) do PCP* (Lisbon: Edições Avante! 1990) p.209.
43. Peter Mair, 'Party Organizations: From Civil Society to the State', in Richard S. Katz and idem (eds.) *How Parties Organize: Change and Adaptation in Party Organizations in Western Democracies* (London: Sage 1994) p.16; emphasis in original.
44. For a more detailed analysis of the relationship between parties and unions in Franco's Spain, see Gunther *et al.* (note 21). An analysis on the initially close and later disintegrating relations between the PSOE and the UGT can be found in: Richard Gillespie, *The Spanish Socialist Party: A History of Factionalism* (Oxford: Clarendon 1989); and idem, 'The Break-up of the 'Socialist Family': Party–Union Relations in Spain, 1982–1989', *West European Politics* 13/1 (Jan. 1990). For the relationship between the PCE and the CCOO, see Miguel Martínez Lucio, 'Trade Unions and Communism in Spain: the Role of the CCOO in the Political Projects of the Left', *Journal of Communist Studies* 6/4 (1990). For the emergence and development of the Portuguese trade unions, see Manuel de Lucena and Carlos Gaspar, 'Metamorfoses Corporativas? Associações de Interesses Econonómicos e Institucionalização da Democracia em Portugal', *Análise Social* 26/114 (1991).
45. In 1995, the UGT executive consisted of 29 socialists, 24 social democrats, 1 communist and 1 member of the CDS-PP. According to an unwritten rule, the secretary general traditionally is a member of the PS, and the president is usually a member of the PSD.
46. See Alan D. Stoleroff, 'Between Corporatism and the Class Struggle: the Portuguese Labour Movement and the Cavaco Silva Governments', *West European Politics* 15/4 (Oct. 1992) p.125.
47. *VII Congresso (Extraordinário) do PCP* (Lisbon: Edições Avante! 1974) p.82.
48. Javier Astudillo Ruiz, 'The Transformation of Social Democracy: the Decomposition of Party-Union Ties in Socialist Spain', paper prepared for the Tenth International Conference of Europeanists, Chicago, 14–16 March 1996, p.12.
49. PSOE (note 38) pp.213–4.
50. For example, the PSOE furnished the UGT with executives and public office holders of the party, supported the UGT with human and financial resources during its electoral campaigns, provided education and formation for the UGT cadres, and sustained the trade union's organisational infrastructure. See *Memoria de Gestión de la Comisión Ejecutiva Federal al 29 Congreso*,'1981, pp.257–60.
51. In 1980, 41 per cent of the PSOE members fulfilled their obligation of affiliating to the UGT. After rising to 48.5 per cent in 1983, the figure dropped to 46.4 per cent in 1986 and further declined to 38.6 per cent in 1989. See *Los Afiliados Socialistas en 1989: Informe de Resultados* (Madrid: Instituto INED) p.36.
52. *Resoluciones del 31 Congreso*, 1988, p.81.
53. Ibid.
54. *Memoria de Gestión de la Comisión Ejecutiva Federal al 32 Congreso*, 1990, p.10–11.
55. The desire for loosening the relationship with the party is also discernable within the UGT. At its 34th congress in 1986, the union still defended its favourable position towards the PSOE, because '[t]he PSOE is the only political option capable of offering acceptable solutions for the problems of our society. [...] Only the political project that the PSOE symbolises coincides essentially with the objectives of transformation and self-emancipation

that the UGT advocates.' See *Resoluciones del 34 Congreso Confederal*, 1986, p.85. Four years later, the UGT had abandoned its antagonistic attitude towards the CCOO, and has clearly moved towards a more autonomous position *vis-à-vis* the political parties. See *Gestión de la Comisión Ejecutiva Confederal al 35 Congreso*, 1990; *Gestión de la Comisión Ejecutiva Confederal al 36 Congreso*, 1994; *Resoluciones del 36 Congreso Confederal*, 1994.

56. *Resoluciones del 33 Congreso*, 1994, p.167.
57. See Otto Kirchheimer, 'The Transformation of West European Party Systems', in Joseph LaPalombara and Myron Weiner (note 9) pp.177–200.
58. See Richard Gunther *et al.* (note 21); Richard Gunther, 'Los Partidos Comunistas de España', in José Ramón Montero and Juan J. Linz (eds.) *Crisis y Cambio: Electores y Partidos en la España de los Años Ochenta* (Madrid: Centro de Estudios Constitucionales 1986) pp.493–523; Hans-Jürgen Puhle, 'El PSOE: un Partido Dominante y Heterogéneo', in ibid., pp.289–344.
59. Gunther *et al.* (note 21) p.203.
60. Richard Gillespie, 'Thirteenth Congress of the PCE: the Long Goodbye', *Journal of Communist Studies* 8/2 (1992) p.170.
61. Idem, 'Spain: Crisis and Renewal in the PCE', ibid. 4/3 (1988) p.339.

Expert Judgements of the Left–Right Location of Political Parties: A Comparative Longitudinal Study

ODDBJØRN KNUTSEN

The purpose of this article is to study the changing left–right location of parties by means of expert judgments from 1982 and 1993. The analysis concentrates on 13 Western European countries, based on data from 1982 and 1993. According to the 'experts', there was a strong centrist tendency in the party systems of Western Europe from 1982 to 1993. This tendency was strongest for the socialist parties, but applies also to the non-socialist parties, although to a lesser degree. On the other hand, the 'New Politics' parties became more firmly located on the extreme left and right, contributing to a new polarisation in the party systems. The analysis supports the notion that left–right semantics have a substantial absorptive capacity in the sense that New-Politics conflicts seem to be incorporated in these semantics.

The language of 'left' and 'right' helps citizens as well as élites to orient themselves in a complex political landscape. It helps to reduce the complexity of the world of politics: for individuals it has primarily functions of orientation; for the political system, functions of communication. It can be used to summarise the programme of political parties and groups, and to label the important political issues of a given era. The left–right schema is thus a taxonomic system, an efficient way to understand, order and store political information.[1]

Party competition tends to take place along the left–right dimension. Several studies have documented that the left-right continuum is the most important dimension in this respect. Two studies based on expert judgements of spatial dimensions, from different time periods, have documented that the left–right dimension is much more important than others. One study, based on the period 1945–73, found that the left–right dimension was overwhelmingly the most salient in all ten Western European countries studied.[2] In a more recent study of 42 countries, Huber

West European Politics, Vol.21, No.2 (April 1998), pp.63–94
PUBLISHED BY FRANK CASS, LONDON

and Inglehart[3] found that left and right were used to define the major poles of political conflict in all countries apart from one. The left–right dimension was particularly important in the 22 most advanced countries, where on average 87 per cent of the experts used the terms left and right to define the major poles of political party conflicts, compared with 70 per cent in the 20 poorest democracies.

The latter finding is important. The collapse of the communist systems and the emergence of a series of new political issues that have become divisive in the party systems, such as environmental concern, immigration and law-and-order issues, do not appear to have changed the political landscape in the sense that other spatial dimensions have become important. The left–right ideological continuum, then, is still a central dimension of political conflict in advanced industrial society.

On the other hand, the language of left and right may have an impressive absorptive power. It has been considered to be an overarching spatial dimension capable of incorporating a variety of salient political issues and conflicts.[4] Since left and right can have a great absorptive capacity, it is possible that these new issues and other conflicts have been incorporated into the left–right division.

The research objective in this article is to analyse the placement of individual parties and party families along the left-right dimension in a comparative longitudinal perspective by using two data sets in which political experts placed the political parties on the left–right dimension. How are parties placed on the left–right scale within different countries? Is there a basic similarity in left–right location between parties grouped in the same party families across countries? Are there systematic changes over time for given party families? Where are the new party families that have emerged since the 1970s located on the left–right dimension?

The two expert judgements are from 1982 and 1993, and are documented in publications by Francis G. Castles and Peter Mair, and John Huber and Ronald Inglehart, respectively.[5] Castles and Mair administered a questionnaire asking 'leading political scientists' to locate political parties in 'their' system on an 11-point left–right scale from 0 (left) to 10 (right). They reported data from 17 countries, 13 Western European countries and 4 additional Anglo-American democracies. Huber and Inglehart conducted a more elaborate survey. They asked 'political scientists, political sociologists and survey researchers' to place the 'main parties' on a 10-point left–right scale from 1 (left) to 10 (right),[6] and they managed to get data from 42 countries, of which 16 were Western European countries.[7]

This analysis will concentrate on the 13 Western European countries from which I have data for both 1982 and 1993. Since the scales comprise 11 and 10 points, respectively, the scores on the scales have to be adjusted.

Here, scores on the 11-point scale is transformed to scores on the 10-point scale by a simple formula.[8] Castles and Mair reported in their tables the mean scores on the scale and the range, while Huber and Inglehart reported the standard deviations in addition to the means and the range. In this analysis I will rely on only the mean scores.[9]

THE SUBSTANTIVE MEANING OF THE LEFT–RIGHT DIMENSION

The idea that the left–right semantics have a large absorptive power implies that the ideological and programmatic meaning of the left–right dimension varies, over time and across cultures. The placement on the left–right scale of parties by experts will be interpreted here to mean that the experts have not only expert knowledge of the policy positions of the various parties on the left–right scale, but also that their expertise extends to interpreting the meaning of the left–right dimension in a given national political culture. The placement of parties reflects the culturally defined meaning of the left–right dimension. Changing positions on the scale reflect, then, both changing policy positions and changing meaning of the left–right scale. Since we do not know exactly how the meanings of left and right are changing in each country, it might be difficult to interpret the changing positions.

The general interpretation of how the left–right dimension has changed is nevertheless as follows: in a typical industrial society, left and right have been associated with the line of class (labour market) and religious conflict, and with issues and values associated with these structurally defined conflicts. For example, the central political issues associated with class conflict were issues related to control over the economy and the degree of economic equality.[10] The placement of parties on the left–right scale reflected the position of the traditional party families on these central lines of conflict – communist and socialist parties on the left, and conservative, liberal and Christian parties on the right and partly in the centre.

In advanced industrial society, 'New Politics' have become a significant line of conflict, and new parties and party families have polarised the party system along a new line of conflict. This new line has been conceptualised somewhat differently by different authors: as materialist/post-materialist,[11] libertarian/authoritarian,[12] or left-libertarian versus right-authoritarian conflict.[13] The parties that polarise the party system along this new line of conflict are first and foremost the new party families – leftist socialist and greens versus radical rightist parties.[14] The theory of the New Politics also assumes that the new dimension is working to transform the meaning of left and right,[15] or at least to incorporate these new meanings into the various meanings of left and right.[16] The three party families that are associated with

New Politics will be called the new party families below, and we will argue that first and foremost these party families correspond to the new meanings of left and right.

EXPERTS' EVALUATION OF THE MEANING OF THE LEFT–RIGHT DIMENSION

Assuming that the experts are the best source for the exact meaning of the left–right dimension, we might ask if we know how they interpret the dimension in their own countries. The Huber and Inglehart study is extremely useful in this respect. After the experts had placed the parties on the left–right scale, they were asked to list the key issues that divide the parties on the left–right dimension. The question was open-ended, and the answers were organised into ten broad categories. The categories to some extent reflect the issues of the Old versus the New Politics. One of these categories is economic issues related to the class conflict, and it turned out to be the most frequently cited category in all of the 13 countries in this study, and in 38 of the 43 countries examined.[17] Two other categories clearly reflect New Politics issues, namely 'authoritarianism versus democracy' and 'xenophobia'. Another category, 'traditional versus new culture', partly reflects the religious/secular cleavage and partly New Politics issues, such as environmental concerns, participation and pacifism.[18] Table 1 presents the percentage breakdown of the issue categories mentioned in the 13 countries.[19]

The countries are ranked according to the percentages of the issues related to the economic or class issues. Although the economic and class conflict category is the most important in all countries, there are interesting differences between the countries with regard to the dominance of the economic issues as the substantive content of the left–right dimension. We note that there are only two countries in which the economic category accounts for less than 50 per cent of the answers. In all West European countries the second most frequently cited category is one of the three New Politics categories. From the table we note that the second most important category varies between 'authoritarianism versus democracy' (in Denmark, Britain and Belgium), 'xenophobia' (in Sweden, France, Italy, Belgium[20] and Germany) and 'traditional versus new culture' (in Ireland, Norway, Spain, the Netherlands, Finland and Austria).

The percentages of New Politics issues are then summed, first only for the two pure categories, and then also including the more dubious category 'traditional versus new culture'. There are large variations in the percentages of the issues that are grouped under the New Politics categories. The pure New Politics categories are most frequently mentioned in

TABLE 1

EXPERTS' ANSWERS THAT IDENTIFIED ECONOMIC CONFLICTS AND ISSUES OF THE NEW POLITICS AS 'THE KEY ISSUES THAT DIVIDE LEFT FROM RIGHT TODAY' (%)

	Economic or Class Issues	Authori-tarianism	Xeno-phobia	Traditional/ New Culture	Other	Number of Coded Issues	New Politics 1[1]	New Politics 2[2]	New/Old Politics 1[3]	New/Old Politics 2[3]
Ireland	88	0	0	8	4	24	0	8	0.00	0.09
Sweden	82	4	7	0	7	28	11	11	0.13	0.13
Denmark	79	11	0	5	5	19	11	16	0.14	0.20
Norway	76	0	0	7	17	29	0	7	0.00	0.09
France	68	5	11	5	11	19	16	21	0.24	0.31
Italy	68	0	16	0	16	19	16	16	0.24	0.24
Spain	67	4	0	21	8	24	4	25	0.06	0.37
Netherlands	66	3	10	17	3	29	14	31	0.21	0.47
Belgium	60	15	15	5	5	20	30	35	0.50	0.58
Britain	57	18	2	9	11	44	21	30	0.37	0.53
Finland	50	8	3	18	21	38	11	29	0.22	0.58
Austria	46	5	9	18	8	22	14	32	0.30	0.70
Germany	36	7	24	21	9	42	31	52	0.86	1.44
Average	65	6	7	10	10	27	14	24		

Notes: 1 Total of the percentages of the categories autoritarianism and xenophobia.
2 Total of the percentages of New Politics 1 and Traditional/New culture.
The percentages for the three New Politics categories do not always sum up exactly to New Politics 1 and 2 in the table due to rounding off.
3 Percentage of the New Politics categories divided by the percentage of economic or class issues.

Source: Data set from the project reported by Huber and Inglehart (1995). The data have kindly been made available by John Huber.

Germany and Belgium, and the same applies to the extended New Politics categories where 'traditional versus new culture' is included. Austria and the Netherlands have about the same percentage as Belgium. The right-hand side of the table shows the New Politics categories as a percentage of the Old Politics categories. Germany stands out as the country where New Politics meanings of left and right are most significant compared with Old Politics meanings. In the extended version of New Politics, the new meanings are even more important than Old Politics meanings. For all the other countries, Old Politics meanings are still the most important.

We can thus conclude that the traditional meaning of the left–right dimension is still salient, and in fact dominant in most countries, but New Politics issues are significant in several countries. This implies that the experts, as interpreters of the dominant trends in their respective countries, will emphasise both traditional economic issues and New Politics issues when they place the parties on the left–right scale, but this will vary across countries in accordance with the results from Table 1.

PARTY FAMILIES

To be able to perform a comparative analysis of the location of various parties on the left–right continuum, I have to rely on some classification of political parties into several *'familles spirituelles*. The classification of parties in different countries into party families is based on a more thorough discussion of classification of parties in another work.[21] I will operate with the following party families: communists, left socialist (or new left), socialist/social democratic, liberal, green, Christian, ethnic (nationalist), conservative and radical-right parties. In the Appendix the abbreviations used for parties in different countries are shown; these abbreviations are used in the text below and in Figure 1.

Table 2 shows the various parties that are grouped in the various party families at the two time points. We note the increase in the number of parties in the green, radical-right and the liberal party families from 1982 to 1993.[22] In Table 3A I have shown the average support for the various party families across countries.[23]

The table illustrates the trends that are fairly consistent from country to country.[24] The support for the old party families has decreased substantially. This applies in particular to the social-democratic, Christian and conservative parties. On the other hand, the support for green and radical-right parties increased and became significant in more countries from the early 1980s to the early 1990s. The same does not apply to the third group of New Politics parties, the left-socialist parties, which have suffered a small decline. In the early 1990s significant green parties were found in the

TABLE 2
GROUPING OF POLITICAL PARTIES INTO NINE PARTY FAMILIES IN WEST EUROPEAN COUNTRIES

	Communists	Left Socialist	Socialist/ Social Democratic	Green	Nationalist/Ethnic	Agrarian	
Austria	KPÖ[1]	–	SPÖ	Green Alternative[2]	–	–	
Belgium	PCB/KPB1	–	PS/SP	Ecolo and Agalev	Volksunie		
Britain	–	–	Labour	–	SNP[1] and Plaid Cymru[1]	-	
Denmark	DKP[1]	SF	Social Democrats	–	–	Agrarian Liberals	
Finland	–	Left-Wing Alliance	Social Democrats	Green League[2]	Swedish People's Party	Agrarian Party	
France	PCF	–	PSF	Generation Ecologie and Les Verts	–	–	
Germany	DKP[1]/PDS[2]	–	SPD	Green Party	–		
Ireland	–	WP	Labour	–	–	–	
Italy	PCI[1]/PDS[2] (or PCR[2])	Proletarian Dem.[1]	PSI	Radical Party[1]/Verdi[2]	Lega Nord[2]	–	
Netherlands	CNP[1]	PSP[1]/Green Left[2]	Labour (PvdA)	–	–	–	
Norway	Red Alliance[2]	SV	Labour (AP)	–	–	Agrarian Party	
Spain	–	United Left (IU)	Socialists (PSOE)	–	CiU and PNV	–	
Sweden	–	Left Party	Social Democrats	Green Party (Miljøpartiet)[2]	–	Agrarian Party	
Number of parties	7/4	8/7	13/13	4/7	4/4	4/4	
	Liberal	**Christian**	**Conservative**	**Radical Right**	**Other Significant Parties**	**Other Parties' Share of the Vote 1982**	**1993**
Austria	Liberal Forum[2]	ÖVP	–	FPÖ	–	–	–
Belgium	PRL/PVV	PSC/CVP	–	Flemish Block	RAD,[1] RW[1] and FDF[1]	4.6	–
Britain	Liberal Party/Liberal Dem.	Conservatives	–	Social Democrats[1]	–	11.8	–
Denmark	Radical Liberals	Christian People's Party	Conservative People's Party	Progress Party	Centre Democrats, Left Socialists	9.2	6.4
Finland	Liberal Party	Christian League	National Coalition Party	–	Rural Party	7.2	3.1
France	UDF	–	RPR	National Front	MRG, Extreme left Parties[2]	1.3	2.6
Germany	FDP	CDU and CSU	-	Republikaner Party[2]	–	–	–
Ireland	Progressive Democrats[2]	Fine Gael	Fianna Fáil	–	–	–	–
Italy	PLI and PRI	Christian Democrats	–	MSI	PSDI	4.0	2.7
Netherlands	VVD	CDA	–	Centre Democrats[2]	D'66, Calvinist fundamentalists (GPV, RPF and SGP)	8.5	16.4
Norway	Liberal Party	Christian People's Party	Conservative Party	Progress Party	–	–	–
Spain	CDS[2]	–	–	Partido Popular	EE,[1] EA,[2] ERC,[1] UDC,[1] UN/FN[1]	11.4	0.6
Sweden	People's Party	Christian Democrats[2]	Conservative Party	New Democracy[2]	–		
Number of parties	10/13	9/10	8/8	6/9			

Notes: 1 Data available only for 1982. 2 Data available only for 1993.

TABLE 3

SUPPORT FOR VARIOUS PARTY FAMILIES IN 1982 AND 1993*

A. Average Support for Various Party Families in the Early 1980s and Early 1990s

	All parties in the various party families			Parties with left-right scores in both 1982 and 1993		
	1980s	1990s	Change	1980s	1990s	Change
Left socialist	6.4 (8)	6.2 (7)	-0.2	7.1	6.2	-0.9 (7)
Socialist	32.5 (13)	26.9 (13)	-5.6	32.5	26.9	-5.6 (13)
Green	3.3 (4)	6.5 (7)	3.2	3.3	6.3	3.0 (4)
Ethnic	5.2 (4)	5.6 (5)	0.4	5.2	4.9	-0.3 (4)
Agrarian	12.5 (4)	16.7 (4)	4.2	12.5	16.7	4.2 (4)
Liberal	10.7 (10)	9.1 (13)	-1.6	10.7	11.0	0.3 (10)
Christian	26.2 (9)	19.2 (10)	-7.0	26.2	21.5	-4.7 (9)
Conservative	29.3 (8)	26.2 (8)	-3.1	29.3	26.2	-3.1 (8)
Radical rightist	5.1 (6)	7.4 (9)	2.3	5.1	9.9	4.8 (6)

B. Support for the New Party Families in the Early 1980s and Early 1990s

	Support for radical-right parties			Support for new left parties (green and left-socialist parties)			Change Radical Right minus New Left	Support for New Politics parties (radical-right, green and left-socialist parties)		
	1982	1993	Change	1982	1993	Change		1982	1993	Change
Austria	5.6	19.6	14.0	–	7.0	7.0	7.0	5.6	26.6	21.0
Belgium	3.3	8.9	5.6	5.6	8.4	2.8	2.8	8.9	17.3	8.4
Britain	–	–	–	–	–	–	–	–	–	-
Denmark	6.3	6.4	0.1	11.6	7.8	-3.8	3.7	17.7	14.2	-3.5
Finland	–	–	–	17.8	17.3	-0.5	-0.5	17.8	17.3	-0.5
France	5.0	12.9	7.9	1.2	7.6	6.4	1.5	6.2	20.5	14.3
Germany	–	2.0	2.0	3.6	6.2	2.6	-0.6	3.6	8.2	4.6
Ireland	–	–	–	3.3	3.5	0.2	-0.2	3.3	3.5	0.2
Italy	6.1	5.4	-0.7	4.4	2.8	-1.6	-0.9	10.5	8.2	-2.3
Netherlands	–	1.5	1.5	2.3	3.8	1.5	0.0	2.3	5.3	3.0
Norway	4.1	6.3	2.2	5.2	7.9	2.7	0.5	9.3	14.2	4.9
Spain	–	–	–	4.1	9.6	5.5	-5.5	4.1	9.6	5.5
Sweden	–	4.0	4.0	5.6	9.6	4.0	0.0	5.6	13.6	8.0

* How the support for various parties are calculated on the basis of results in general elections is outlined in note 23. The figures in parentheses in Table A are the number of parties which the average scores are based on

same number of countries as left-socialist parties and with about the same average support. Another group of parties that have increased their support significantly are the agrarian parties in the Nordic countries.

Since we are interested in the mobilisation and strength of the new party families in a comparative setting, Table 3B shows the support of these parties in the early 1980s and early 1990s. It should be emphasised that the parties grouped under the left-socialist umbrella in Finland and Spain are dominated by communist parties, while the radical rightist party in Italy is the MSI. These classifications are dubious. The table presents the support for the radical-right parties and the green and left-socialist parties combined. The latter parties are called new-left parties below.

With regard to the radical-right parties, we see that such parties were significant, with three–six per cent level of support in six countries in the early 1980s (Austria, Belgium, Denmark, France, Italy and Norway). If we define radical rightist mobilisation from the early 1980s to the early 1990s as the increase in support for such parties, we note from Table 3B that such mobilisation was definitely largest in Austria, followed by France, Belgium and Sweden, while such mobilisation was small in three other countries, namely Germany, the Netherlands and Norway. In the early 1990s support for radical-right parties was largest in Austria, France and Belgium, followed by Italy and the three Nordic countries, Denmark, Norway and Sweden.

With regard to the new-left parties (green and socialist-left parties), these were strongest in Finland and Denmark in the early 1980s, and considerably weaker in Belgium, Italy, Norway, Spain and Sweden. The new-left mobilisation from 1982 to 1993 was strongest in Austria, France, Spain and Sweden. In the early 1990s new-left parties were strongest in Finland, followed by Spain, Sweden, Norway, Denmark, France, Austria and Germany. In the early 1980s the left-socialist parties were the dominant new-left parties in most of the countries with significant new-left parties. However, the strongest mobilisation took place among the green component of new-left parties; and in the early 1990s green parties constituted the new-left parties in Austria, Belgium, France and Germany, while left socialists were dominant in Denmark, Norway and Spain. In Sweden and Finland both groups of parties constituted the new left.

The table also shows the total support for the new party families at the two time points. If we establish limits of five per cent and ten per cent for the early 1980s, we can divide the countries into three groups: one in which the new parties have a strong support (Denmark, Finland and Italy), one in which these parties have small support (Britain, the Netherlands, Ireland, Spain and Germany), and one in which the support is moderate (the remaining five countries). The development over time in the three groups is as follows. In the first group the support declined somewhat (Denmark and Italy) or remained fairly stable (Finland). In the second group, there was a large increase in four of the five countries (Austria, France, Belgium and Sweden) and a more modest increase in the fifth country (Norway). In the third group there was an increase in the support for the new parties, but the increase was modest and was lower than ten per cent in 1993 in all countries.

The relative size of new right and new left mobilisation is also calculated in the table. In Austria the mobilisation of the radical right is much larger than the mobilisation of the new left. The same applies to a much more modest degree in some other countries (Belgium and France as well as Denmark, where the difference is obtained by demobilisation concentrated on the left). Only in Spain is a significant larger mobilisation found on the new left than on the new right.

HYPOTHESES

I will first formulate some hypotheses about the placement of the old party families and then go on to outline the expectations related to the new party families and changes in left–right placement from the early 1980s to the early 1990s.

I expect that liberal, Christian and conservative parties will be placed on the 'right' end of the left–right scale. These parties have strongly emphasised at least one of the types of issues and values traditionally associated with the 'right' (economic liberalist or Christian values). In addition, all of these party families define themselves or are defined by neutral observers (mass media and other political leaders) as being on the right. I also expect that the ethnic parties will be located on the right. These parties clearly belong to the non-socialist, or bourgeois, group of parties. The terms 'left' and 'right' are, however, not very central to the way they define themselves, and they are not extremist with regard to the left–right division.

It is difficult to have clear expectations about the relative left–right location of these party families. To a large extent, modern conservative parties and liberal parties in continental Europe have their main identity connected to economic liberalism with an aversion to economic regulation, planning and a strong welfare state. These parties are also identified as the modern 'right' within their respective political systems. In Britain and the Scandinavian countries, the liberal parties have another origin, and have for a long time defined themselves as 'centre' parties between the conservative and social democratic parties.[25] I, therefore, hypothesise that the liberal parties will be located closer to the centre than the liberal parties on the

Continent. The Christian democratic parties stressed class integration and their nature as broad-based *Volksparteien* or catch-all and centrist parties when they emerged after World War II, and they have focused on moderate state intervention and redistribution. Christian democracy has been seen as a distinct force separate from traditional conservative and liberal parties also outside the religious cleavage.[26] On the other hand, given that religious values and interests in continental Europe have been strongly identified with the right – both historically and at present – it might be hypothesised that they are located close to the rightist pole. Given that the economic class issues constitute the most important substantive content of the left–right dimension also in these countries, I expect that the liberal parties in continental Europe will definitely be located clearly to the right of the Christian parties. In the Nordic countries, the situation is quite different from that in continental Europe in this respect. Here the Christian People's parties as well as the liberals emerged from the old pre-industrial 'left' alliances and have identified themselves as being close to the political centre in the industrial cleavage structure.[27] Similarly, the Nordic agrarian parties have also placed themselves in the centre on the left–right dimension. This is expressed by the fact that the parties in Finland, Norway and Sweden are called 'centre parties'.

There are, however, some exceptions to these expectations that should be mentioned. The Christian parties in Austria and Germany have a less distinct centre location, and are difficult to differentiate from conservative parties.[28] Also the Danish Agrarian Liberal Party is considered as 'something of a special case' among the agrarian parties, having a much more right-wing orientation on economic issues than the others.[29]

The parties that are expected to be located closer to the left are first and foremost the social-democratic, communist and left-socialist parties. These parties all label themselves as leftist, they are considered as such by experts and the mass media, and their political programmes favour economic regulation, a strong welfare state and economic equality. It is first and foremost the economic leftist orientations which define these parties as leftist, although historically their anti-clericalism has also contributed in this respect.

The period from 1982 to 1993 saw the emergence of and increased support for green parties in several countries, as we have seen above. Previously, the left-socialist parties in some countries had focused on postmaterialist or left-libertarian issues, and during the 1980s and early 1990s some of the communist parties changed profile or became part of electoral alliances that can be considered as left-socialist (not communist) forces. According to several authors these parties compete on a new conflict dimension. For example, Herbert Kitschelt, who conceptualises the new dimension as a left-libertarian/right-authoritarian dimension describes this as follows:

> In a structural perspective, the New Right constitutes the mirror image and opposite pole of a New Left that began to mobilize in the 1960s... On the one hand, the New Left stands for 'leftist' income redistribution by way of encompassing social policies in the economic sphere, and 'libertarian' democratic participation and maximum individual autonomy in politics and the culture sphere. The New Radical Right ..., on the other hand, advocates rightist free market economics and 'authoritarian' hierarchical arrangements in politics, together with a limitation of diversity and individual autonomy in culture expression.[30]

Does the absorptive capacity of the left–right semantics imply that these New Politics party conflicts are also incorporated in the left–right scale? According to New Politics theory, we should expect so, and given Kitschelt's emphasis on the fact that these parties combine traditional leftist and rightist values with New Politics libertarian and authoritarian issues, there should be two reasons why the green and left-socialist parties, and radical-right parties, respectively, should be placed to the left and right. They emphasise both traditional economic left–right concerns and new non-economic issues that reflect the new meanings of left and right.

Thus, I believe that these parties will be located closer to the left and right than the established socialist, liberal, conservative and Christian parties. These new party families have contributed to a new left–right polarisation.

On the other hand, radical economic leftist positions concerning nationalisation, economic planning and income levelling have become less popular and less central for the traditional parties on the left. In this respect I expect that the established left-wing parties will have moved towards the right. This is particularly true for the socialist parties, the major party family associated with economic left-wing positions. These parties have moved towards the centre, but to some degree they have also increasingly focused on new issues (i.e. left-libertarian issues) to be able to compete on the New Politics dimension.[31]

In addition to expecting that the leftist parties have moved towards the centre, I might generally anticipate that the established parties have moved closer towards the centre along the left–right scale, because of the new meanings attached to left and right. On the New Politics dimension, the established party families often have more modest or centrist positions, and when left and right are increasingly associated with New Politics issues, they may be located closer to the centre.

The data allow us to study left–right changes of the party system as a whole. From the centrality of the economic conflicts of the left–right dimension I expect that the party systems have moved towards the right. Traditional economic leftist policies have become less central for the parties on the left. However, the New Politics parties on the right and the left have contributed to a new left–right polarisation. Whether this contributes to a left-oriented or a right-oriented trend in the party system depends, however, on the relative size of the radical right and new-left mobilisations in the party system. From the discussion about the support for new right and new left mobilisation above, I expect that the new party families will be contributing to a trend to the right first and foremost in Austria, but also in Denmark, Belgium and France, and to a trend to the left in the only country with a relatively larger new-left mobilisation, namely Spain.

The hypotheses about changes over time can be summed up as follows:

(1) A centrist tendency is expected for the old party families. This should apply in particular to the socialist parties.

(2) Radical-right and new-left (green and left-socialist) parties will increasingly be the dominant parties among those located at the extreme left and right.

(3) The party systems will have generally moved towards the right from the early 1980s to the early 1990s.

(4) Given the relative mobilisation of new right and new left parties, I expect that the tendency to the right should be particularly large in Austria, Belgium, Denmark and France, while the new left mobilisation in Spain should contribute to a more leftist trend in that country.

EMPIRICAL ANALYSIS

Placement of Parties in Party Families in Various Countries

The comparison below will use the party families to compare the placement of parties in various countries and in a comparative setting. To get a first impression of the location of the parties from the various party families across countries, the average left–right location for the various party families has been calculated in Table 4 on the basis of the political experts' placement of the various parties within each country. The averages are shown for the two time points.

From the mean scores for the various party families in 1982, we find an expected grouping of parties from left to right: communist and left-socialist to the extreme left, then socialists and greens with a more moderate leftist

TABLE 4

AVERAGE LEFT–RIGHT PLACEMENT FOR THE VARIOUS PARTY FAMILIES IN 1982 AND 1993

	Communist	Left Socialist	Socialist/ Social Democrat	Green	Nationalist	Agrarian	Liberal	Christian	Conservative	Radical Right
A. *All parties*										
1982	2.1 (7)	2.3 (8)	3.7 (13)	4.0 (4)	6.2 (4)	6.3 (4)	6.2 (10)	6.6 (9)	7.8 (8)	9.0 (6)
1993	1.90[2]/1.52[3] (4)	2.63 (7)	4.26 (13)	3.50 (7)	6.68 (4)	6.61 (4)	6.30 (13)	6.71 (10)	7.52 (8)	9.33 (9)
Change[1]		0.3	0.6	-0.5	0.5	0.3	0.1	0.1	-0.3	0.3
B. *The same (number of) parties*										
1982	-[4]	2.4 (7)	3.7 (13)	4.0 (4)	6.6 (3)	6.3 (4)	6.2 (10)	6.6 (9)	7.8 (8)	9.0 (6)
1993	-	2.63 (7)	4.26 (13)	3.34 (4)	6.41 (3)	6.61 (4)	6.19 (10)	6.68 (9)	7.52 (8)	9.35 (6)
Change[1]		0.2	0.6	-0.7	-0.2	0.3	0.0	0.1	-0.3	0.4

Notes: Number of parties in parentheses.

1. + means changes to the right, - means changes to the left.
2. Calculation based on the Italian PDS.
3. Calculation based on the Italian PCR.
4. It is impossible to compare the scores for the communist parties. Of the four parties in 1993, only the French PCF is the same party as the parties grouped under in the communist party family in 1982.

placement. On the rightist side we find ethnic, agrarian, liberal and Christian parties with very similar mean scores, and then conservative and radical rightist parties with more extreme placement.

In Figure 1 the placement of the parties on the left–right scale is shown on two horizontal lines in such a way that it is possible to see the relative positions of the various parties in the respective party systems in 1982 and 1993 and the changing positions over time of individual parties. The figures also show an overall mean score for the party system of each country (in bold type). The initial comments below will focus on the relative positions of parties in party systems in 1982, then on changes from 1982 to 1993.

Communist and left-socialist parties are in all countries placed to the left of the socialist parties. The green parties are located to the right of the socialist parties in two of the four countries (Belgium and France) where such parties existed, and to the left in the other two countries (Germany and Italy).

It is among the non-socialist party families that we find the greatest variations in the placement of the various party families. In all six countries with significant radical-right parties, they are located clearly to the right of other parties, with the Austrian party as a somewhat deviant case. If we ignore the (then) quite small right-wing parties, the conservative parties are, in seven of the eight countries where such parties existed, located closest to the right pole. In Ireland the party under the Christian umbrella (Fine Gael) is placed somewhat more to the right than the conservative party (Fianna Fáil). The Christian Party is the furthest to the right party (apart from the radical-right parties) in respective party systems in Austria, Germany, and Ireland; and the liberal parties occupy the same position in Belgium and the Netherlands. The Italian pattern is discussed below.

The liberal party family appears to be the one that is grouped most differently in different party systems. These parties are all placed to the left of the conservative parties in countries where such parties existed (Britain, France and the four Nordic countries). In countries where both party families existed, they are also placed to the left of the Christian parties (Germany and the Nordic countries). The liberal party family in the Italian case is represented by two parties; one is located to the right of the Christian Democrats (PLI), and one to the left (PRI). Only in Belgium and the Netherlands are the liberal parties placed to the right of the Christian parties.

The Nordic agrarian parties are placed near the centre in Finland, Norway and Sweden. In Finland and Sweden they are grouped close to the liberal parties, while the Norwegian Agrarian Party is more rightist than the Norwegian Liberal Party. The Danish Agrarian Liberal Party is, as expected, a somewhat deviant case, being placed closer to the conservative party than to the Liberal Party.

FIGURE 1

LEFT–RIGHT PLACEMENT OF PARTIES 1982 AND 1993

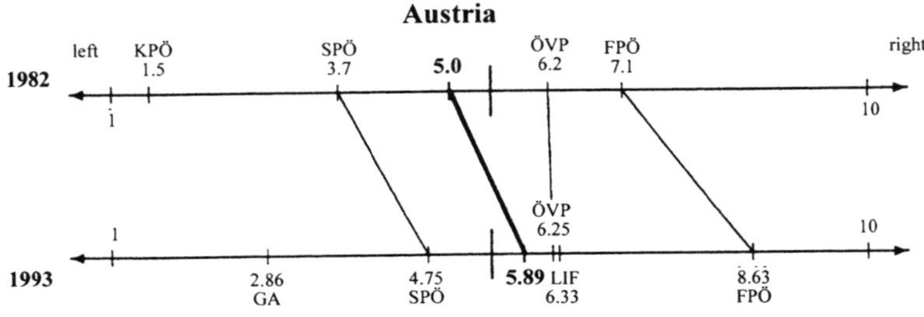

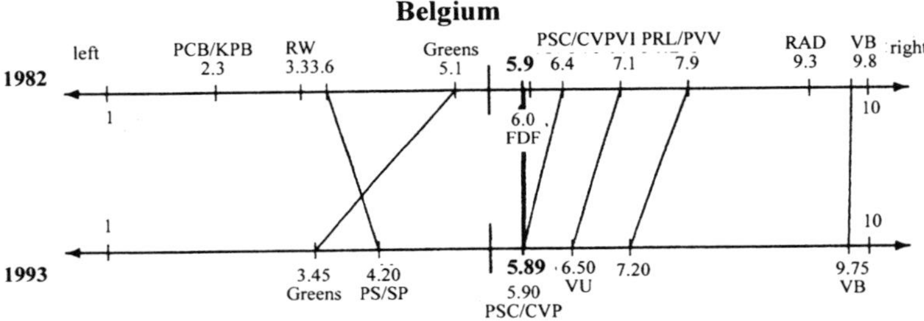

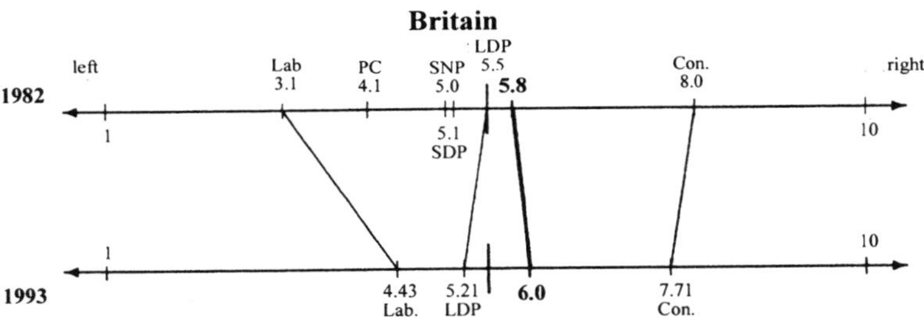

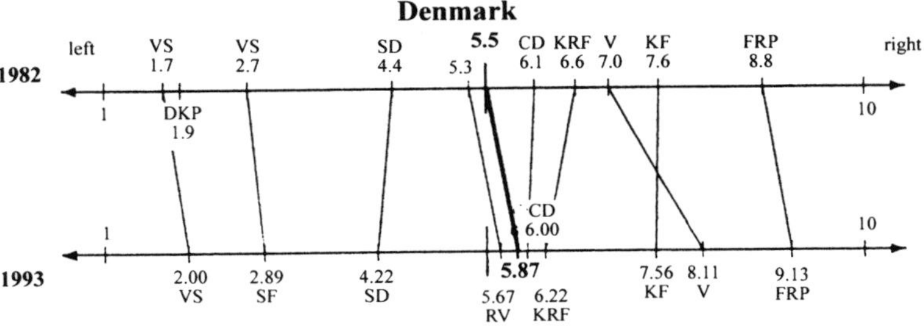

Note: For key to abbreviations, see Appendix.

FIGURE 1 (Contd)

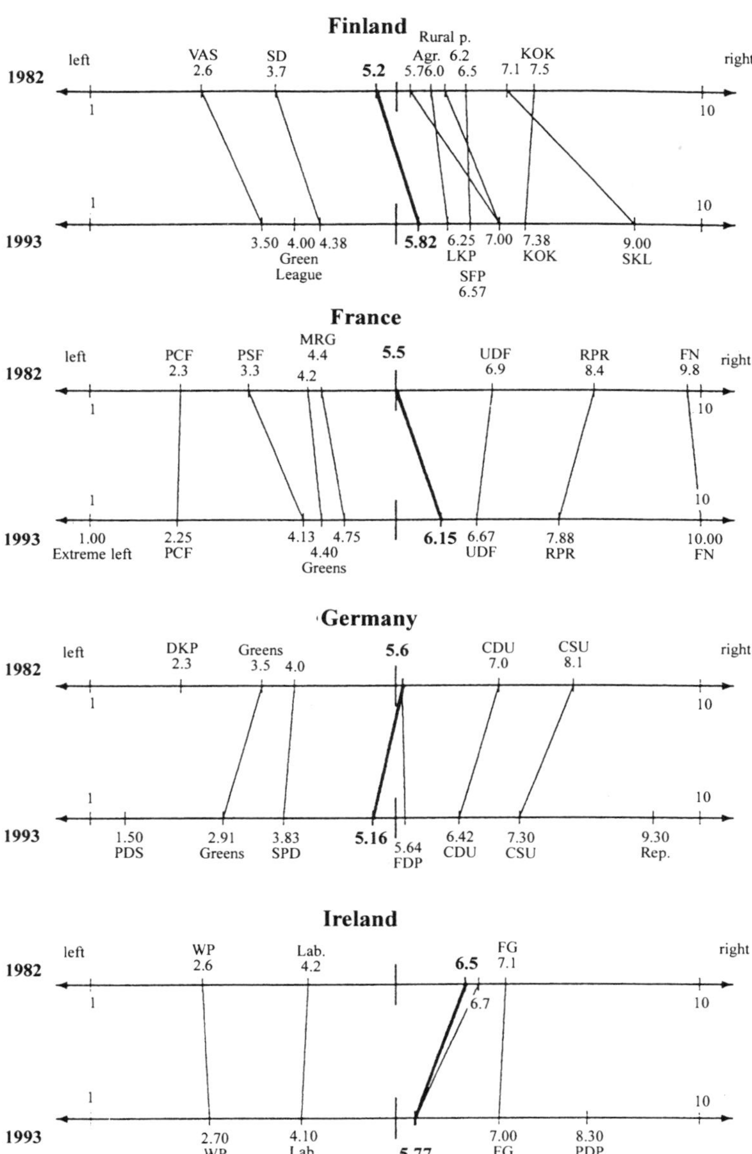

Note: For key to abbreviations, see Appendix.

FIGURE 1(Contd)

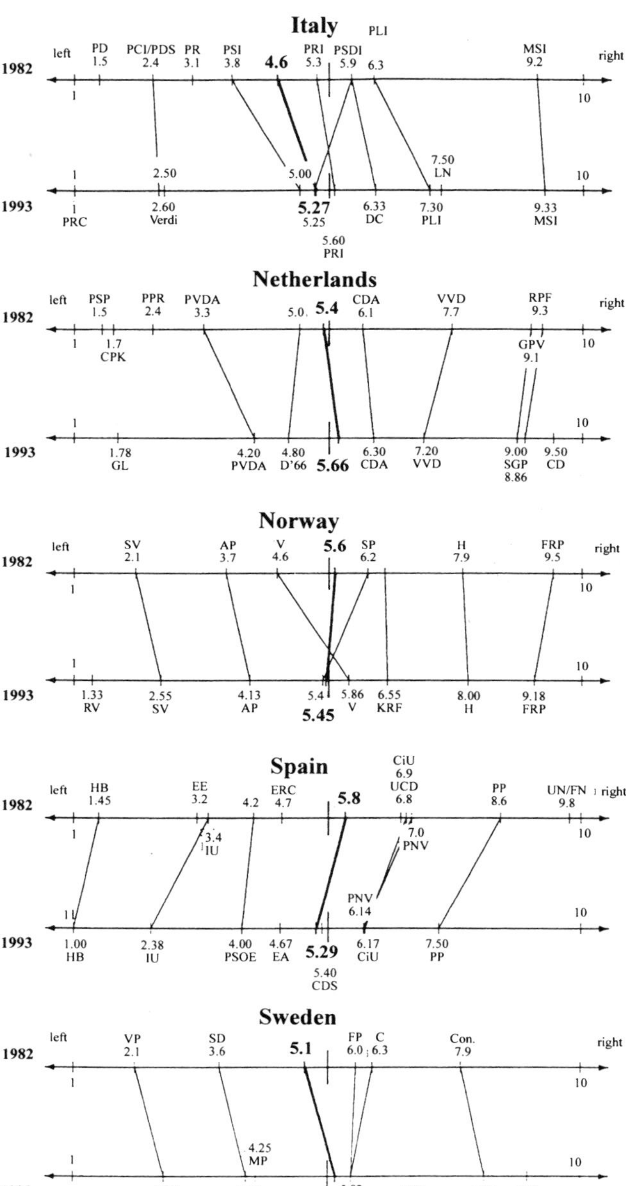

Note: For key to abbreviations, see Appendix.

The ethnic parties are denoted as parties of the moderate right in Belgium,[32] Spain and Finland, while the British nationalist parties are placed to the left of the Liberal Party, which is located exactly in the centre. The Italian Lega Nord was located clearly on the right in 1993, close to the PLI, but away from the radical-rightist MSI, and far from the parties of the radical right in other countries. According to the left–right location of that party, it is clearly not a party of the radical right. These findings are basically in accordance with the general hypotheses.

Thus, let us examine to what extent and how the placement of the various party families changed from the early 1980s to the early 1990s. The main impression from the data is that there is an impressive stability in the way parties are ranked on the left–right scale. The comments below will focus on the changes, but the stability is the dominant impression. This can be illustrated by the average scores for the various party families, which basically rank the party families in the same order in 1993 as in 1982 (see Table 4).

From the average scores for the various party families, we note that the green parties on average are located to the left of the socialist parties in the early 1990s, contrary to the early 1980s. In fact, all green parties apart from the French and Swedish parties are located to the left of the socialist parties. Because of the decline or dissolution of the communist parties, the left-socialist or green parties are now the most significant leftist parties in most cases.

The somewhat complicated location of parties among the non-socialist party families are impressively stable. The changes that can be observed are partly due to new parties and partly caused by some different location of the same parties.

Let me start by commenting on the new parties. The additional right-wing parties that gained some electoral support have all been located at the extreme right. This applies to Germany, the Netherlands and Sweden. Three new liberal parties emerged in Austria, Ireland and Spain. These parties are, however, located very differently. The new Irish Liberal Party is located to the right of the existing parties, the Austrian Liberal Party close to the Christian Party, and the Spanish party in the centre of the party system. Three new green parties has emerged, and they are located somewhat differently. In Austria and Finland they are located to the left of the socialist parties, while the opposite occurs in Sweden.

With regard to the changing positions of parties, the most significant changes are found in the Nordic countries with respect to some of the non-socialist parties: In Denmark the Agrarian Liberal Party, which increased its support significantly, is located to the right of the Conservative party. In Finland the small Christian Party moved to a more extreme right-wing position, and the Agrarian Party also moved further to the right. In Norway the Agrarian and the Liberal parties have changed positions. In 1993 Agrarian Party was to the left of the Liberal Party, while the opposite was true in the early 1980s. Both parties crossed the centre (5.5), but in opposite directions!

A main change from 1982 to 1993 was that parties of the radical right occupied the space to the extreme right in more party systems than in 1993. The radical right-wing parties occupied the rightmost position in six countries in 1982 and nine countries in 1993. In several of the countries where the radical right-wing parties already occupied the rightmost position in 1982, their electoral support increased significantly (Austria, Belgium, France and Norway). Their location is more extreme than the parties previously occupying the rightist position in the left–right dimension, and they are consequently contributing to a higher degree of polarisation in the party system.

CHANGES OVER TIME

The changes from 1982 to 1993 in left–right placement of individual parties can be seen in Figures 1A and 1B. Two types of changes will be examined more systematically. First I will examine changes in a left versus right direction, then changes towards or away from the centre.

Left–Right Changes

In the section of Table 4 which shows the average left–right changes for the various party families for the same parties at both time points, the following trends can be observed: socialist, agrarian and radical-right parties moved towards the right, while green and conservative parties moved leftwards. The largest changes are found for green and socialist parties.

These average trends might cover different trends in different countries. In Table 5 left–right changes are calculated for parties in the various party families. At the bottom of the table, I have shown the number of changes and the number of significant changes. All leftist and rightist changes are simply changes of 0.1 or more, while 'significant' changes are changes of least 0.5. On the lower right-hand side of the table, the total numbers of parties that have been placed to the right and the left in 1993 compared with 1982 have been calculated.

Calculations based on all changes and only significant changes show that there was nearly exactly the same number of changes to the right as to the left. We note that there was a significant change in left–right placement for nearly half of the parties (46 per cent).

Looking more closely at the changing left–right placement of party

TABLE 5

LEFT–RIGHT CHANGE FOR PARTIES IN VARIOUS PARTY FAMILIES, 1982–93

Party Families

	Commu- -nist	Left Socialist	Socialist/ Social Democrat	Green	Ethnic	Agrarian	Liberal	Christian	Conser- vative	Radical Right	Other Parties		
Austria		–	1.1	–	–	–	–	0.1	–	1.5	–		
Belgium	–	–	0.7	-1.6	-0.6	–	-0.7	-0.5	–	0.0	–		
Britain	–	–	1.3	–	–	–	-0.3	–	-0.3	–	–		
Denmark	–	0.2	-0.2	–	–	1.1	0.4	-0.4	0.0	0.3	-0.1, 0.3		
Finland	–	0.8	0.7	–	0.1	1.3	0.3	1.9	-0.1	–	0.8		
France	0.0	–	0.8	0.2	–	–	-0.2	–	-0.5	0.2	0.4		
Germany	–	–	-0.2	-0.6	–	–	0.0	-0.6, -0.8	–	–	–		
Ireland	–	0.1	-0.1	–	–	–	–	-0.1	-0.9	–	–		
Italy	0.1	–	1.2	-0.5	–	–	0.3, 1.0	0.4	–	0.1	-0.6		
Netherlands	–	0.0	0.9	–	–	–	-0.7	0.2	–	–	-0.2,-0.2,-0.3,-0.3		
Norway	–	0.5	0.4	–	–	-0.8	1.3	0.1	0.1	-0.3	–		
Spain		-1.0	-0.2	–	-0.7, -0.9	–	–	-1.1	–	-0.5			
Sweden	–	0.5	0.5	–	–	-0.4	-0.1	–	0.4	–	–		
												Total	Percentage
Changes to right	1	5	9	1	1	2	5	5	2	4	3	38	48
Changes to left	0	1	4	3	3	2	5	5	5	1	7	36	46
No change	1	1	0	0	0	0	1	0	1	1	0	5	6
Significant changes to right	0	3	8	0	0	2	2	1	0	1	1	18	23
Significant changes to left	0	1	0	3	3	1	2	3	3	0	2	18	23
No significant change	2	3	5	1	1	1	7	6	5	5	7	43	54

Notes: + changes to the right.
– changes to the left.
A significant change is defined as a change of at least 0.5.

families, we find that a high portion of the parties among the leftist party families were placed more to the right in 1993 than in 1982. This is particularly evident for the socialist parties, a group in which eight of 13 parties were placed significantly more to the right while none were placed significantly more to the left. The rightist change was large (1.0 or higher) in Britain, Italy and Austria), more modest in Belgium, Finland, France and the Netherlands (0.7–0.9), and smaller in Norway and Sweden (0.4–0.5).

Several of the left socialist parties also moved towards the right (in Finland, Norway and Sweden), while the opposite occurred for the green parties. Three of the four green parties for which I have 1982 data moved significantly towards the left.

Among the parties in the non-socialist party families, the trends were more mixed, but at least among the Christian and conservative parties, the trend was to the left or no significant change. The largest non-socialist parties moved significantly towards the left in Belgium, France, Germany, Ireland and Spain, but in the Netherlands the right-wing Liberal Party also moved towards the left. On the other hand, in Denmark and Finland, two of the largest non-socialist parties, the Agrarian Liberals and the Agrarian Party, respectively, moved towards the right. Italy nearly belongs to this group: The Christian Democrats moved slightly towards the right, and the small Liberal Party (PLI) became significantly more right-wing.

These findings are basically in accordance with the general hypotheses. There was a marked trend from the left towards the centre among the socialist parties. There were also some trends from right to centre for the non-socialist parties.

Although the numbers of parties changing in the two directions were nearly equal, the leftist and rightist trends were not evenly distributed among the 13 countries. This can be seen in Table 6.

According to the table, which includes only significant changes, more parties moved to the right than to the left in Austria, Britain, Denmark, Finland, Italy, Norway and Sweden, while the opposite occurred in Belgium, Germany, Ireland and Spain.

From the left–right placement of the various parties in each country, it is possible to calculate a left–right average for the party system as a whole.[33] These mean scores are shown in Table 6B and on the right-hand side of Table 6A.

In 1982 the Irish party system was the furthest to the right, followed by those of Belgium, Spain and Britain. On the leftist side we find the Italian party system and then those of Austria, Sweden and Finland. The ranking of countries is quite different for 1993, indicating that there was considerable change in the left–right orientation of the various party systems. The cross-national differences in mean scores were smaller in 1993 than in 1982. We

TABLE 6

LEFT–RIGHT CHANGE FOR PARTIES IN VARIOUS COUNTRIES AND FOR PARTY SYSTEMS, 1982–93

A. Number of Changes to Left or Right Parties in Various Countries

	All Changes			Significant Changes			Mean*		
	To right	To left	No change	To right	To left	No sign change	1982	1993	Change
Austria	3	0	0	2	0	1	5.0	5.9	0.9
Belgium	1	4	1	1	4	1	5.9	5.9	0.0
Britain	1	2	0	1	0	2	5.8	6.0	0.2
Denmark	5	3	1	1	0	8	5.5	5.9	0.4
Finland	7	1	0	5	0	3	5.2	5.8	0.6
France	4	2	1	1	1	5	5.5	6.2	0.7
Germany	0	4	1	0	3	2	5.6	5.2	-0.4
Ireland	1	3	0	0	1	3	6.5	5.8	-0.7
Italy	6	1	0	2	1	4	4.6	5.3	0.7
Netherlands	2	5	1	1	1	6	5.4	5.7	0.3
Norway	5	2	0	2	1	4	5.6	5.5	-0.1
Spain	0	6	0	0	5	1	5.8	5.3	-0.5
Sweden	3	2	0	2	0	3	5.1	5.6	0.5
Total	38	35	5	18	17	43	5.5	5.3	0.2

B. Ranking of Countries According to Left–Right Mean Scores of the Party Systems and Changes, 1982–93

1982		1993		Changes 1982–1993	
Ireland	6.5	France	6.2	Austria	0.9
Belgium	5.9	Britain	6.0	France and Italy	0.7
Britain and Spain	5.8	Belgium, Denmark and Austria	5.9	Finland	0.6
Germany and Norway	5.6	Finland and Ireland	5.8	Sweden	0.5
Denmark and France	5.5	Netherlands	5.7	Denmark	0.4
Netherlands	5.4	Sweden	5.6	Netherlands	0.3
Finland	5.2	Norway	5.5	Britain	0.2
Sweden	5.1	Italy and Spain	5.3	Belgium	0.0
Austria	5.0	Germany	5.2	Norway	-0.1
Italy	4.6			Germany	-0.4
				Spain	-0.5
				Ireland	-0.7

* How the support for various parties necessary for calculating the mean scores are obtained on the basis of results in general elections, is outlined in note 23.

note a small average change in rightist directions in accordance with the expectation, when an average left–right location is estimated across the various countries. The party systems, on average, became more rightist, but the change was small, and there were large cross-national variations.

I have ranked the countries according to the strength of the changes on the right-hand side of the table. If we establish a significant change as a change of 0.4 or more, several party systems moved significantly towards the right, namely those of Austria, France, Italy, Finland, Sweden and Denmark, while there were significant changes towards the left in only Ireland, Spain and Germany.

There is no single explanation for the left–right changes of the party systems. If we decompose the changes in the averages for the party systems (not shown in detail here),[34] we find that the radical rightist parties account for almost all changes towards the right in Austria and France. The main causes of the rightist tendency in Sweden were the emergence of the radical right-wing New Democracy on the extreme right and the Christian Democrats on the moderate right. In Italy the rightist tendency had several components: the declining support for the communists (PDS and PRC), the significantly more centrist orientation of the socialists and the emergence of the Lega Nord on the moderate right. In Denmark the changing position (and increased support) of the Agrarian Liberals account for all the rightist changes, and in Finland the main factor was the more rightist location of the socialist and agrarian parties.

The trends in three countries with a leftist tendency in the party system are all explained by the more centrist location of the main parties among the non-socialist parties: Fianna Fáil in Ireland, CDU and CSU in Germany, and *Partido Popular* in Spain. In Spain all parties moved towards the left; in Ireland the Labour Party also gained support at the expense of the two larger non-socialist parties.

In Belgium, where a strong rightist tendency was expected because of the increased support for the radical rightist Flemish Block, the centrist tendency among the other non-socialist parties cancelled out the effect of the increased support for the radical right.

These findings are only partly in accordance with the hypotheses. There was an average trend towards the right in the party systems in Western Europe from 1982 to 1993. The rightist trend was strongest in Austria, and was also significant in France and Denmark, but not in Belgium. The increased support for the radical right is a main explanation for the rightist trends in Austria, France and, to a lesser extent, Sweden. In other countries the rightist trends were caused by a more centrist location of the parties of the left. On the other hand, some of the other left–right changes cannot be explained by the factors incorporated in the hypotheses, as indicated above.

Changes Towards and Away from the Centre

The parties of the left moved to the right and a significant number of parties of the right moved to the left. This implies that there was an important change, not towards the right or the left, but towards the centre. This can be seen in Table 7. It contains the same absolute figures as Table 5, but positive values now indicate movement towards the centre of the scale (5.5), while negative values indicate trends away from the centre.

At the bottom of the table, we note that a much greater number of parties moved towards the centre than away from the centre. If all changes, including minor changes, are examined, more than half of the 79 parties that we have 1982 and 1983 data for moved towards the centre, while about a third moved away from the centre. If we examine the significant changes, 30 per cent of all parties became more centrist, 14 per cent moved away from the centre, while 56 per cent were fairly stable or moved across the centre line. The centrist tendency was strongest among the parties of the left, and in particular among the socialist parties, about 60 per cent of which moved significantly towards the centre. Among the major non-socialist party families (liberal, Christian and conservative), the significant centrist tendency applied to about 30 per cent of all parties.

Table 7 and Figure 1 can also be analysed by examining the parties moving towards and away from the centre. We note the following trends for the various countries:

In Austria the centrist tendency was found for the SPÖ, but at the same time the FPÖ moved far to the right and increased its support significantly. In Belgium the three major parties, socialist, liberals and Christians, all moved towards the centre. The green parties on the other hand, moved towards the left, and the radical-right Flemish Block, being stably located at the extreme right, increased its support significantly. In Britain the Labour Party moved a long distance from the left towards the centre, and there was no significant trend in the opposite direction. In Denmark there was a slight move towards the centre for many parties, but one party moved significantly in the opposite direction: the Agrarian Liberals, the largest non-socialist party in the 1990s. In Finland the parties on the left (Left-Wing Alliance and Social Democrats) moved towards the centre, while the Agrarian Party and some small non-socialist parties moved to the right, away from the centre. In France the main parties on the left and right, socialist and conservative RPR, moved significantly towards the centre. The National Front at the extreme right did, however, increase its support, and parties on the extreme left also gained some support in elections. In Germany the larger parties moved closer towards each other because of the centrist movement of the two Christian-democratic parties. On the other hand, parties appeared on the

TABLE 7

CENTRIST CHANGE FOR PARTIES IN VARIOUS PARTY FAMILIES, 1982–93

Party families

	Com-munist	Left Socialist	Socialist/ Social democrat	Green	Ethnic	Agrarian	Liberal	Christian	Conser-vative	Radical Right	Other Parties		
Austria	–	–	1.1	–	–	-	–	-0.1	–	-1.5	–		
Belgium	–	–	0.7	-1.6	0.6	–	0.7	0.5	–	0.0	–		
Britain	–	-	1.3	–	–	-	-0.3	–	0.3	–	–		
Denmark	–	0.2	-0.2	–	-	-1.1	(0.4)	0.4	0.0	-0.3	0.1, 0.3		
Finland	–	0.9	0.7	–	-0.1	-1.3	-0.3	-1.9	0.1	–	-0.8		
France	0.0	–	0.8	0.2	–	-	0.2	–	0.5	-0.2	0.4		
Germany	–	–	-0.2	-0.6	–	-	0.0	0.6, 0.8	–	–	–		
Ireland	–	0.1	-0.1	-	–	–	–	0.1	0.9	–	–		
Italy	0.1	–	1.2	-0.5	–	–	(0.3), -1.0	-0.4	–	-0.1	(0.6)		
Netherlands	–	0.0	0.9	–	–	–	0.7	-0.2	–	–	-0.2, 0.2, 0.3, 0.3		
Norway	–	0.5	0.4	–	–	0.8	1.3	-0.1	-0.1	0.3	–		
Spain	–	-1.0	-0.2	–	0.7, 0.9	–	–	–	1.1	–	-0.5		
Sweden	–	0.5	0.5	–	–	0.4	0.1	–	-0.4	–	–		
											Sum	Percentage	
Changes towards centre	1	5	9	1	3	2	5	5	5	1	6	43	54
Changes away from centre	0	1	4	3	1	2	3	5	2	4	3	28	35
No change	1	1	0	0	0	0	3	0	1	1	1	8	10
Significant changes towards centre	0	3	8	0	3	1	3	3	3	0	0	24	30
Significant changes away from centre	0	1	0	3	0	2	1	1	0	1	2	11	14
No significant change	2	3	5	1	1	1	7	6	5	5	8	44	56

Notes: + change towards centre, – change away from centre.
Changes for parties that have crossed the centre (5.5), are placed in parentheses.
A significant change is defined as a change of at least 0.5.

extreme left and right (PDS and the Republican Party), and the Green Party moved towards the left. In Ireland the conservative Fianna Fáil moved towards the centre, but, on the other hand, the Labour Party gained larger support and remained firmly on the left, and the new Progressive Democrats occupied a new rightist position in the party system. The left–right location of the Italian parties was fairly stable. The Socialist Party is the only one that moved towards the centre, but Communist Refoundation occupied an extreme left-wing position in 1993. In the Netherlands, Labour and Liberals, the main antagonists along the left–right dimension, moved towards the centre. There was no significant change away from the centre, but a party of the radical right, the Centre Democrats, emerged and gained some support. In Norway three parties, the Socialist Left, The Liberals and the Agrarian Party, moved towards the centre, and only the tiny Red Alliance emerged at the extreme left. In Spain the conservative Partido Popular and the two right-wing ethnic parties moved closer to the centre, while the left socialists and a small, extreme ethnic party moved away from the centre. Finally, the Swedish parties on the left, the Social Democrats and the Left Party, became more centrist, while a new radical rightist party emerged on the right.

CONCLUSIONS

The purpose of this article has been to study the changing left–right location of parties by means of expert judgements. The analysis supports the notion that left–right semantics have a substantial absorptive capacity in the sense that New Politics conflicts seem to be incorporated in these semantics. This can be concluded from the meanings the experts attach to the left–right continuum, and from the fact that the New Politics parties are consistently are located on the left and right.

According to the experts, there was a strong centrist tendency in the party systems of western Europe from 1982 to 1993. This tendency was strongest for the socialist parties, but applies also to the non-socialist parties, although to a lesser degree. On the other hand, the New Politics parties became more firmly located on the extreme left and right, contributing to a new polarisation in the party systems.

In terms of left–right location of the party systems, there was generally a trend to the right. This trend was greatest in the countries where mobilisation of the New Right had been the strongest, but several factors contributed to left–right trends in the party systems.

APPENDIX

Abbreviations for the various political parties in Figure 1 and comments on some of the parties and numbers estimated in those figures

Names are used when no abbreviation is indicated.

Austria	Abbreviation
Communist Party	KPÖ
Green Alternative	GA
Socialist Party	SPÖ
People's Party	ÖVP
Liberal Forum	LIF
Freedom Party	FPÖ

Britain	Abbreviation
Labour	Lab.
Plaid Cymru	PC
Scottish National Party	SNP
Social Democratic Party	SDP
Liberal Democrats*	LDP
Conservative Party	Con.

* Liberal Party in 1992.

The scores for the two nationalist parties (SNP and PC) are lacking for 1993. It is assumed that their location on the scale was constant from 1982 to 1993.

Denmark	Abbreviation
Left Socialists*	VS
Communists	DKP
Socialist People's Party	SF
Social Democrats	SD
Radical Liberals	RV
Centre Democrats	CD
Christian People's Party	KRF
Agrarian Liberals	V
Conservative People's Party	KF
Progress Party	FRP

* For 1993: Left-Green Alliance.

Finland	Abbreviation
Left-Wing Alliance*	VAS
Green League	
Social Democrats	SD
Agrarian Party	Agr.
Liberal Party	LKP
Rural Party	Rural Party
Swedish People's Party	SFP
Christian League	SKL
National Coalition Party	KOK

* People's Democratic League in 1982.

Belgium	Abbreviation
Communists	PCB/KPB
Walloon Gathering	RW
Socialist Party	PS/SP
Greens*	
Democratic Front of French Speakers	FDF
Christian Socials	PSC/CVP
Volksunie	VU
Liberals**	PRL/PVV
Respect for Work and Democracy	RAD
Flemish Block***	VB

The Flemish and Francophone parties are included in all data that are presented in this article.

* Only one average score was reported for the two green parties, Ecolo and Agalev, in 1982, but two in 1993. The average scores for these parties were obtained for 1993 by weighting the two scores according to the support for the two parties in the 1991 and 1995 elections.

** Huber and Inglehart do not report any score for the Flemish Liberal Party. In the 1995 national election, the Flemish Liberals and the FDF constituted one federation. Thus, it is not possible to break down the electoral results for these parties. I have, therefore, combined the results for FDF and the Flemish Liberals and added the support for these parties to the support for the Walloon Liberals, assuming that they have the same location. The score for the FDF in 1993 is 7.00, according to Huber and Inglehart.

*** Huber and Inglehart do not report any score for the Flemish Block, a significant party in the Belgian party system. The score for 1993 was reported by John Huber in a private communication. The support for another right-wing extremist party – the National Front is added to the support for the Flemish Block.

Appendix (continued)

France	Abbreviation
Extreme Left*	
Communist Party	PCF
Socialist Party	PSF
Greens**	
Left Radicals	MRG
Union for French Democracy	UDF
Rally for the Republic	RPR
National Front	FN

* The mean positions are based on two parties reported by Huber and Inglehart, namely the Republican Communist Front and the Workers' Front.
** The Greens in 1993 comprised both Generation Ecologist and Les Verts Ecologists.

Germany	Abbreviation
Communist Party	DKP
Democratic Socialist Party	PDS
Greens	
Social Democrats	SPD
Free Democratic party	FDP
Christian Democratic Union	CDU
Christian Social Union	CSU
Republican Party	Rep.

Italy	Abbreviation
Proletarian Democrats	PD
Communist Refoundation	PRC
Communist Party/ Democratic Party of the Left	PCI/PDS*
Verdi	
Radical Party	PR
Socialist Party	PSI
Republican Party	PRI
Social Democrats	PSDI
Lega Nord	LN
Christian Democrats	DC
Liberal Party	PLI
Italian Social Movement	MSI

* Communist Party (PCI) in 1982 and Democratic Party of the Left (PDS) in 1993.

Because several parties split and merged from 1992 to 1994, it was not possible to include the results for the 1994 national election.

Ireland	Abbreviation
Workers' Party*	WP
Labour Party	Lab.
Fianna Fail	FF
Fine Gael	FG
Progressive Democrats	PDP

* The Democratic Left Party, which splintered off from the Workers' Party in 1993. The percentage is based on the Workers' Party together with the Democratic Left Party.

Netherlands	Abbreviation
Pacifist Socialist Party	PSP
Communist Party	CPN
Green Left	GL
Labour Party	PVDA
Democrats '66	D'66
Christian Democratic Appeal	CDA
Liberal Party	VVD
Reformed Political Union	GPV
Reformed Political Federation	RPF
Political Reformed Party	SGP
Centre Democrats	CD

Norway	Abbreviation
Red Alliance	RV
Socialist Left Party	SV
Labour Party	AP
Agrarian Party	SP
Liberal Party	V
Christian People's Party	KRF
Conservative Party	H
Progress Party	FRP

Appendix (continued)

Spain	Abbreviation
Herri Batasuna	HB
Euskadico Esquerra	EE
United Left*	IU
Socialist	PSOE
Basque Solidarity	EA
Esquerra Republicana de Catalonya	ERC
Convergence and Unity	CiU
Partido Nacionalista Vasco	PNV
Union del Centro Democratico	UDC
Centro Democratico y Social**	CDS
Partodo Popular***	PP
Union Nacional/Fuerza Nueva	UN/FN

* Communist Party in 1982.
** The support of the splinter party Centro Democratico y Social, which was founded in 1982, is included.
*** Alianza Popular in 1982.

Sweden	Abbreviation
Left Party*	VP
Social Democrats	SD
Green Ecology Party	MP
Liberal Party	FP
Agrarian Party	C
Christian Democrats	KDS
Conservative Party	Con.
New Democracy	ND

* Left Party Communists (VPK) in 1982.

NOTES

1. Dieter Fuchs and Hans-Dieter Klingemann, 'The Left–Right Schema,' in M. Kent Jennings and Jan van Deth *et al.* (eds.) *Continuities in Political Action* (Berlin and NY: de Gruyter 1990) p.205; Ronald Inglehart and Hans-Dieter Klingemann, 'Party Identification, Ideological Preference and the left–right Dimension among Western Mass Publics', in Ian Budge, Ivor Crewe and Dennis Farlie (eds.) *Party Identification and Beyond. Representations of Voting and Party Competition* (London: John Wiley 1976) pp.244–5.
2. Michael-John Morgan, 'The Modelling of Governmental Coalition Formation: a Policy-Based Approach with Interval Measurement' (U. of Michigan) PhD thesis, reported in Michael Laver and Norman Schofield, *Multiparty Government: The Politics of Coalitions in Europe* (Oxford: OUP 1990) pp.248, 250.
3. John Huber and Ronald Inglehart, 'Expert Interpretations of Party Space and Party Location in 42 Societies', *Party Politics* 1/1 (1995) p.81.
4. John D. Huber, 'Values and Partisanship in Left–Right Orientations: Measuring Ideology', *European Journal of Political Research* 17 (1989) pp.611–15; Oddbjørn Knutsen, 'Value Orientations, Political Conflicts and Left–Right Identification: A Comparative Study', *European Journal of Political Science* 28/1 (1995) pp.63–93; Giacomo Sani and Giovanni Sartori 'Polarization, Fragmentation and Competition in Western Democracies', in Hans Daalder and Peter Mair (eds.), *Western European Party Systems: Continuity and Change* (Beverly Hills and London: Sage 1983) pp.310–16.
5. See Francis G. Castles and Peter Mair, 'Left–Right Political Scales: Some "Expert Judgements"', *European Journal of Political Research* 12 (1984) pp.73–88; Huber and Inglehart (note 3) pp.73–111.
6. The location of the parties on the left–right scale was one of several questions in the survey. The respondents were also asked to identify the key issues that divided left and right, and whether there was some other important dimension in addition to the left–right dimension; see Huber and Inglehart (note 3) p.91.

7. In addition to the 13 western European countries in Castles and Mair's study, Huber and Inglehart's study includes data from Iceland, Portugal and Switzerland.
8. The scores on the 11-point scale (from 0–10) used by Castles and Mair has been transformed to scores on a 10-point scale (from 1 to 10) by the following formula. If we name the score on the 11-point scale v_{11}, the corresponding score on the 10-point scale is: $v_{11} * 0.9 + 1.0$. Castles and Mair report the average scores with one decimal place, while Huber and Inglehart report two decimal places. This difference is reflected in the tables in this article. The scores are reported with one and two decimal places, respectively, but with only one decimal places when differences between the scores in 1982 and 1993 are calculated.
9. One deficiency in both questionnaires is that they did not include pre-defined lists of parties. In Huber and Inglehart's study, the respondents were even asked to place 'the main parties' on the scale. This implies that some parties may have been omitted because few respondents placed them on the scale, and this may have caused the number of parties placed on the scale to vary. This is particularly problematic for the data from 1993 for a few parties, but it is generally a problem that we do not have data for all the parties in both data sets. To calculate the left–right mean scores in given party systems (see Figure 1 and Table 6), it is essential that the parties accounted for as large a percentage of the votes in elections close to 1982 and 1993 as possible. It is, therefore, important that all significant parties are reported in the two data sets. In most countries the parties for which the mean scores are reported, account for 95 per cent or more of the vote in both data sets. In only four countries, namely Ireland, Italy, Spain and France was the support lower than 95 per cent in 1993. Apart from France (89.4 per cent), the support in the other countries was above 90 per cent (91–92 per cent).
10. See Ronald Inglehart, 'The Changing Structure of Political Cleavages in Western Societies', in Russell J. Dalton, Scott C. Flanagan and Paul Allen Beck (eds.) *Electoral Change in Advanced Industrial Societies* (Princeton UP 1984) p.25; Oddbjørn Knutsen, 'Left–Right Materialist Value Orientations', in Jan van Deth and Elinor Scarbrough (eds.) *The Impact of Values*, Vol.4 in the European Science Foundation series 'Beliefs in Government' (Oxford: OUP 1995).
11. Ronald Inglehart, *The Silent Revolution – Changing Values and Political Styles among Western Publics* (Princeton UP 1977); Idem, *Cultural Shift in Advanced Industrial Society* (Ibid. 1990).
12. Scott C. Flanagan, 'Changing Values in Advanced Industrial Societies – Inglehart's Silent Revolution from the Perspective of Japanese Findings', *Comparative Political Studies* 14 (1982) pp.403–44; Idem, 'Value Changes in Industrial Societies', *American Political Science Review* 81 (1987) pp.1303–19.
13. Herbert Kitschelt, *The Transformation of European Social Democracy* (Cambridge: CUP 1994); Idem, *The Radical Right in Western Europe – A Comparative Analysis* (Ann Arbor: U. of Michigan Press 1996).
14. Inglehart, *Cultural Shift* (note 11) pp.275–7; Kitschelt, *Radical Right* (note 13) Chs. 1–2.
15. Inglehart, ibid. pp.289–300; Ronald Inglehart and Jacques-René Rabier, 'Political Realignment in Advanced Industrial Society: From Class-Based Politics to Quality-of-Life Politics', *Government and Opposition* 21 (1986) pp.472–73.
16. Herbert Kitschelt and Staf Hellemans, 'The Left–Right Semantics and the New Politics Cleavage', *Comparative Political Studies* 23 (1990) pp.210–38; Knutsen (note 4) pp.63–93.
17. Huber and Inglehart (note 3) pp.83–90.
18. Ibid. p.78, Table 1.
19. A description of the ten categories is presented in Inglehart and Huber (note 3) p.78, Table 1. Another category that is part of the economic meanings of the left–right dimension is named 'property rights'. However, there are no issues grouped in that category in any of the 13 countries. The other categories are 'centralisation of power', 'isolation versus internationalism', 'conservatism versus change', 'constitutional reform' and 'national defense'. From the description of the last category, it is evident that it could be grouped in the New Politics group, but some of the issues reflect more traditional economic left–right concerns, for example defence spending. This category was mentioned by experts in only three of the countries: Austria (14 per cent), Britain and Germany (both 2 per cent).
20. 'Authority' and 'xenophobia' were of equal importance in Belgium.

21. Oddbjørn Knutsen 'Value Orientations and Party Choice: A Comparative Study of the Relationship between Five Value Orientations and Voting Intention in thirteen West European Democracies', in Oscar W. Gabriel and Jürgen W. Falter (eds.) *Wahlen und politische Einstellungen in westlichen Demokratien* (Frankfurt: Peter Lang 1996) pp.258–66.
22. The table illustrates that, in some countries, parties other than those that belong to the three 'new' party families are 'new' in the sense that they have recently been established, but they do not belong to any of the new party families. Most of them have, in fact, been grouped into some of the old party families. When I use the terms old and new party families or only old and new parties below, I refer to the party families, not individual parties.
23. In order to calculate the figures in Table 3 and the mean scores of the party system in Figure 1 and Table 6, it is necessary to obtain the percentages of the vote for the various parties in the closest elections. As a rule, when a general election was held in 1982 or 1993, I have relied on only that election. Where the year was not an election year, I have calculated the average support in the closest elections, held before and after 1982 or 1993.
24. The parts of Table 3A and Table 4B that include only the same parties control for the fact that parties for which I have data for only one point in time might misrepresent the average score for cross-time comparisons.
25. Michael Steed and Peter Humphreys, 'Identifying Liberal Parties', in Emil J. Kirchner (ed.) *Liberal Parties in Western Democracies* (Cambridge: CUP 1988) pp.416–17.
26. R.E.M. Irving, 'Christian Democracy in Post-War Europe: Conservatism Writ-Large or Distinctive Political Phenomenon?', *West European Politics* 2/1 (Jan. 1979) pp.53–68.
27. Neil Elder, Alistair H. Thomas and David Arter, *The Consensual Democracies? The Government and Politics of the Scandinavian States* (Oxford: Martin Robertson 1983) pp.30–1.
28. Irving (note 26) pp.54, 66; Wolfgang C. Müller and Barbara Steininger, 'Christian Democracy in Austria: The Austrian People's Party', in David Hanley (ed.), *Christian Democracy in Europe – a Comparative Perspective* (London: Pinter 1994) p.95.
29. Elder, *et al.* (note 27) pp.39, 42.
30. Kitschelt (note 13) p.2.
31. Kitschelt (note 13) pp.30–9, 149–206.
32. The figures for Belgium are based on the Flemish Volksunie, while the other two ethnic parties FDF and RW are not included since I lack data from 1993. For 1982 there appear to be large differences in the left–right placement of the three ethnic parties (see Figure 1), Volksunie to the right, FDF in the centre and RW to the left.
33. This is done by simple multiplying the left–right placement of each party by the party's share of the vote expressed as a proportion, then summing these figures for the various parties.
34. This is done by first multiplying the left–right score for each party by the voter support for the party for in the early 1980s and early 1990s, then comparing the scores for each party for the two time points.

Postmaterialism and Electoral Choice before and after German Unification

DIETER FUCHS and ROBERT ROHRSCHNEIDER

This article examines the implications of German unification for the relationship between postmaterial values and voters' party preference. Based on longitudinal data covering 1983 through to 1995, the article argues and shows empirically that, in the post-communist context: economic, immigration, and security issues became more salient to voters, while postmaterial issues, such as environmentalism are reduced in salience; as a result, the proportion of materialists increased sharply while the proportion of postmaterialists decreased substantially; which affects the competitive position of parties. In particular, while the CDU/CSU is in a favourable position to address materialist issues without upsetting a delicate balance between materialist and postmaterialist constituencies, the SPD faces a strategic quandary in trying to satisfy both types of constituencies. These developments at least temporarily reduce the effect of postmaterialism on voters' partisanship. Against this backdrop, we assess the continuous relevance of postmaterialism for the future of electoral politics in Germany.

The theory of postmaterial value change has had a fundamental affect on how analysts interpret political attitudes and behaviour in Germany (and other industrial democracies) in the post-war decades.[1] By the time the Berlin Wall fell in 1989, western Germany was frequently cited as a particularly suitable example of how postmaterialism may lead to the evolution of social movements, the formation of Green parties and the spread of unconventional modes of participation.[2] Even established parties, such as the Social Democratic Party (SPD), began to adopt policy positions about environmental protection and gender equality, for instance, which is an indication of the importance of these new issues as a force in Germany's party system. Despite the continuing controversies over whether life-cycle or generational processes dominate this process of value change,[3] most analysts would agree that far-reaching changes in citizens' basic political values took place in western Germany before unification revamped the backdrop of German politics.

West European Politics, Vol.21, No.2 (April 1998), pp.95–116
PUBLISHED BY FRANK CASS, LONDON

Germany's unification in 1990, however, raises the issue of whether postmaterial values continue to influence citizens' political behaviour with the same force, given the changed context in the unified Germany. Due to the enormous cost of unification, eastern and western Germany are experiencing economic problems which may temporarily reduce the relevance of postmaterial issues and increase the importance of 'bread-and-butter' issues over the economy. We began elsewhere to examine the impact of unification and the changing issue context on voters' partisanship with regard to the 1994 federal election.[4] This article continues to explore the impact of Germany's unification on the electoral process by examining the impact of postmaterialism on citizens' electoral choice. In order to assess the degree to which unification affects the link between postmaterialism and electoral behaviour, we adopt a long-term perspective and study the linkage between postmaterialism and partisanship during the period 1983–95.

We begin by suggesting that the unified electorate represents a merger of two different electorates. We then argue that the unified electorate's structural characteristics and the changed issue context in post-communist Europe create conditions which reduce the relevance of postmaterial values for voters and parties over the medium term. Next we document empirically that (1) voters' policy priorities changed after Germany's unification; (2) the proportion of voters holding postmaterial value priorities declined after Germany's unification which, in turn, (3) has influenced the relationship between postmaterial values, party policies and voters' party preferences.

POSTMATERIALISM AND THE ELECTORAL PROCESS IN EASTERN AND WESTERN GERMANY

As a starting point for this discussion, it is useful to separate the unified electorate in Germany into its constituent eastern and western German components (Figure 1). This figure reflects our belief that the formally unified electorate is actually composed of two electorates which adhere to different electoral logics. The figure should not be misread as depicting a strict temporal sequence. Obviously, competitive elections did not take place in eastern Germany before unification occurred. Rather, the figure represents a heuristic device to differentiate the various processes that exist in the formally unified electorate. We first discuss the developments in western Germany in order to assess the specific role of postmaterialism in the western German party system at the time of Germany's unification. We then summarise what is known about the eastern German electorate after which we examine how the merger of the two electorates might affect the relevance of postmaterialism in this changed issue context.

FIGURE 1
THE LOGIC OF TWO ELECTORATES

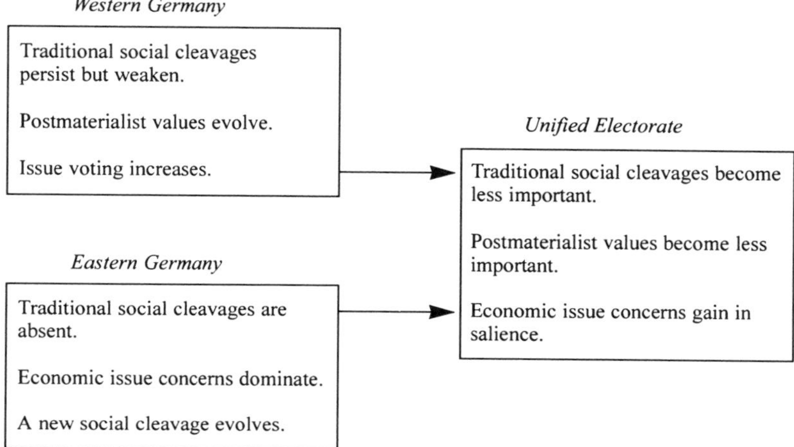

Source: R. Rohrschneider and D. Fuchs, 'A New Electorate?', *German Politics and Society* 13/1 (1995) p.103.

Postmaterialism and Electoral Choice in the West

Analysts of voters' choice in industrialised democracies frequently place the interpretation of electoral behaviour within a cleavage framework. One important account of this perspective can be found in Lipset and Rokkan[5] who argue that the establishment of the nation-state and the industrial revolution produced societal divisions which formed the foundation for western European party systems of the twentieth century. These divisions establish: (a) the centre–periphery cleavage leading to ethnic and regional parties; (b) a cleavage between religious denominations, primarily Protestants and Catholics; (c) a division between the industrial and agrarian sectors; and (d) the industrial cleavage which provides the foundation for socialist and centre-conservative parties. Although nation-specific developments as well as institutional differences and variations in élite behaviour influenced how societal divisions were translated into party systems, both the industrial and religious cleavages became important determinants of electoral behaviour in the twentieth century in most advanced industrial societies.[6]

The western German party system provides no exception to this general scenario. After the first competitive federal election in 1949, the behaviour of voters, as well as the number of parties, were stable throughout the 1950s. Until the early 1970s, the party system and the electoral choice of voters primarily reflected the industrial and the religious cleavages.[7] Likewise, economic and welfare issues frequently constituted one important theme in most election campaigns, in addition to the election-specific context such as Brandt's *Ostpolitik* in 1972. Until the early 1970s, then, voters' choice was frequently interpreted along class and religious cleavages: the SPD was primarily seen as a representative of the working class, especially the unionised and less religious sectors, while the Free Democrat Party (FDP) and the Christian Democratic Union/Christian Social Union (CDU/CSU) were predominately supported by the middle class and, in case of the CDU/CSU, the religious sector.[8]

By the early 1970s, however, the first signs of change emerged.[9] Partially as a result of Germany's continuous transformation from an industrial society to a post-industrial one (i.e., the growing new middle class, the growing proportion of well educated, the decline of the religious sector), the division between the working and middle class alone became less satisfying as an explanatory tool of voters' decision making. Because the new middle class lacked a clear position in the traditional cleavage space of the German party system, these voters lacked a clear partisan representative within the established party spectrum and consequently had to be attracted by parties' programmatic appeals. For example, Brandt's *Ostpolitik* successfully attracted a disproportionate share of the new middle class.[10] While this success helped the Social Democrats (SPD) to win the 1972 election, it also increased the range of constituencies that the SPD had to satisfy from then on, setting the stage for heated intraparty debates in the ensuing decade over environmental, peace, and women's issues.

In addition to the weakening of traditional cleavages, the evolution of postmaterial values has contributed to fundamental changes in the political agenda and structure of Germany's party system. The main proponent of this approach, Ronald Inglehart, argues that the conditions of affluence and international stability, which prevailed during the post-war years, lead to a basic shift in value priorities among western European publics and élites.[11] Building upon Maslow's hierarchy of needs, Inglehart's scarcity hypothesis maintains that individuals first satisfy basic material needs (for food, shelter, etc.) before they turn their attention to satisfying the so-called higher-order needs (e.g., a clean environment and greater participation in the political process). The socialisation hypothesis posits, in turn, that economic conditions during an individual's formative years of socialisation are crucial in forming that individual's value priorities. Thus, Inglehart's theory predicts that postmaterial value priorities emerge along generational lines when economic affluence prevails and international stability predominates. Consistent with these expectations, Inglehart documented in several analyses that postmaterialists are less likely to prioritise economic and security issues.

Inglehart provides ample evidence consistent with the predictions derived from the theory of postmaterialism,[12] as follows: (1) with the exception of Belgium, there has been a net shift towards postmaterialism in most western European countries; (2) younger cohorts have a higher proportion of postmaterialists than older cohorts; and (3) short-term fluctuations in this overall increase towards postmaterialism tend to occur during economic recessions, as during the late 1970s. Despite this evidence, several analysts criticised the conceptual and empirical foundations of this theory. Although most agree that values are changing, it is especially controversial whether the observed changes represent long-term generational change or shorter-term life-cycle effects[13] and whether they are caused by measurement problems.[14] Despite this onslaught on postmaterialism, Inglehart and Abramson conclude: 'It is apparent that there has been a trend toward postmaterialism in seven of the eight European societies, as well as in the United States.'[15]

Established parties were initially reluctant to integrate new issues into their programmes because these orientations are not easily integrated in a party system which primarily represents alternative economic and religious policies. Additionally, since postmaterialists are concentrated among the younger, better educated voters whose socio-demographics predisposed them to support centre-conservative parties in the past, the postmaterial cleavage cuts across established partisan alliances. Consequently, the Green party was founded in the late 1970s. Although the Greens failed to clear the five-percent threshold in the 1980 election, they jumped this hurdle in the 1983 and 1987 elections. While the (western) Greens did not enter the Bundestag in 1990 – only the eastern Alliance 90/Greens garnered enough votes to obtain parliamentary representation – the pragmatic reorientation of the Alliance 90/Greens may help this party to become a permanent feature of the German party system.[16] At the same time, the SPD began to address policy demands made by social movements which resulted in their enhanced ability to attract environmentally concerned voters.[17] By the time of Germany's unification, the SPD had begun to synthesise material and postmaterial policies, whereas the governing parties of the CDU/CSU and the FDP by and large continued to focus on economic and security issues.

In sum, it is widely accepted in the electoral politics literature that the evolution of postmaterial values has transformed western Germany's party system. This development is reflected in the evolution of non-economic issues onto the political agenda throughout the 1980s. Subsequently, these new policy issues significantly altered western Germany's party system. A new party was founded, established parties responded to new issue challenges, and established parties even began to experiment with democratic intraparty procedures.[18]

Electoral Choice in the Eastern German Electorate

Given the relatively short history of competitive elections in eastern Germany, we know considerably less about the eastern German electorate. But if one compares the developments in the West with those in the East as they evolved over the past years, there are both similarities, but also striking differences. The first important difference concerns the linkage between traditional social cleavages and electoral choice. Four decades of socialism largely eradicated traditional social cleavages from eastern German society, although there is some evidence that the eastern German electorate is slowly approaching the employment structure of the western German electorate.[19] Still, given that traditional cleavages were eradicated and party competition was restrained under the socialist system, the development of a stable linkage between occupational groups and party preference in the East probably requires that citizens in the East experience the electoral process a few times before the linkage between occupational groups and party preferences is in parallel with that of the western electorate. Therefore, voters' choice in the East is likely to remain less structured by voters' occupations than in the West, even though the two electorates may eventually converge in their behaviour in the long run.[20]

The collapse of the socialist system also created a division between those who supported or at least benefited from the perished socialist system and those who did not. 'Unification losers' frequently held positions in the non-industrial sector, such as the government administration, universities, or the party bureaucracy in the GDR. Although these voters frequently do not suffer materially from Germany's unification, they disproportionately support the PDS. These voters are typically classified as white-collar employees in electoral analyses. In turn, working-class individuals lacking a habitual attachment to any major party in the East endorse parties which represent economic prospects and German unification – the CDU/CSU and the FDP. Consequently, the relationship between eastern German voters' electoral choice and their class status in the 1990 and 1994 federal elections and the March 1990 Volkskammer election differs substantially from that observed in the West.[21] The working class disproportionately supported the CDU/CSU,[22] which continued to hold true for the 1994 election.[23] Simultaneously, the SPD in eastern Germany, and especially the PDS, obtain more support from the new middle class than from the working class, almost in reverse of the historical link between the working class and left-wing parties, although this relationship is weakening too. Finally, while the religious sector disproportionately supports the centre-conservative party spectrum – which runs parallel to the relationship between religiosity and partisanship in the West – the large number of nonbelievers in the East means that religiosity is not a major influence on eastern German voters.[24]

Coinciding with the weak influence of the class and religious cleavage on eastern voters' party preference, the policy expectations of the eastern German electorate are substantially driven by economic policies. After all, one central motivation for the revolution in 1989 was the prospect for eastern Germans to replace the command economy with a market system, promising a way out of eastern Germany's economic malaise. The promise of the governing coalition in 1990 to achieve economic prosperity in the East (in addition to the enthusiasm over achieving unification) undoubtedly helped the governing parties to win the first election after unification in 1990. The economic policy emphasis among the eastern German electorate is reinforced by the fact that eastern Germany does not qualify as an advanced industrial society in terms of its basic societal characteristics (e.g., with a large middle class, the existence of an elaborate information infrastructure, economic affluence). However, a change from a material to a postmaterial policy agenda is typically associated with the presence of these conditions.[25] Thus, the baseline expectations of eastern Germans and the nature of eastern German society increase the salience of economic issues to voters, while such New Politics themes as environmentalism or women's' issues are of secondary importance to eastern Germans.

POSTMATERIALISM AND THE ELECTORAL PROCESS IN THE UNIFIED GERMANY

Given the different character of the eastern and western electorates, in what ways, if at all, does the changed context in the unified Germany affect the relationship between postmaterialism and voters' party preference? It is difficult to anticipate precisely how the confluence of these various forces in the eastern and western electorate reinforce and counterbalance each other in the long run. But the unified electorate probably contains the following characteristics, at least over the medium term.

For one, we expect that the unification of Germany further weakens the relationship between traditional social cleavages and voters' partisanship, despite the fact that eastern Germany is not yet an advanced industrial economy. In essence, the absence of traditional social classes in the eastern electorate reinforces the dealignment in the West. Likewise, the religious cleavage should become less important as a predictor of electoral behaviour for the unified electorate, given the declining proportion of religious voters in the West and the large group of non-believers in the East. Combining the eastern and western German electorates, then, accelerates the decline of the class and religious cleavage as a predictor of electoral behaviour. This, in turn, increases the odds that a new cleavage, such as postmaterialism, takes the place of traditional social cleavages in structuring the voter–party relationship, provided that contextual conditions remain conducive to the formation of postmaterialist values. However, the changed context in post-communist Europe raises the question whether these conditions continue to generate a shift toward postmaterialism over the short term.

Consider that the collapse of socialist systems in East-Central Europe created a different political environment in Europe which affects the salience of economic, immigration, and security issues relative to New Politics issues.[26] A first important shift in the salience of issues in Germany developed as a result of the economic baseline expectation of eastern German voters. The prospects for economic affluence undoubtedly represented one central reason why eastern Germans favoured quick unification after the Wall fell in November 1989. Further, both eastern and western Germans now feel the financial pressures (through increased taxes or reports about the massive financial transfers from the West to the East, for instance), and may, therefore, prioritise economic policies. Consequently, parties are now called upon to provide policies that provide solutions to the economic problems whereas policies for New Politics issues are less relevant in attracting voters who are concerned with economic policies.

A second important change concerns the renewed emphasis on international security issues in Europe. While the division of Europe after 1949 led to unprecedented regional stability, despite the tensions of the Cold War, the collapse of socialist systems revived traditional resentments among various ethnic, social, and political groups in East-Central Europe with sometimes dramatic consequences (e.g., in the former Yugoslavia). This increase in regional conflict has repercussions for West European nations which are called upon to provide the means (political or military) to secure peaceful stability in Europe. In Germany, for example, the increased salience of security issues is manifested in the recent decision by the government to provide troops to the UN mission in the Balkans. The first military mission of German troops after the Second World War caused an agonising debate in Germany over the acceptability of such military missions which undoubtedly created a heightened sense for international (in)security issues.

Finally, the dissolution of the Iron Curtain reinforces the salience of immigration issues. Greater freedom of movement in East-Central Europe increased the opportunities for individuals to seek asylum in Germany. The dramatic increase of immigrants after the fall of the Wall prompted Germany to change its Basic Law in 1993 to reduce the number of immigrants. Further, ethnic-Germans from the former Soviet Union now have the opportunity to emigrate to Germany. Consequently, the immigration issue has become an even more pressing issue now than it was when the Iron Curtain prevented any significant East–West migration into Germany.

These changes in the post-communist Europe are reflected in the issue salience of various issue areas (Table 1). In western Germany, preunification concerns were defined, in this order, by unemployment and environmental protection. However, after unification, the order of policy priorities changed substantially after Germany's unification. First, unemployment was temporarily reduced because unification and immigration issues overwhelmed the political agenda in Germany during 1991 and 1992. By 1994, however, unemployment had regained its status as the main issue concern for the western German public, and it remained the most important issue in 1995. Second, other issues, like law and order, immigration, or international security issues are much more often mentioned after unification than before – in fact, some of them, such as law and order, were not mentioned at all before 1989. In stark contrast, environmental protection is less important than it used to be. Overall, although the specific mix of salient issues varies somewhat over time, the overwhelming message is that economic and immigration issues, in particular, became more salient to western German voters than they used to be, while issues such as environmentalism presently appear less pressing to voters.

TABLE 1
THE MOST IMPORTANT PROBLEMS IN WESTERN GERMANY 1986–95 (%)

	1986	1987	1991	1992	1993	1994	1995
Unemployed	61	64	12	10	44	61	60
Environmental protection	45	44	16	8	9	12	14
International security issues	22	28	14	6	–	–	14
Economic issues	13	11	18	12	14	10	16
Social security issues	16	24	–	3	7	12	12
Immigrants, foreigners	–	–	45	78	32	21	21
Unification related problems	–	–	40	27	8	6	–
Law and order/Right-wing extremism	–	–	–	5	19	19	–
Housing problems	–	–	7	7	6	7	–

Source: Forschungsgruppe Wahlen (FGW), *Politbarometer* Surveys.

The eastern German electorate is even more preoccupied with economic, security, and immigration issues than the western electorate (Table 2). This is, for example, reflected in the irrelevance of environmental issues to eastern German voters which appear on this list for the first time in 1995. Instead, the policy agenda throughout the initial years after Germany's unification have been dominated by material issues. In sum, although the relative salience of issues may change again as economic conditions improve, the change in issue salience between the mid-1980s and 1995 reflects the dramatic shock wave created by the upheavals in 1989.

TABLE 2
THE MOST IMPORTANT PROBLEMS IN EASTERN GERMANY 1991–95 (%)

	1991	1992	1993	1994	1995
Unemployed	60	62	72	74	77
Environmental protection	–	–	–	–	8
International security issues	11	–	–	–	8
Economic issues	41	29	24	13	5
Social security issues	15	10	15	16	9
Immigrants, foreigners	8	35	9	9	6
Unification related problems	20	14	16	12	9
Law and order/Right-wing extremism	–	17	27	28	10
Housing problems	13	12	7	10	8

Source: Forschungsgruppe Wahlen (FGW), *Politbarometer* Surveys.

Postmaterialism and the Changed Environment

These developments raise two questions. First, given the importance of postmaterial issues to German voters before the fall of the Berlin Wall, how strongly do postmaterialist values structure voters' electoral choice during this period of upheaval? Second, what are the odds that postmaterialism will continue to influence voters' choice given the changed issue context?

In answering these questions, it is useful to recall that Inglehart's theory of postmaterial value change rests on two key hypotheses: scarcity and socialisation.[27] Given the theoretical premises of postmaterialism, one would predict that levels of postmaterialism decline at least temporarily during a transitional period. This expectation is clearly confirmed (Figure 2). In following the tradition of presenting these trends, Figure 2 presents

FIGURE 2
PERCENTAGE OF POSTMATERIALISTS MINUS PERCENTAGE OF MATERIALISTS IN GERMANY AND EUROPE, 1976–95

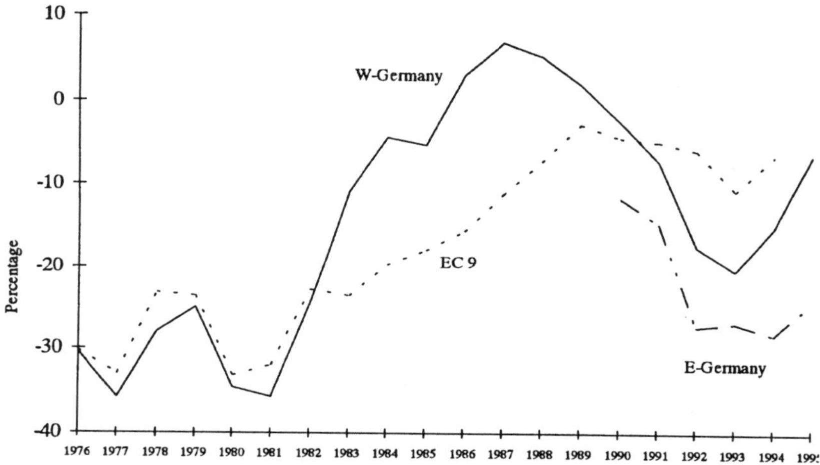

Notes: Europe/EC9 consists of Belgium, Britain, Denmark, Germany, Ireland, Italy, Luxembourg, and the Netherlands. The database are the average of the countries. The country data are weighed.

Source: Eurobarometer, Nos. 6–42 (1976–94), KSPW-BUS 1995.

the net percentage of postmaterialists (i.e., the percentage of materialists is subtracted from the percentage of postmaterialists). We also present the pooled West European results for those countries for which data exist for 1976–95. The much shorter time series in eastern Germany begins in 1990.

Let us begin with western Germany. After a 'bumpy start' at the beginning of the time series which coincides with the economic recession at the end of the 1970s, there is a steady shift toward postmaterialism until about 1988, but declines substantially thereafter. This decline coincides with the changed economic and security context in the unified Germany. As during the recession at the end of the 1970s, short-term fluctuations in economic (and security) conditions may reduce overall levels of postmaterialism. These findings are, therefore, generally consistent with the premises of postmaterialism which would predict this decline, given the economic conditions in Germany at the time of unification. At the same time, it is surprising from a generational perspective how quickly the changed context in western Germany reduced aggregate levels of postmaterialism, a point we will take up below. The declining trend is reversed in 1993 and aggregate levels of postmaterialism begin to return to previous levels by 1995. It appears that as the eastern economic sector bottoms out of the economic recession, levels of postmaterialism may rise again to pre-unification levels.

The shorter time span covered in eastern Germany also generates results consistent with postmaterialism. The net proportion of postmaterialists is lower in the East which undoubtedly reflects the lower level of economic prosperity in eastern Germany. Furthermore, like in the West, the downward trend appeared to be levelling off by 1995, perhaps signalling the onset of a rise of postmaterialism as economic conditions began to improve somewhat throughout 1994 and early 1995. Overall, the changed context after Germany's unification created unfavourable conditions for the formation of postmaterial values.

Postmaterialism and Electoral Choice Before the Fall of the Wall

The rise of postmaterialism in western Germany changed the party landscape in two important ways throughout the 1980s. First, postmaterial values led to the formation of a viable Green party which entered the federal parliament for the first time in 1983, winning 27 seats. Although the (western) Greens did not manage to pass the threshold of five per cent in the 1990 election, they regained entry to the federal parliament in 1994 in an alliance with its eastern German counterpart. By now, the Alliance 90/Greens are a well-established party based on its stronghold in the western electorate. Second, the evolution of the Greens in the West prompted established parties to address postmaterial issues. The SPD in particular made a substantial effort to attract voters with New Politics orientations, such as support for environmental issues or women's issues.[28] While the CDU–CSU also attempted to cater for the environmental sentiment of voters, the main party outlets for postmaterial issues are located predominately at the Old and New-Left end of the party spectrum.

The general relationship (gamma) between voters' party preference and postmaterial values reflects the growing importance of this dimension for western German voters in the 1980s (Figure 3). After a significant increase in the strength of the relationship in the early 1980s following the formation of the Green Party, the relationship slowly levelled off and decreased somewhat by the end of the 1980s, although it stayed at a relatively high level. In short, when the Greens began to offer a partisan outlet and the SPD began to address these issues, postmaterialism had a substantial impact on voters' party preference. (The development after 1989 is discussed below).

While this relationship confirms the overall importance of postmaterialism for electoral behaviour, we suspect that postmaterialist voters may side with different parties at different times, depending on the

FIGURE 3
CORRELATION BETWEEN VALUE PREFERENCES AND VOTE INTENTION 1976–95 (GAMMA)

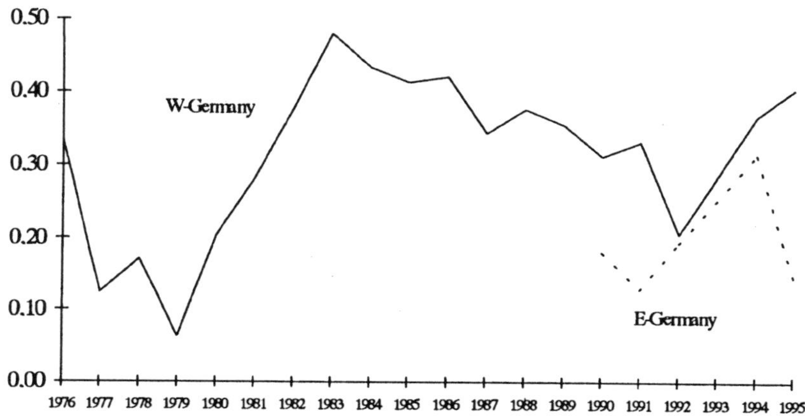

Notes: Vote intention is treated as an ordinal variable. The parties are ordered according to the left-right self-placement of the respective party supporters: 1 = Republikaner, 2 = CDU/CSU, 3 = FDP, 4 = SPD, 5 = Grüne/B90, 6 = PDS.

Source: Eurobarometer, Nos.6–38 (1976–92), Post-election Survey 1994, KSPW-BUS 1995.

programmatic positions of parties (Table 3). Between 1983 and 1989, the CDU/CSU is clearly the major party for materialists, even though this proportion is reduced from a high of 63.9 per cent in 1983 to 49.2 per cent in 1989. The relatively low percentage in 1989 is probably due to the fact that the right-wing Republikaner Party attracts a comparatively larger share of materialists (9.3 per cent) than in previous (and subsequent) years. In contrast, postmaterialists are substantially less likely to support the CDU/CSU. The highest proportion never exceeds 23.9 per cent (in 1987), and more often fluctuates around 20 per cent between 1983 and 1989.

The main opposition party, the SPD, also attracts a substantial share of materialists, ranging from a low of 33.2 per cent in 1983 to a high of 41.0 per cent in 1985, after which the proportion of postmaterialists within the SPD's constituency decreases by a small margin. In contrast to the CDU/CSU, however, the proportion of postmaterialists with a party preference for the SPD is larger than the corresponding materialist percentage. The fact that the SPD did not lose – in the aggregate – postmaterialists to the Greens throughout the late 1980s is undoubtedly attributable to the SPD's effort to cater for postmaterial constituencies by, for example, opposing the further expansion of nuclear power as an energy source. This mix of materialists and postmaterialists in the SPD constituency also reflects the programmatic difficulties for the SPD: if it focuses too much on postmaterial issues, it may lose materialist voters to the CDU/CSU; if it overly emphasises materialist policies, it may lose voters to the Greens.

TABLE 3
VALUE PRIORITIES AND VOTE INTENTION IN WESTERN GERMANY, 1983–89

	Materialists						
	1983	1984	1985	1986	1987	1988	1989
Republikaner	0.3	0.0	0.5	0.1	0.5	0.8	9.3
CDU/CSU	63.9	56.6	53.6	54.7	53.0	57.1	49.2
FDP	1.7	2.2	4.0	3.2	5.0	2.4	4.1
SPD	33.2	38.3	41.0	40.5	37.0	39.0	35.0
Grüne	0.9	2.9	0.9	1.5	4.5	0.7	2.4
Total	100%	100%	100%	100%	100%	100%	100%
(N)	(442)	(333)	(357)	(277)	(271)	(309)	(556)

	Postmaterialists						
	1983	1984	1985	1986	1987	1988	1989
Republikaner	0.0	0.0	0.0	0.1	0.4	1.8	2.2
CDU/CSU	19.6	16.0	20.7	19.9	23.9	23.8	23.3
FDP	3.3	2.3	3.0	4.5	6.3	4.5	5.3
SPD	46.5	55.2	51.1	49.4	46.9	49.5	50.2
Grüne	30.6	26.5	25.2	26.1	22.5	20.5	19.0
Total	100%	100%	100%	100%	100%	100%	100%
(N)	(271)	(264)	(279)	(304)	(349)	(386)	(689)

Source: Eurobarometer, Nos.19–31 (1983–89).

Finally, the Green Party was another central partisan outlet for postmaterial voters during this time.[29] Note, however, that the percentage of postmaterialists almost without exception declined steadily from the high of 30.6 per cent in 1983 to a low of 19.0 per cent. This proportion is substantially lower than the percentage of postmaterialists who preferred the SPD (50.2 percent). In addition to the intra-organisational debates over the future course of the Greens, the effort of the SPD to attract postmaterialists is clearly one important factor for this weakening support of postmaterialists for the Greens.

Postmaterialism and Electoral Choice After Unification

As we discussed earlier, the new issue context after the fall of the Berlin Wall led to a decline of postmaterial values. The new issue context affects parties' competitive position relative to each other which, in turn, influences the relationship between postmaterialism and voters' party preferences.

Let us start with the unification 'winner' at the party level. The CDU/CSU undoubtedly benefited from the events surrounding unification because these parties were the champions of Germany's unification. Further, the focus on economic, immigration, and security issues after Germany's unification is consistent with the party's past policy emphasis on material issues. Unification thus created a short and a medium-term electoral 'boost' for the CDU/CSU. In the short term, Chancellor Kohl's political skills in achieving unification helped this party win the 1990 election. Over the medium term, the focus on materialist issues has helped this party because it has been able to offer an established programmatic canon for materialist policy issues without jeopardising a delicate balance between material and postmaterial constituencies.

In contrast to the CDU/CSU, Germany's unification created a dilemma for the SPD. This quandary ironically originates, in part, with the successful attempts made by the SPD to attract material and postmaterial voters before unification. After unification, the SPD faced the difficult choice between emphasising materialist policies and developing a programmatic synthesis between material and postmaterial policies. It soon became clear that the SPD shifted its programmatic emphasis towards material issues when, for example, the SPD decided to support a change in the refugee clause of the constitution to reduce the influx of foreigners. This programmatic adjustment was evidently motivated by the SPD's desire to increase its appeal to the material preferences of centrist voters and to document its willingness to adopt government responsibility. Further, the willingness of the SPD to reach a compromise with the governing coalition in terms of long-term nursing care also indicated that the SPD sought to appeal to centrist voters. But these programmatic developments also suggest that the SPD for now de-emphasises postmaterial issues.[30]

Finally, the Greens, while facing difficulties to coming to terms with the renewed nationalist component in German politics, were unwilling to abandon the postmaterial platform. Thus, they became the central party representative for postmaterial voters.

In the western German electorate, the changing programmatic profile of the SPD after unification is clearly manifested in the increase of materialists and the declining proportion of postmaterialists which supported the SPD (Table 4). In fact, by 1994, the proportion of materialists supporting the SPD

(49.4 per cent) is larger than the proportion of postmaterialists siding with the SPD (35.0 per cent); and this balance continued to favour materialists in 1995. This was the only point in time between 1983 and 1995 when a greater percentage of materialists than postmaterialists preferred the SPD. Correspondingly, the percentage of postmaterialists supporting the Greens increased substantially between 1990 (13.5 per cent) and 1995 (41.2 per cent), even exceeding the high levels of 1983. Whether this trend will continue, depends on the SPD's policy decisions over the next years. Expectedly, the CDU/CSU continues to be supported by voters having materialist values. Regarding the relationship between postmaterialism and party preferences, unification has returned the western German party system to the competitive situation of 1983!

TABLE 4
VALUE PRIORITIES AND VOTE INTENTION IN WESTERN GERMANY, 1990–1995

	Materialists					*Postmaterialists*				
	1990	1991	1992	1994	1995	1990	1991	1992	1994	1995
Republikaner	3.3	2.3	6.3	0.6	2.0	0.4	2.6	5.7	0.0	0.7
CDU/CSU	52.2	50.3	42.1	43.4	47.6	26.4	14.7	16.8	22.5	17.6
FDP	5.4	6.2	4.2	4.8	2.0	7.4	12.6	4.4	1.9	5.1
SPD	36.7	39.1	42.4	49.4	44.2	51.7	50.0	48.1	35.0	31.6
Grüne/B'90	2.3	2.1	4.9	1.8	4.1	13.5	18.7	23.4	35.6	41.2
PDS	0.0	0.0	0.0	0.0	0.0	0.5	1.4	1.6	5.0	3.7
Total	100%	100%	100%	100%	100%	100%	100%	100%	100%	100%
(N)	(125)	(323)	(394)	(166)	(146)	(150)	(237)	(176)	(160)	(136)

Source: Eurobarometer, Nos.33–38 (1990--92); Post-election Survey 1994; KSPW-BUS 1995.

In the eastern electorate, the CDU/CSU was the main party representative of materialists, as was the case in the West (Table 5). The similarity of the link between postmaterialism and CDU/CSU partisanship in the East and West indicates that the centre-conservative party bloc had little difficulty in adjusting to the new issue context. Further, as in the West in 1994 and 1995, the eastern SPD is also predominately supported by materialists, although the proportion of postmaterialists approaches that of materialists. This result is clearly consistent with the programmatic developments of the SPD towards emphasising materialist policies and the predominant materialist orientation of the eastern electorate.

Importantly, there are two parties to the left of the SPD in the eastern electorate, which compete for postmaterial and, to a lesser degree, materialist voters. First, the Alliance 90/Greens attracts a disproportionate share of postmaterialists. Although this percentage was at its low point in 1994 (13.9 per cent), it had increased again by 1995 (22.4 per cent). Certainly, the Alliance 90/Greens represents one important partisan representative for postmaterial voters. The decline of materialists supporting the Alliance 90/Greens reflects the fact that the groups constituting the eastern Alliance 90 are more concerned with 'bread-and-butter' issues than the western Greens. After the merger of the eastern Alliance 90 and the western Greens, the growing dominance of western Greens within this new-left party led to a shift towards postmaterial policies which, in turn, has reduce the attraction of this party to materialist voters. Thus, as in the western electorate, the Alliance 90/Greens competes with the SPD for postmaterial voters.

In contrast to the western electorate, however, the PDS attracts both a significant minority of materialists and a substantial proportion of postmaterialists. The percentage of postmaterialists increased from a low of 10.6 per cent in 1990 to a huge 41.8 per cent in 1994. Although the

TABLE 5
VALUE PRIORITIES AND VOTE INTENTION IN EASTERN GERMANY, 1990–1995

			Materialists		
	1990	1991	1992	1994	1995
Republikaner	0.0	2.0	5.1	0.0	0.5
CDU/CSU	53.7	33.2	30.4	49.0	40.8
FDP	10.2	11.1	11.2	3.3	5.8
SPD	21.5	33.7	32.8	36.1	34.0
Grüne/B'90	10.4	12.6	12.8	1.7	5.8
PDS	4.1	7.4	7.8	10.0	13.1
Total	100%	100%	100%	100%	100%
(N)	(169)	(324)	(374)	(241)	(191)

			Postmaterialists		
	1990	1991	1992	1994	1995
Republikaner	0.0	2.8	1.0	0.0	3.4
CDU/CSU	34.4	21.0	13.3	24.1	20.7
FDP	6.3	10.8	8.3	1.3	5.2
SPD	29.5	28.0	36.8	19.0	22.4
Grüne/B'90	19.3	25.7	19.5	13.9	22.4
PDS	10.6	11.6	21.1	41.8	25.9
Total	100%	100%	100%	100%	100%
(N)	(106)	(165)	(89)	(79)	(58)

Source: Eurobarometer, Nos.33–38 (1990–92); Post-election Survey 1994; KSPW-BUS 1995.

proportion was reduced to 25.9 per cent in 1995, it is fair to note that the PDS established itself as a main postmaterial party in the eastern electorate. Further, unlike the Alliance 90/Greens, the PDS also continues to attract a significant materialist proportion. The percentage of materialists increased from 4.1 per cent in 1990 to 13.1 per cent in 1995. Evidently, then, the PDS's attempt to cater to a rainbow constituency (e.g., younger generation, direct democracy, social-egalitarian and ecologically oriented) seems to have paid off among eastern German postmaterialists and, to a lesser degree, materialists.

The existence of the PDS and its ability to appeal to both materialists and postmaterialists further exacerbates the difficulties of the SPD to project a coherent policy message to the two electorates. If the SPD appeals to centrist materialist voters, which would appear to be a reasonable strategy with predictable electoral payoffs in the western electorate, it loses postmaterialist voters and it may lose materialist voters in the East: dissatisfied leftist materialists may support the PDS. If, on the other hand, the SPD moves towards the postmaterialist end of the spectrum, it will lose on the materialist side in the West and may not necessarily be able to establish itself as the main postmaterialist alternative among eastern voters, given the presence of the Bündnis 90/Greens and, especially, the PDS.

Summary

Overall, these results indicate that the reordering of parties' competitive position after unification predominately has been felt on the left side of the party spectrum. The CDU/CSU has clearly benefited from the changed issue environment because of its traditional position as the main representative of materialist issues, which has matched the greater emphasis on 'bread-and-butter' issues. In stark contrast, the SPD faces a strategic dilemma: if it responds to the changed environment by emphasising materialist issues, it may be more attractive to those voters in the East and the West who are concerned with economic issues while also losing ground to the postmaterialist left. If, however, it continues to hold on to the carefully developed balance between materialists and postmaterialist policies, the SPD is likely to lose ground to the materialist centre while not necessarily becoming the most attractive partisan outlet for postmaterial voters. Instead of the SPD, they may prefer the Greens in the West and the PDS in the East.

Among the smaller left-wing parties, the Alliance 90/Greens is well established due to its core of support in the West. Finally, while the PDS is in a strategically good position in the eastern electorate, its weak standing among western German voters remains a serious problem for this party.

The changing relationships between postmaterialism and partisanship

(Figure 3 and Tables 3–5) also suggest the importance of party behaviour – in addition to voters' issue concerns – as a mediating influence on the link between postmaterialism and partisanship. The overall relationship (Figure 3) increased in the mid-to late 1980s in western Germany because parties increasingly offered viable alternatives as well as postmaterialism. However, because the 1990 election was dominated by unification-related concerns among the level of parties and voters, the impact of postmaterialism was reduced significantly in 1990 and 1991. In turn, the growing impact of postmaterialism after 1991 indicates that traditional dimensions again influenced voters' party choice following the unusual events in 1989–90, which overshadowed traditional determinants of citizens' partisan choice.

POSTMATERIALISM AND ELECTORAL BEHAVIOUR IN THE FUTURE

The formal unification of Germany merged two electorates that exhibit different structural characteristics. Theoretically, the general characteristics of the unified electorate lead us to expect that (1) traditional social cleavages will further lose their influence on voters' party preferences; (2) economic, security, and immigration issues gain in salience, at least over the medium term; and (3) postmaterial issues will become temporarily less important than material issues. These predictions are consistent with the scarcity hypothesis of postmaterialist theory which indeed predicts the temporary decline of postmaterial issue priorities under the prevailing conditions in post-communist Europe.

At the same time, the quick pace at which the changing context in Germany affects aggregate levels of postmaterialism revitalises the debate over the validity of the socialisation premise of postmaterialism theory. A sceptic might plausibly note that the extent and pace of the decline in levels of postmaterialism observed in Germany and elsewhere in Europe appears inconsistent with the notion of generational change.[31] A sceptic might thus suggest that contemporary economic conditions appear to shape voters' value priorities. Indeed, Inglehart would agree with this criticism by conceding that generational effects may be modified upwards or downwards through life-cycle and period effects.[32] The theoretical premises of the postmaterialist model would thus allow for some period and life-cycle effects as long as substantial generational components occur as well. Further, one may argue that especially in turbulent political times where a large number of citizens are politically mobilised, individuals may reassess their political views. Consequently, economic problems in contemporary Germany may prompt a young postmaterialist to refocus attention on economic issues. Likewise, these events may redefine the issue priorities of older individuals. During the exceptional circumstances created by Germany's unification, issue priorities may be significantly altered even after an individual's formative years of socialisation. Because postmaterialism theory was developed against the backdrop of the (comparatively) tranquil post-war decades in Western Europe, a temporary dominance of period effects in this rapidly changing context would not automatically invalidate the conceptual foundations of postmaterialism.

If these speculations about the longevity of postmaterialism are correct, we expect that levels of postmaterialism and their influence on partisan choice will return to pre-unification levels, provided that the economic context in Germany improves and the international situation remains peaceful. From a long-term perspective, then, the substantial changes observed in this article may turn out to be as temporary as the period effects observed in the later 1970s.

Over the short term, however, it is important to recognise that Germany's electoral process has taken a different turn since 1990. One important consequence is that material issues became more salient relative to postmaterial issues with important ramifications for the competitive situation between parties. Most important, while the persistent emphases of centre-conservative parties on material issues require comparatively minor adjustments in this new issue context, the SPD's carefully wrought policy compromises between material and postmaterial policies suddenly represent a strategic quandary. The 1994 election is a case in point because it clearly documents the importance of economic conditions as predictors of electoral behaviour after the fall of the Berlin Wall. Most analysts agree that while the poor economic projection hurt the governing coalition in public opinion polls taken before 1994, the improving economic forecasts that emerged in the early months of 1994 helped the CDU/CSU–FDP coalition carry the day on 16 October 1994.[33] At the same time, these improving economic conditions may also reverse the trend towards materialist orientations. Economic recessions in Western Europe during the second half of the 1970s and the 1980s have led to temporary declines in levels of postmaterialism, with rises thereafter throughout the 1980s as the economy improved. Over the medium term, therefore, traditional economic, security, and immigration issues will play a greater role than they would have without unification, until the German economy grows stronger and the European context becomes less volatile.

NOTES

1. See Ronald Inglehart, *The Silent Revolution* (Princeton UP 1977), idem, *Cultural Shift* (Princeton UP 1990).

2. See Max Kaase and Hans-Dieter Klingemann, *Der mühsame Weg zur Entwicklung von Parteiorientierungen in einer 'neuen' Demokratie: Das Beispiel der früheren DDR*, in Hans-Dieter Klingemann and Max Kaase (eds.) *Wahlen und Wähler. Analysen aus Anlaß der Bundestagswahl 1990* (Opladen: Westdeutscher Verlag 1994) pp.365–96; Samuel H. Barnes and Max Kaase *et al.*, *Political Action* (Beverly Hills, London: Sage 1979).
3. See Wilhelm P. Bürklin, Markus Klein and Achim Ruß, 'Dimensionen des Wertewandels: Eine empirische Längsschnittanalyse zur Dimensionalität und der Wandlungsdynamik gesellschaftlicher Wertorientierungen', *Politische Vierteljahresschrift* 35/4 (Dec. 1994) pp.579-606; Ronald Inglehart and Hans-Dieter Klingemann, 'Dimensionen des Wertewandels. Theoretische und methodische Reflexionen anläßlich einer neuerlichen Kritik', ibid. 37/2 (June 1996) pp.319–40.
4. Robert Rohrschneider and Dieter Fuchs, 'A New Electorate? The Economic Trends and Electoral Choice in the 1994 Federal Election', *German Politics and Society* 13/1 (Spring 1995) pp.100–22.
5. Seymour Lipset and Stein Rokkan, 'Cleavage Structures, Party Systems, and Voter Alignments: an Introduction', in idem (eds.) *Party Systems and Voter Alignments* (NY: Free Press 1967) pp.1–67.
6. See Stefano Bartolini and Peter Mair, *Identity, Competition, and Electoral Availability* (Cambridge: CUP 1990); Arend Lijphart, 'Religious vs. Linguistic vs. Class Voting. The "Crucial Experiment" of Comparing Belgium, Canada, South Africa, and Switzerland', *American Political Science Review* 73/2 (June 1979) pp.442–58; Russell J. Dalton, *Citizen Politics in Western Democracies* (Chatham, NJ: Chatham House 1988).
7. Kendall Baker, Russell J. Dalton and Kai Hildebrandt, *Germany Transformed* (Cambridge: CUP 1981).
8. Franz Urban Pappi, 'Sozialstruktur, gesellschaftliche Wertorientierungen und Wahlabsicht', *Politische Vierteljahresschrift* Jahrgang18/2/3 (1977) pp.195–229.
9. See Russell J. Dalton, Scott C. Flanagan and Paul A. Beck, *Electoral Change in Advanced Industrial Democracies* (Princeton UP 1984); Mark Franklin, T. Mackie and Henry Valen *Electoral Change* (Cambridge: CUP 1992).
10. Baker *et al.* (note 7).
11. Inglehart (note 1).
12. See most recently, Paul R. Abramson and Ronald Inglehart, *Value Change in Global Perspective* (Ann Arbor: U. of Michigan Press 1995).
13. E.g. Wilhelm P. Bürklin, 'Einstellungen und Wertorientierungen ost- und westdeutscher Eliten 1995', in Oscar W. Gabriel (ed.), *Politische Orientierungen und Verhaltensweisen im vereinigten Deutschland* (Opladen: Leske + Budrich 1997) pp.235–61; Raymond M. Duch and Michael A. Taylor, 'Postmaterialism and the Economic Condition', *American Jnl of Political Science* 37/3 (Aug.1993) pp.747–79; Scott C. Flanagan, 'Changing Values in Advanced Industrial Societies: Inglehart's Silent Revolution from the Perspective of Japanese Findings', *Comparative Political Studies* 14/4 (Jan. 1982) pp.403–44.
14. Harold D. Clarke and Nitish Dutt, 'Measuring Value Change in Western Industrialized Societies: the Impact of Unemployment', *American Political Science Review* 85/3 (Sept. 1991) pp.905–20.
15. Ronald Inglehart and Paul Abramson, 'Economic Security and Value Change', ibid. 88/2 (June 1994) p.337.
16. Russell J. Dalton and Wilhelm Bürklin, 'The Two German Electorates: The Social Bases of the Vote in 1990 and 1994', *German Politics and Society* 13/1 (Spring 1995) pp.79–99.
17. See Robert Rohrschneider, 'New Party versus Old Left Realignments: Environmental Attitudes, Party Policies, and Partisan Affiliations in Four West European Countries', *Journal of Politics* 55/3 (Aug. 1993) pp.682–701; Dieter Fuchs, 'Zum Wandel politischer Konfliktlinien: Ideologische Gruppierungen und Wahlverhalten', in Werner Süß (ed.) *Die Bundesrepublik in den Achtziger Jahren* (Opladen: Leske + Budrich 1991) pp.69–86.
18. Robert Rohrschneider, 'How Iron is the Iron Law of Oligarchy? Robert Michels and National Party Delegates in Eleven West European Democracies', *European Journal of Political Research* 25/2 (Feb. 1994) pp.207–38.
19. Wolfgang G. Gibowski, 'Germany's General Election in 1994: Who Voted for Whom',

German Studies Review, special election issue (1995) pp.91–114.
20. Kaase and Klingemann (note 2).
21. Dieter Roth, 'Die Wahlen zur Volkskammer in der DDR. Der Versuch einer Erklärung', *Politische Vierteljahresschrift* 31/3 (1990) pp.369–93.
22. Russell J. Dalton and Wilhelm Bürklin, 'The German Party System and the Future', in Russell J. Dalton (ed.), *The New Germany Votes* (Providence: Berg 1993) pp.233–56.
23. Dalton and Bürklin (note 16).
24. Russell J. Dalton, *Politics in Germany*, 2nd ed. (NY: HarperCollins 1992).
25. Inglehart and Abramson (note 15); Inglehart (note 1).
26. Dieter Fuchs and Hans-Dieter Klingemann, 'Citizens and the State: A Relationship Transformed', in Hans-Dieter Klingemann and Dieter Fuchs (eds.) *Citizens and the State* (Oxford: OUP 1995) pp.419–43.
27. Abramson and Inglehart (note 12).
28. Rohrschneider (note 17).
29. Herbert Kitschelt, *The Logics of Party Formation* (Ithaca, NY: Cornell UP 1989).
30. Gerard Braunthal, 'The Perspective from the Left', *German Politics and Society* 13/1 (Spring 1995) pp.36–49.
31. See Bürklin (note 13); Raymond and Taylor (note 13).
32. Abramson and Inglehart (note 12); Inglehart and Klingemann (note 3).
33. E.g., Rohrschneider and Fuchs (note 4); Christopher Anderson and Carsten Zelle, 'Helmut Kohl and the CDU Victory', *German Politics and Society* 13/1 (Spring 1995) pp.12–35; David Conradt, 'The 1994 Campaign and Election: An Overview', *German Studies Review* special election issue (1995) pp.1–18.

Between Deepening and Widening: Role Conflict in Germany's Enlargement Policy

HENNING TEWES

Although Germany is the principal proponent of the EU's eastern enlargement, it has at times found it difficult to reconcile this aim with its desire to promote deeper EU integration. The use of role theory illustrates these conflicting priorities. West Germany's post-war role in European politics was that of a promoter of deeper integration; the deepening of West European integration thus became part of the self-conception of West German foreign policy-making élites. The changed situation after 1990 placed new demands on German foreign policy makers. West Germany's traditional self-conception as an integration deepener conflicted with the desire on behalf of unified Germany to press for EU enlargement. However, although German policy makers employed a variety of strategies in order to pursue their incongruous foreign-policy aims, their principal concern remained with the deepening of western integration.

Although it has become increasingly popular to argue that identities matter in the study of foreign policy and international relations, precisely how they do is often unclear.[1] In particular, little is known on how identities affect a state's choices and preferences, and in turn, how a state's actual foreign policy feeds back into the definition of its identity. In the case of Germany, the relationship between national identity and foreign policy goes back to the nineteenth century, when the 'national question' was frequently subject to the so-called *Primat der Außenpolitik*, the doctrine of the primacy of foreign policy.[2] The relationship between national identity and foreign policy lies at the heart of this article, which traces the link between Germany's European identity, its foreign-policy culture, and its policy towards the EU's eastern enlargement between 1990 and 1994. The main questions examined here are these: what strategy did Germany pursue with regard to the eastern enlargement of the EU, and why did it pursue the strategy it did? The answer is that Germany's promotion of EU enlargement was hesitant since, within Germany's European diplomacy, the deepening

West European Politics, Vol.21, No.2 (April 1998), pp.117–133
PUBLISHED BY FRANK CASS, LONDON

the EU took priority over its widening. As the desire to deepen the EU was not obviously reconcilable with the desire to enlarge it to Central and Eastern Europe, deepening and widening were conflicting priorities. I will argue that these different priorities created a *role conflict* for German foreign policy, in which (West) Germany's traditional role conception as an 'integration deepener' prevailed. German policy makers attempted to solve the increasingly acute role conflict by employing three strategies. The first was a strict denial that a conflict existed; the second was a segregation between the roles of 'deepener' and 'widener'; the third was an attempted merger of the two. At no stage, however, did a fundamental redefinition of Germany's role in the integration process take place. Thus, the main priority in Germany's European diplomacy continues to be the primacy of integration. On these grounds, I contend that the definition of German interests in the enlargement process can only be understood against the background of Germany's European identity and its foreign-policy culture, which were marked by an instinctive commitment to Western integration.

ROLE THEORY

The usefulness of role theory for the study of foreign policy lies in the conceptual tools it provides to trace the link between a state's identity, the development of its foreign-policy culture and the particular policies it pursues on a persistent basis. Role theory was developed in social psychology and micro-sociology and is much more prolific there than in the study of foreign policy. Here, a role is defined as a persistent pattern in a state's foreign-policy behaviour. This pattern is shaped by *role expectations* from others, which attach norms and expectations to particular positions. Role expectations thus serve as the conceptual bridge between social structure and role behaviour in general, and, focused on foreign- policy analysis, between the international system, on the one hand, and its influence on state behaviour on the other. Any state's foreign policy is thus influenced by expectations external to the state, such as system-wide values, general legal principles and treaty commitments.

In social psychology and micro-sociology, role theory has been split between a structuralist and an interactionist school. Structuralists argue that *alter part* influences virtually determine an individual's behaviour.[3] Thus, behaviour becomes little more than an individual's compliance to external expectations. The interactionist school regards the influence of social structure as less rigid. The making of a role is seen as a creative process between agent and structure at the heart of which is a constant negotiating and renegotiating of the role.[4] This view has prevailed in the use of role theory for foreign-policy analysis. Here, policy makers are seen to be influenced not only by external expectations, but also by domestic factors like popular opinion, historical memory and a whole host of domestic norms, values and expectations. These influences lead to *role conceptions* which are particular to a national polity and its foreign-policy culture. The combination between a state's *alter part* role expectations and its *ego part* role conceptions thus leads to its *role performance*, or actual behaviour in a particular situation.

Role expectations, role conceptions, and a state's actual role performance influence a foreign-policy culture. The concept of foreign-policy culture questions the approach to the definition of state interests advanced by traditional theories of international relations. In contrast to theories such as realism, liberal institutionalism and rational choice theory, it views interests not as a given but as contingent on norms, beliefs and values.[5] These make up identities that may vary from state to state. By way of definition, we can refer to foreign-policy culture as 'a set of attitudes, beliefs and sentiments which give order to the foreign-policy process and which provide the underlying assumptions and rules that govern behaviour in the international system'.[6] At a time when students of international relations and foreign policy are becoming increasingly alert to the fact that identities shape the definition of state interests, the concept of foreign-policy culture can serve as an intermediate object of analysis.[7] The use of role theory facilitates this analysis. Through the concepts of role expectations and role conceptions it can identify the influences on a state's foreign-policy culture.[8] As role expectations and role conceptions can change, a state's foreign-policy culture can change, too. An example for such change was the development of West Germany's foreign policy in the 1950s and 1960s.

WEST GERMANY'S ROLE IN EUROPEAN INTEGRATION

The division of Germany and the dynamics of the Cold War generated a chronic tension between the Federal Republic's 'state' and 'national' identities. As a 'new' state in a divided Europe, 'West Germany constructed its identity through its diplomacy and particularly its European policy.'[9] In this construction the accession to Western institutions was of critical importance. As Jeffrey Anderson and John Goodman pointed out, 'in the eyes of German political élites, institutional memberships were not merely instruments of policy but also normative frameworks for policy-making'.[10] This explains that the foreign-policy culture of the Federal Republic, which unified Germany inherited, was greatly shaped by *alter part* influences, in particular on behalf of the Western allies. It was expected that West Germany would refrain from exercising the foreign policy of a great power;

unilateral diplomatic initiatives, let alone military adventures, were, therefore, impossible. With time, these external expectations were internalised by West Germany's political élite, and after a while, by the population, too, so that the multilateral and economistic nature of Bonn's foreign policy became a veritable foreign-policy culture.[11] The consensus that existed between the Western allies, the political class and the population may have been subject to occasional strains, such as over rearmament in the 1950s or over *Ostpolitik* in the 1970s, but there was virtually uninterrupted agreement over the fact that the Federal Republic was a principal promoter of European integration.[12]

It was thus a recurrent feature of West Germany's European diplomacy that it accompanied every gain of sovereignty with closer integration at West European level. The Federal Republic's foundation was followed by the foundation of the European Coal and Steel Community in 1951; the attainment of sovereignty in 1955 was directly dependent on the accession to NATO, and followed by the foundation of the EEC in 1957; the initiation of *Ostpolitik* in 1969 came just prior to the foundation of European Political Co-operation; and of course, German unification was followed by the Maastricht Treaty. Thus for the Federal Republic, state building went hand in hand with Western European integration.

Indeed, the link between West Germany's identity and Western European integration transcended the practice of state building, since a lot of what the Federal Republic came to stand for was inseparable from Western integration: anti-communism and economic success, democratisation and social stability. The Federal Republic became a Western state, not only in its political system and foreign-policy orientation, but also in terms of economic governance, culture and society.[13] This Western European identity fed into the role conceptions of its foreign policy makers, who pursued the path of deeper integration. Hence at the end of the 1980s, *alter part* role expectations and *ego part* role conceptions corresponded very closely to one another. West Germany was seen as a promoter of deeper European integration, and its role performance in completing the single European market and preparing for monetary union testified to this.

NEW ROLES FOR UNIFIED GERMANY

The watershed of 1989/90 challenged the congruence of *alter part* role expectations and Germany's *ego part* role conception. The newly democratising states in Central and Eastern Europe (CEE) placed demands on Germany which partially conflicted with its traditional role as a promoter of deeper integration. To be sure, Germany did not at first react to these new role expectations. As argued above, the Maastricht Treaty, signed in December 1991, was, in a sense, a submission of newly-won German sovereignty to Western institutional structures, and, therefore, corresponded to the pattern of West Germany's post-war European policy. But this is not to deny that the new situation, both through Germany's unification and through new challenges from CEE, affected the way German policy makers defined German interests. Although a rigid distinction is inevitably artificial, one can identify three influences that shaped Germany's emergent role conception towards CEE: Germany's domestic policy debate, expectations from CEE and expectations from Western Europe.

The Domestic Policy Debate

The end of the Cold War and German unification provided a double trigger for the opening of debate on foreign policy in Germany which challenged traditional role conceptions. On one level, Germany's policies towards CEE were subject to a wider debate about the kind of foreign policy that a unified Germany should conduct.[14] Some commentators advocated a much more active, unilateral policy towards CEE, which would take account of, but be uninhibited by, Germany's Western commitments.[15] On another level, this debate was concerned with the Soviet legacy in CEE. As long as the Soviet Union existed, Germany saw it as a guarantor of stability and security in CEE, and thus made it the priority of its Eastern policy. After the Moscow coup in August 1991, this changed. CEE came to be seen as a potentially unstable backyard, which, through immigration, organised crime and environmental risks could threaten the security and well-being of German society. Thus, although German business may have seen CEE primarily in terms of export opportunities and cheap labour, German policy makers saw it primarily in terms of its potential for instability. As Ludger Kühnhardt pointed out: 'For good reasons it is especially up to Germany to promote the *Westbindung* of its immediate eastern neighbours. Germany will only be redeemed of its old, often conjured up *Mittellage*, if it has but Western countries on its immediate Eastern border.'[16] EU membership was a crucial element of this stabilisation strategy.

Role Expectations from Central and Eastern Europe

Second, there were expectations from the CEE countries, for whom the integration into the institutional structures of the West became the overarching foreign-policy goal after 1989/90.[17] Their most significant step in this early period was the signing of the 'Europe Agreements' in December 1991, a date from whence a veritable race towards the earliest possible achievement of full membership began. The view of Germany in CEE was largely ambiguous. On the one hand, there were fears of

Germanisation, which played a significant part in the quest for EU membership. It was hoped that although membership in the EU would hardly reduce Germany's importance in terms of economic relations and cultural affinity, it would at least dilute the strategic importance it had politically.[18] On the other hand, it was clearly recognised that without active German support, EU membership would be even more difficult to attain. Given Germany's self interest in enlargement, and the CEE's own interest in enlargement, it is not surprising that Germany ensured its support for their eventual accession to the EU in the bilateral treaties, which it signed with the CEE countries in 1991/92. Hence, one may argue that from the viewpoint of the CEE states, the most significant element in their diplomatic relations with Germany was the German promise to support their future application to the EU.

Expectations from Western Europe

Role expectations in Western Europe were contradictory in a sense, since obviously Germany was expected to ratify the Maastricht Treaty and to join EMU in 1997 or 1999. However, there were also increasing expectations in Western Europe as to the strategy Germany would pursue towards CEE, and German support for enlargement towards the East was seen with rather more wariness. Occasionally, this wariness took the form of the 'Germanisation' thesis of the EU, according to which Germany was going to increase its weight substantially within the EU by the two rounds of enlargement towards the North and the East. Due to economic links, cultural affinity, and a number of preferences in foreign and domestic policy, so the argument ran, Germany would lead a northern bloc in the EU against a southern bloc dominated by France.[19] However, this view was only the extreme of a more general incertitude about Germany's European intentions. In any case, for most of 1992 and 1993, EU member states were sufficiently occupied by internal problems, such as the ratification problems of the Maastricht Treaty, the collapse of the EMS, and a deep and painful recession. Few governments made the Eastern enlargement of the EU their top priority. In this context it is understandable how significant the fact was that German politicians addressed the issue at all.

ROLE CONFLICT FOR GERMANY'S *EUROPAPOLITIK*

Considering that Germany came to see itself, and came to be seen as, the CEE countries' advocate *vis-à-vis* the European Union, it may be argued that the importance of these countries for Germany's foreign-policy orientation had grown. This is probably true. Yet it would be false to assume that the importance of the West had therefore declined. This was not a matter of either/or; it was a both-the-one-and-the-other situation. Although there was considerable speculation about Germany's potential 'drifting off to the East', the Kohl government never ceased to emphasise its entirely Western orientation. 'The Federal Government renews its loyalty to the Atlantic Alliance. (...) We want to open new ways for the unification of Europe', Kohl had said in 1982.[20] Eleven years later he stated quite unequivocally: 'The two pillars of German policy are the European Community and the Atlantic Alliance.'[21] Yet although the Kohl government's Western orientation could never be in serious doubt, its activities towards the East, in particular towards its Visegrad neighbours, were so intense that the planned reconciliation between these potentially conflicting foreign policy aims merits discussion. If it was Germany's explicit aim to promote the eventual accession of the CEE countries to the EU, what did this mean for the EU? Would it be able to absorb another round of enlargement? Would the institutional structures created for 6 members continue to work for 20? And perhaps most importantly, would the CAP and the Regional Development Fund not increase exponentially the size of the EU budget if extended to the new members? To discuss these questions in any detail would distort the proportions of this article. But it can be pointed out that the deepening and widening the EU were not as evidently reconcilable as maintained by German policy makers. Policies to the East and policies to the West had become two sides of the same coin, both of them belonged to *Europapolitik*. Yet, the German vision of that Europe remained unclear. On the one hand, the Western partners were assured that EMU would go ahead. On the other hand, however, it remained ill-defined how the Eastern European states would be able to catch up with a group of states that had advanced so far down the road of integration.

I therefore suggest that Germany found itself in a *role conflict* between its roles as an 'integration deepener' and an 'integration widener'. In role theory, a role conflict refers to a situation where new role expectations and conceptions are incompatible with already existing ones. In micro-sociology, role theory has identified approaches in which an individual can deal with a role conflict, not all of which are relevant here. Three of these approaches, however, can serve to understand Germany's convoluted policy on enlargement to the East. The first is the denial of role conflict.[22] This does nothing to alter the external environment and, therefore, cannot solve the tension at the heart of role conflict. For much of the 1990s, German policy makers failed to acknowledge that a conflict between EU deepening and widening existed. This denial was particularly pronounced in the first two years after unification, and coincided with Germany's more hesitant support of Eastern enlargement. Inevitably, the more enlargement moved up the EU's agenda, the less possible it became to deny that it was gong to have severe implications for the future of the Union. As the need to conceive of one single *Europapolitik* became stronger, German policy makers tried to solve the role conflict by strategies two and three, namely by segregating roles and then by attempting to merge them. Both the strategy of role segregation and that of role merger are geared at the external environment and so have a larger chance of solving the tensions that lie at the heart of role conflict. They are thus automatically more sophisticated policy instruments than the mere denial that a conflict exists. To an extent, all three strategies to solve this role conflict – denial, segregation, and merger – coexisted with one another throughout the period under consideration. None dominated completely, and none was wholly successful. At the end, however, there was at least the attempt at merging the roles which, though building on the primacy of Western integration, outlined a single vision of German *Europapolitik.*

Denial of Role Conflict

Especially in the first two years after unification, German policy makers did not publicly acknowledge that a conflict existed between deepening and widening. In a sense, this was probably accurate, because the deepening of western integration was so clearly the priority, and because Germany's promotion of Eastern enlargement was so non-committal. On the other hand, it must have been apparent to German policy makers, as it was to others, that in the not-too-distant future, deepening and widening were likely to be conflicting dynamics. In the early 1990s, no serious strategy had been employed for the CEE countries' eventual accession to the EU. In March 1991, Chancellor Kohl said no more on the topic than 'Of course the countries of Central, Eastern, and South-Eastern Europe would have to fulfil the necessary conditions. All of us hope that they will reach this aim soon; we have to make our contributions, too.'[23] In the bilateral treaties, Germany's pledge to support an eventual EU accession of its Eastern neighbours was relatively discretionary.[24] In October 1992 Kohl said in a speech on the basic principles of his thinking on Europe: 'The fact that there are candidates for membership says something favourable about the European Community. These countries do not reject it; they want to be part of it. I also mean Poland and Hungary, the Czechs and the Slovaks, and the Baltic States. Even though not in this decade, I regard an enlargement towards these countries as possible at some point early in the next century.'[25] As noted above, this rhetoric was not without effect. By 1992 Germany was regarded as the CEE countries' natural advocate in the EU.[26] With increasing disappointment about the protectionism of the Europe Agreements, German encouragement of accession was like a sparkle in a gloomy picture. One area where both Germany's role conflict and the efforts to deny it were illustrated very clearly was the Maastricht Treaty. On the one hand, the treaty promoted very tight integration between the 12 EU member states, even though the negotiations had resulted in a union more loosely knit than aspired to by the Germans. This by itself can be taken as a hint as to where German priorities lay. A part of this logic can be explained as a continuation of Adenauer's politics of strength, proposing to build up a magnet in Western Europe that would inevitably attract the Eastern European countries away from the Soviet orbit. Not surprisingly, however, the CEE governments responded to the Maastricht Treaty by complaining that it would render it even more difficult to attain the high standards of development necessary to accede to the EU. To these complaints German policy makers reacted by squaring the circle: Maastricht, they argued, was in fact a treaty for the CEE countries. In a masterpiece of this rhetoric, Kohl explained:

> After the end of the East-West conflict, Germany and Europe face new challenges. The radical change in Central, Eastern and South-Eastern Europe entails recognisable risks and imponderabilities. The whole of Europe needs a secure anchor now more than ever before. This role and this task can only be assumed by a strong European Community. This brings me to one, if not to the essential aim of the Maastricht Treaty. This treaty is not least a European answer to the collapse of the Communist dictatorships in Central, Eastern and South-Eastern Europe. With it we take up our responsibility for the whole of the European continent.[27]

This statement exemplifies the habitual conflation between Europe and Western Europe which is typical of the language of German politicians. Not only does this obscure what the Czech or Polish input into this 'European answer' called the Maastricht treaty actually consisted of, it also obscures which elements of the Treaty were going to be so obviously beneficial to the CEE countries. The rhetoric of the Chancellor, although it denies the role conflict between Germany's aim to both deepen and widen the EU, could hardly conceal the tension in Germany's foreign-policy aims.

Role Segregation

The concept of role segregation refers to a situation where a state has not actually solved its role conflict, but oscillates between roles in order to avoid role change, that is, the completely new inception of its international role. To an extent, German enlargement policy never quite ceased to be affected by an alternation between Germany's roles as a deepener and widener of integration. The recipe by which Germany tried to segregate the conflicting roles in its *Europapolitik* in the early 1990s consisted of the desire to stabilise the CEE countries, which meant working towards their full membership of the EU, without at the same time weakening the functioning of existing EU policies and institutions. This strategy had a rhetorical and a practical component. Rhetorically it was of paramount importance to increase awareness in the West that potential Eastern instability was not just a threat to Germany but instead would affect the whole continent. The Chancellor said in 1991: 'I hope that this contribution (i.e. towards stability in CEE), which we pay out of our budget, will be recognised as a contribution in the interest of the whole of the West. By promoting reforms and especially the transition to a social market economy, we contribute to security and stability in the whole of Europe.'[28] Or in more simple terms he said in 1993: 'Central, Eastern and South-Eastern Europe is not just a matter for the Germans but for all Europeans'.[29] In practice this rhetoric was translated into the attempt to engage the member states of the EU into a more active policy towards the East.

The key event here was the Copenhagen summit in June 1993, in the commmuniqué of which an eventual accession of the CEE countries to the EU was mentioned for the first time. At Copenhagen, the EU states also decided in favour of initiating a permanent political dialogue with the associated states. This included regular meetings between representatives of the associated countries on the one hand, and Commission officials and representatives of the countries holding the EU Presidency on the other. In addition the heads of government of the associated states began to partake in one of the two annual European Council summits. This facilitated their gradual incorporation into the CFSP, and was thus both a preparation of full EU membership and the attempt to work towards a common stance in international organisations like the UN or the CSCE. On the other hand, however, the Copenhagen summit clarified that a condition for enlargement was that new members would not only fulfil the necessary criteria to accede, but that they would then have to be able to sustain and reinforce the development towards closer integration. The outcome of the Copenhagen summit thus illustrated the segregation and alternation between the roles of deepening and widening in German *Europapolitik*. It was an advance towards the eventual enlarge to the East of the Union. However, it also left untouched the entire thrust of already existing EU institutions and policies. Germany had at this stage not shed its traditional role as 'integration deepener', as in fact it never quite did during the period under discussion. More importantly, it had not attempted to merge conflicting role expectations and role conceptions into a new role. However, since it had not done so, the role of 'integration deepener' was exposed to increasing tension by Germany's newly acquired role as an 'integration widener'.

Attempted Role Merger

The first response to this tension came with the publication of the so-called Schäuble-Lamers paper in September 1994.[30] Published under the modest name 'Reflections on European Politics' by the CDU/CSU caucus in the Bundestag, its authors were the immensely influential leader of the CDU/CSU caucus, Wolfgang Schäuble, and its foreign policy spokesman Karl Lamers. The Schäuble-Lamers paper was not primarily concerned with CEE. Its principal proposal was a two-tier EU, consisting of a core of very tightly integrated countries and a periphery with those countries who were either not willing or not able to become part of the core. It argued that the EU found itself in a pre-crisis situation because of an increasing divergence of interests, economic recession, a regressive nationalism and the prospective enlargement to the East. This, the authors argued, could only be overcome by allowing those countries that were willing to go ahead with closer integration to do so. The Schäuble-Lamers paper foresaw the accession of the Visegrad countries (plus Slovenia) for the year 2000. Since such an early accession would put economic and financial strain on both old and new members, it had to be managed by long periods of transition and practices of 'variable geometry'. The precondition for the enlargement towards the East was a tightly integrated core. If, Schäuble and Lamers warned, the 'five to six core countries' (i.e. the founding member states, depending on developments in Italy) did not dare to take the next step to integration, centrifugal tendencies would lead to an eventual loosening of ties. This is the crunch of the argument. The creation of a group of core countries was not seen as an aim in itself, but as a means to resolve the tension between deepening and widening. The acknowledgement that such a tension actually existed was in itself breathtaking, as was the proposal that the Visegrad countries would not have to adopt the full *acquis communautaire* upon their accession to the EU.[31] But the coherent plan for a way out of the role conflict by advocating geographically limited but functionally intensive deepening on the one hand, and rapid, geographically limited widening on the other was a watershed in German *Europapolitik*.

A point of caution should be included at this juncture. The Schäuble-Lamers paper was not a government proposal. It came neither from the Chancellery nor from the Foreign Office, but from two parliamentarians who were interested in foreign policy. Yet Schäuble's domestic status added substantial weight to the proposals of the paper. In addition it is commonly accepted wisdom that Kohl had read and accepted the paper in June but had asked the authors to postpone its publication for fear it would be mistaken as the government's agenda for Germany's EU presidency.[32] It can, therefore, be assumed that the ideas expressed in the paper, although not official German policy, reflected the thinking of the closest governmental circles. As such they can be taken as an important background information on the government's *Europapolitik*, since here for the first time, a coherent strategy for the two sides of German *Europapolitik* was presented. For the present discussion, the paper leads to three conclusions. The first is that the Schäuble-Lamers paper underlined the primacy of western integration: 'the core of the hard core are France and Germany'.[33] The second is that the proposals do not completely escape the strategy of role segregation discussed above, reinforcing the argument that German *Europapolitik* sought to maintain the workability of the EU while at the same time encouraging the stabilisation of CEE. Finally, and perhaps most importantly, the concern with the Eastern enlargement reflected on the proposals for the reform of the Union. For the first time it became clear that the government's Eastern concerns affected its policies in the West. Put differently: The desirable outcomes in the East were at the heart of the proposals for the future of the West. This in itself was new.

EXCURSUS: THE LIMITS OF FOREIGN-POLICY CULTURE

The role conflict between deepening and widening the Union, however, does not explain all complexities of German *Europapolitik*. It has to be supplemented by a consideration of Germany's fragmented institutional structure and the Kohl government's domestic political considerations. It has been noted before that the policy making process of German European policy is highly fragmented.[34] This view is reinforced by policies concerning the EU's Eastern enlargement. The role conceptions of 'integration deepener' and 'integration widener', namely, though shared by the grand strategists of European policy, affected other policy makers to a lesser extent. Germany's foreign policy is increasingly determined by functional interests which transcend the traditional distinction between foreign and domestic politics. Conflicting aims, therefore, increase the extent to which societal actors take an interest in foreign policy.[35]

Indeed one could take this argument further and point out that at least at EU level, the functional interpenetration between the German and the EU's political systems is of a density which the term 'foreign policy' can no longer account for.[36] Thus, German enlargement policy was not at all times dominated by the chancellery or the foreign ministry. These belonged to a group of ministries that saw CEE primarily in terms of its security-political, economic and moral significance for the idea of European union, that is, in terms of stabilisation, markets and the growing together of the continent, which also included the defece ministry and to a lesser extent the economics ministry. On the other hand, there were those ministries that had domestic clientele, in particular the agriculture ministry. Since German agriculture is not very competitive, the agricultural lobby strong and the agriculture minister as a CDU member vulnerable to its pressure, the German government did not push to prepare the CAP for an Eastern enlargement of the EU. The same is true for other ministries that had to account for powerful domestic lobbies, such as for transport or construction. The input of the clientele ministries was strongest during the negotiations for the Europe agreements in 1991. The fact that the Europe Agreements put restrictions on the Visegrad countries' access to EU markets in the agricultural, textile and steel sectors was not only due to French or Portuguese pressure. German representatives could hide behind French positions, knowing that it would be hard to sell a new CAP reform to German farmers. Hence, the fact that the clientele ministries had such influence reinforces the argument that co-ordination is difficult to achieve in a policy-making process as fragmented as the German one. German enlargement policy was, therefore, influenced not only by the role conflict between deepening and widening, but also by domestic political considerations. This view is reinforced by the calls of Finance Minister Waigel that the Eastern enlargement should not cost one more pfennig more to the German tax payer.[37]

Of course it is illusory to assume that the CAP or the Regional Development Fund could be extended to the new members without being more costly. Yet the need to demonstrate domestically that the German government was not wasting any money was crucial at a time when the country was in obvious financial crisis. This illustrates that German foreign-policy culture, as affecting old and new role conceptions, can only explain the grand schemes of diplomacy. It is less competent to account for the negotiating stances of those ministries with domestic clientele, whose representatives are not primarily concerned with the projection of a particular image of Germany abroad.

CONCLUSION

Leaving aside the details of Germany's European policy-making process, the conclusion returns to Germany's basic European dilemma after unification. On the one hand, Germany had long-standing, actual commitments to the West. On the other hand, it wanted to make commitments to the East. Its primary foreign policy orientation was in the West. Yet, the primary risks to its security and well-being lay in the East. These conflicting foreign policy aims explain that much of what German policy makers did in their *Europapolitik* was indeed contradictory, and that much of what they said attempted to cover this contradiction. Germany's enlargement policy was the heritage of the Federal Republic's foreign-policy culture with its emphasis on deepening European integration. This foreign-policy culture goes to the heart of German identity. For the Federal Republic, Western integration had been a critical component not only of state building, but also of democratisation, economic success and societal stability. Hence, unified Germany inherited a foreign-policy culture which was critically moulded in the 1950s. In the role conflict that emerged in the 1990s between the deepening and widening of integration, the parameters of the 1950s remained in place. The role conflict was denied, and there was the segregation and attempted merger of the two roles, but what never occurred in Germany's policy was the complete change of its European role. What had been a conscious foreign policy decision in the 1950s, was an instinctive foreign policy decision in the 1990s. In order to understand how interests were formulated in Germany's enlargement policy, one, therefore, has to look first at (West) German identity and at the way in which it shaped foreign-policy culture.

The approach employed here has obviously benefited from Alexander Wendt's constructivist approach to the study of international relations, in particular in its treatment of identities as endogenous to the formulation of state interests.[38] However, since the present discussion is a study in foreign policy, its methodology is different from Wendt's. Constructivism in international relations traces the link between the practice of state interaction (the independent variable) and the constitution of state interests (the dependent variable). The present approach, in what could be termed 'constructivism in foreign policy analysis', reverses this methodology in trying to trace the link between already existing state identities (the independent variable), and the formulation of a particular foreign policy in response to a changed environment (the dependent variable). To put it simply: whereas Wendt is interested in how what states *do* affects what they *are*, this author is interested in how what states *are* affects what they *do*. These methodological differences notwithstanding, however, both approaches share an interest in the constructed nature of state identities and interests.

Although role theory does provide conceptual tools which facilitate the observation of links between identity and foreign policy, it also has weaknesses. Its limited predictive ability in particular is one that has long been recognised by those who have employed it for the study of foreign policy.[39] One reason for this poor predictive record is that role performances often diverge from role expectations and role conceptions; another is that foreign-policy cultures are hybrid phenomena that can change as circumstances change. However, despite this weakness, or rather because of it, change in foreign-policy culture deserves more scholarly attention. Little is known for instance about how states change their roles. Assuming that roles are not fixed but negotiable, advances could be made in the understanding of their development, both in terms of internal role conceptions and external role expectations. Related to this is the question of how states learn to accept certain roles, as West Germany for instance did in the 1950s. Little is known about how states are socialised, that is, how they accept norms, values and conducts of behaviour, especially when they are literally new states without experience in the conduct of foreign policy. Equally little is known about how states internalise these norms and about the mechanisms through which they become part of a state's identity. These are questions which mirror the recent interest of the 'English' school in exploring the socially constructed nature of international society.[40] Here, a link is being identified between the norms and values that make up international society, on the one hand, and the identity of states, on the other. A more sophisticated use of role theory, utilising the concepts of socialisation usually employed in micro-sociology, could make an important contribution to this endeavour.

NOTES

1. An earlier draft of this article was presented at the second ASGP Graduate Conference in Birmingham, April 1997. I would like to thank the participants for their comments. For numerous helpful points on an earlier draft I am indebted to Vladimir Handl, Jonathan Lipkin, William E. Paterson and Peter Pulzer.
2. The historical link was pointed out to me by William E. Paterson. For a concise introduction to the relationship between state building, national identity and the use of foreign policy see Peter Pulzer, *Germany 1870–1945, Politics, State Formation, and War* (Oxford: OUP 1997) especially Chs. 1, 2 and 3. [Reviewed on pp.212–14 of this issue.]
3. Erving Goffman, *The Presentation of Self in Everyday Life* (London: Penguin 1990).
4. Ralph H. Turner, 'Unanswered Questions in the Convergence between Structuralist and Interactionist Role Theories', in H.J. Helle and S.N. Eisenstadt (eds.) *Micro-Sociological Theory* (London: Sage 1985).
5. Thomas Schaber and Cornelia Ulber, 'Reflexivität in den Internationalen Beziehungen', *Zeitschrift für Internationale Beziehungen* 1/1 (1994).
6. Hanns W. Maull and Kirste Knut, 'Zivilmacht und Rollentheorie', *Zeitschrift für Internationale Beziehungen*, 3/2 (1996) p.284. Kirste and Maull paraphrase Lucian Pye's 1974 definition of the term 'political culture'.
7. See also Peter J. Katzenstein (ed.), *The Culture of National Security (*NY: Columbia UP 1996); Arthur Hoffmann and Kerry Longhurst, *The Construction and Deconstruction of Germany's Security Identity*, Paper presented at the second ASGP Graduate Conference, Birmingham, April 1997.
8. K.J. Holsti, 'Toward a Theory of Foreign Policy: Making the Case for Role Analysis', in *Role Theory and Foreign Policy Analysis* (Durham, NC: Duke UP 1987) p.7.
9. Simon Bulmer and William E. Paterson, 'Germany in the European Union: Gentle Giant or Emergent Leader?', *International Affairs* 72/1 (1996). For the theoretical argument on the construction of identities see Alexander Wendt, 'Collective Identity Formation and the International State', *American Political Science Review* 88/2 (1994).

10. Jeffrey J. Anderson and John B. Goodman, 'Mars or Minerva? A United Germany in a Post-Cold War Europe', in Stanley Hoffman, Robert Keohane and Joseph Nye (eds.) *After the Cold War* (Cambridge, MA: Harvard UP 1993).
11. Timothy Garton Ash, *In Europe's Name: Germany and the Divided Continent* (London: Vintage 1993); Wolfram Hanrieder, *West German Foreign Policy, 1949–79* (Boulder, CO: Westview 1980).
12. Simon Bulmer, William E. Paterson, *The Federal Republic and the European Community* (London: Allen and Unwin 1987).
13. Reiner Pommerin (ed.) *The American Impact on Postwar Germany* (Providence, RI: Berghahn 1995).
14. For a discussion of this debate see for instance Peter Pulzer, 'Nation-State and National Sovereignty', *Bulletin of the German Historical Institute* (London, Nov.1995; and Gunther Hellmann, 'Goodbye Bismarck? The Foreign Policy of Contemporary Germany', *Mershon International Studies Review* 40 (1996).
15. Arnulf Baring, *Deutschland, was nun?* (Berlin: Siedler 1991).
16. Ludger Kühnhardt, 'Der Osten des Westens und die "russische Frage"', *Europa-Archiv* 9 (1994).
17. The treaty on the foundation of the Visegrad group, signed on 15 Feb. 1991, had the meaningful name of 'Declaration on Co-operation between the Republic of Hungary, the Czech and Slovak Federal Republic and the Republic of Poland on the Way to European integration'.
18. Vladimir Handl, 'Germany and Central Europe: "Mitteleuropa" restored?', *Perspectives* 1 (1993) p.48.
19. For a discussion of this argument see Josef Janning, 'Am Ende der Regierbarkeit? Gefährliche Folgen der Erweiterung der Europäischen Union', *Europa-Archiv* 22 (1993).
20. Cited in Josef Janning and Melanie Piepenschneider, *Deutschland in Europa. Eine Bilanz europäischer Einigungspolitik*, Deutschland-Report 19 (1993) Konrad-Adenauer Foundation, Sankt Augustin, p.34.
21. Kohl's speech at the CDU party conference in *Protokoll* 4 (1993), Parteitag der CDU Deutschlands, 12–14 Sept. 1993 in Berlin, p.30.
22. Role theorists call this 'attention deployment'.
23. The Chancellor's speech is published in *Bulletin* 33, 22 March 1991, pp.241–7.
24. For a general discussion of these treaties see Wolf Oschlies, *Ehe Nachbarschaft zur Nähe wird* (Cologne: Berichte des Bundesinstituts für ostwissenschaftliche und internationale Studien, no. 60 (1991)) and Dieter Bingen, *Deutschland und Polen in Europa: Probleme, Verträge und Perspektiven* (Cologne: Berichte des Bundesinstituts für ostwissenschaftliche und internationale Studien, no. 49 (1991)).
25. Kohl's speech is published in *Protokoll* 3, Parteitag der CDU Deutschlands, Düsseldorf, 26–28 Oct. 1992.
26. See for instance Dieter Bingen, 'Germany and Poland in Europe', *Polish Western Affairs* 1 (1992) p.143. Reinhard Stuth has pointed out that this fact was to a large extent the apathy and inactivity of other Western governments, see Reinhard Stuth, 'Deutschlands neue Rolle im sich wandelnden Europa', *Außenpolitik* 1 (1992) p.29.
27. *Protokoll* 3, Parteitag der CDU Deutschlands, pp.165–6.
28. *Bulletin* 33, 22 March 1991, p.247.
29. *Protokoll* 4, Parteitag der CDU Deutschlands, p.31.
30. CDU/CSU–Fraktion des Deutschen Bundestages, *Überlegungen zur Europäischen Politik*, 1 Sept. 1994.
31. This was at the same time the key difference between the stance of the Foreign Office and that of the Schäuble-Lamers paper.
32. Helmut Hubel and Bernhard May, *Ein 'normales' Deutschland? Die souveräne Bundesrepublik in der ausländischen Wahrnehmung,* Arbeitspapiere zur Internationalen Politik 92 Forschungsinstitut der Deutschen Gesellschaft für Auswärtige Politik (Bonn: 1995) p.109.
33. CDU/CSU–Fraktion des Deutschen Bundestages (note 30) p.10.
34. Simon Bulmer and William Paterson, *The Federal Republic and the European Community*,

(London: Allen and Unwin 1987) pp.18–21.
35. Lothar Buehl, 'Gesellschaftliche Grundlagen der deutschen Aussenpolitik', in Karl Kaiser and Hanns W. Maull (eds.) *Deutschlands neue Außenpolitik* (Munich 1994).
36. Penny Henson and Nisha Malhan, 'Endeavours to Export a Migration Crisis: Policy Making and Europeanisation in the German Migration Dilemma', *German Politics* 4/3 (1995).
37. 'L'Allemagne ne veut plus être la vache à lait de l'Europe', *Le Monde*, 25 June 1995.
38. The seminal essay is Alexander Wendt, 'Anarchy is What States Make of it: The Social Construction of Power Politics, *International Organisation* 46/2 (1992). See also Wendt (note 9).
39. Hanns W. Maull and Kirste Knut, 'Zivilmacht und Rollentheorie', *Zeitschrift für Internationale Beziehungen* 3/2 (1996).
40. Timothy Dunne, 'The Social Construction of International Society', *European Journal of International Relations* 1/3 (1995).

Overlapping Games and Cross-Cutting Coalitions in the European Union

JOSE I. TORREBLANCA

Despite hopes of theoretical convergence between the disciplines of comparative politics and international relations, the integration of explanations of the European policy-making process and of the process of European integration is yet to be accomplished. This article looks at how decision-making crises could be the focal points with which to explore the no-man's land where comparative politics and international relations could meet each other. The article will highlight the structural ambivalence of the EU policy process and the collision of functional areas and territorial politics over multi-dimensional decisions. It will also show that the interplay of overlapping policy games, cross-cutting coalitions and poor co-ordination mechanisms at all levels can go a long way to explaining the oscillations between path-dependency and policy instability.

COMPARATIVE POLITICS AND INTERNATIONAL RELATIONS

This journal has lately encouraged debate on the most suitable theoretical approach to the study of the European Union.[1] Yet, readers have the right to feel disappointed: there have been either winners or losers and the outcome has resembled a friendly agreement leaving things as they stood. As if it was easier with the EU than with any other political system to isolate the levels and sequences of the policy process (when evidence suggests the opposite), the debate has shown a tendency for competing approaches to divide up the field of study and ignore each other.[2]

This outcome does not correspond with the expectations raised. The problems of the grand theories of international relations to explain the process of European integration, together with the ever-increasing volume of policy output in the EU, provided the justification for comparative politics to explain the EU's policy-making process as 'any other political system'.[3]

Yet, as is the case with international relations approaches, over-simplification, sectorialisation, insulation, and unidimensionality might be

West European Politics, Vol.21, No.2 (April 1998), pp.134–153
PUBLISHED BY FRANK CASS, LONDON

the Achilles' heel of comparative politics. As the 'multi-level governance' literature shows, attempts to cast some light on the present theoretical confusion about the European Union may require even more stress on the inherent complexity of the phenomenon. Thus, the moment for simplicity and elegance does not seem to have arrived yet.[4]

Beyond interdisciplinary disputes, a majority of analyses continue to separate the *polity-building* process from the *policy-making* process. The existence of these two processes, and their complex relationship, is not only the most outstanding characteristic of the European Union, but also the most theoretically relevant and the one which should merit empirical attention. Yet, the absence of a research agenda specifically focused on studying how processes of policy making and polity building interact with each other is evident.

Still, there is room for hope. Comparative politics and international relations could meet, and they could do so around actors and institutions, or more precisely, around the relationship between them.[5] Both disciplines should widen their focus away from two of their most beloved research topics. On the one hand, international relations should abandon its emphasis on separating two levels, an international and a domestic one, as if the whole process of European integration was merely a two-level game being played by national governments representing national interests.[6] On the other hand, a good part of comparative politics may also need to abandon those sectorial policy studies which take the European Union's policy-making system as given and deliberately evade the question of what kind of polity policies are helping to shape and how does this polity-building process affect particular policy outcomes.[7]

As an institution-building process, European integration cannot be explained without attention to the two basic questions behind the 'new' institutional approaches, that is, (i) how do institutions originate and change? and (ii) how do they affect individual action and collective outcomes?[8] These two questions enable us to look at the debate between international relations and comparative politics in a completely different manner.

First, by bringing to the forefront the agent-structure debate, they organise the theoretical discussion in terms of questions pertinent to both disciplines. The two resulting views of institutions ('rational-choice institutionalism' and 'historical institutionalism') ask questions about actors and institutions which cut across international relations and comparative politics.[9]

Second, when these two questions become the central elements of the research agenda, the communication between disciplines brings extremely fruitful results and shows that there is enough room for theoretically relevant empirical research. Notwithstanding the fact that the European Union (EU) is more than an international regime, the conclusions of regime theory about how participation transforms the participants are being successfully applied to the EU, as the literature on 'epistemic communities' shows. Similarly, the concept of 'governance' is extremely useful for analysing complex and non-hierarchical systems of political negotiation, at global, regional and national levels.[10]

Third, though this is a larger task which exceeds the scope of this article, theoretical convergence between these two approaches to institutions ('rational choice' and 'historical') cannot be disdained if and when the adequate research questions are posed.[11]

In this sense, the real no man's land is represented by those micro-foundations of actor/institution interaction which would enable us to know why and when actors behave strategically and design institutions to help them maximise their preferences, and why and when those institutions transform the actors and their preferences. Decision-making crises, this article will show, can reveal crucial aspects of policy-making systems. Because they push the system to its limits, they represent excellent focal points with which to study the interconnections between policies, arenas, institutions and actors. Watching first the decision-making system collapse, and then reorganise itself later, offers a good opportunity both to discuss competing theoretical explanations about the EU, as well as to help to establish more adequate research agendas.[12]

MULTIDIMENSIONAL DECISIONS

A Threat of Veto

On 22 November 1991, negotiators from the European Commission and the governments of Poland, Hungary and Czechoslovakia initialled an agreement of wide political and economic content by which these countries would 'associate' themselves to the European Community. After almost one year of formal negotiations, these agreements were to reflect the new relationship between the EC and Eastern Europe after the 1989 changes. Though membership to the EC was not promised, it was evident that these countries had started their (long) accession journey.[13]

The Dutch Presidency had scheduled the ratification of the agreements by the Council of Ministers to take place three weeks later, on 16 December 1991. Ratification by the Council should not have been problematic. Behind the formalities ('the Commission proposes, the Council decides'), ratification by the Council of this type of agreement was purely routine. National governments, through their representatives in the Council's Group on Eastern Europe, had very closely scrutinised the negotiations. In fact, though this was the usual pattern of Council behaviour in external relations, European Commission negotiators complained with special bitterness of the scant margin for negotiation they had enjoyed *vis-à-vis* the Council.[14]

Yet, five days after the Commission had initialled the agreements, the Spanish foreign affairs minister threatened to veto the ratification of association agreements. In a letter to the President of the Commission, Jacques Delors, he encouraged the Commission to find 'a balanced and satisfactory solution' to the problem of future Eastern steel exports to the Community and warned that if Spanish interests were not taken into account 'the Spanish government, in spite of the political importance which it attaches to these agreements, could be obliged to adopt decisions which I believe it is our duty to try to avoid'. As a Spanish official commented later, the idea of a formal appeal to the Luxembourg Compromise was clearly in the air.[15]

The relevance of the crisis could not be underestimated: accepting the Spanish demand would mean reopening (for protectionist reasons) the negotiations with Eastern Europe at a moment when the international prestige of the Community was not at its highest and when criticisms of lack of generosity towards eastern Europe were proliferating.[16]

The questions one could ask are evident. How was it that the negotiating machinery in Brussels had not defused the problem beforehand? How was it that steel imports were threatening the EC's policy path of approximation to central-eastern Europe? How could it happen that *envisaging* the limitation of eastern steel imports had turned out to be a question of national interest for the Spanish government? As will be shown the crisis was the result of the interplay of overlapping policy games, cross-cutting coalitions and very poor co-ordination mechanisms at all levels.

Overlapping Games

Four policy areas converged in the issue of Voluntary Restraint Agreements (or VRAs in the GATT jargon) *vis-à-vis* Eastern Europe.[17] First, and most obviously, there were EC relations with Eastern Europe. As stated, the association agreements were to represent the EC's policy of support for the political, economic and geopolitical transition processes taking place in central-eastern Europe as a result of the 1989 changes. Close dialogue in foreign policy matters, a free-trade area to be built within ten years and a wide economic co-operation framework were its main elements. The agreements were already controversial within the EC: a majority of national governments (France and Spain being the most prominent) did not hide their anxiety concerning the whole process of approximation between the EC and Central-Eastern Europe. The new status of Germany after reunification, the likely eastward shift of the EC's centre of gravity, the 'deepening' versus 'widening' debate and the run-up to Maastricht were already proving to be a source of division within the EC and were affecting very negatively EC policies towards Central-Eastern Europe. Thus, this policy was already very weak and the economic sacrifices which the logic of foreign policy required did not enjoy a very solid consensus within the EC. Hence, though under the logic of collective interests, trade liberalisation with Eastern Europe was imperative, and there was an ongoing discussion about how much sacrifice was required and how it should be distributed.[18]

Then there was the issue of steel. After more than ten years of continuous lay-offs of workers, reductions in production and massive subsidies, the European steel industry was still in very bad shape: with few exceptions it was oversized, expensive, unproductive and grossly unable to compete internationally. At the same time, steel was, together with agriculture, one of the oldest and more privileged policy areas in the EC: it had its own treaty (ECSC), the Commission and the European Court of Justice had ample powers and it still enjoyed major political salience.[19] The European steel industry faced three major threats.

First, there was the prospect that the ongoing Uruguay Round negotiations would force the EC to further open up its steel market to international competition. Significantly, the Commission had already been authorised by the Council to negotiate, within the framework of the Multilateral Steel Agreements, the suppression of VRAs in its steel trade. Thus, policy had to reconcile the fears of European steel industries to open up to international competition with their need to gain better access to the US market.

Second, the association agreements meant the setting up of a full free-trade area in the area of steel trade within five years. The EC's previous timid market openings to eastern Europe had already resulted in large increases in steel imports and many member states were wary of what increased market access for Eastern steel would mean when overproduction and subsidised prices were the rule in the Eastern European steel sector. In this policy dimension, the main priority was to obtain the agreement of Eastern governments to reduce output, cut subsidies and abide by EC competition rules.

The third threat to the European steel sector had its origin in the single market, which required the end of national quotas and trade restrictions within the EC as well as the ending of state aid to steel industries. Obviously, in this policy dimension, the debate was about exceptions to these rules, but also about privatisations, capacity reductions and their social and regional impact.

Cross-Cutting Coalitions

Hence, there were four very deeply interconnected policy games. For example, it was soon to be seen that giving East Europeans longer adaptation periods to abide by EC rules on competition and state aid could trigger parallel demands of EC industries *vis-à-vis* the Commission and that this in turn would weaken the EC's negotiating position in the Uruguay Round and possibly result in US sanctions against EC industries.

Such a policy move meant that coalitions would immediately cut across the Commission, national governments, and even EC industries. At one extreme, foreign ministers and the Commission's Directorate for Eastern Europe (DG I-E) were engaged in a game about how to make the collective foreign-policy interests of the 12 member states (to support democracy and the market economy in Eastern Europe) compatible with their different views about the speed and intensity of the EC's approximation to Eastern Europe. Then, trade ministers and the Directorate for Multilateral Affairs (DG I-D, in charge of the Uruguay Round negotiations) were concerned to maximise the combined weight of the EC in the world market at the same time as taking into account the opportunities and costs for their respective national industries. Meanwhile, industry ministers and DG III (Industry) had to figure out how to make the modernisation of the European steel sector compatible with the minimum of electorally costly job losses.

Other actors had also important roles to play. DG IV (Competition) had to ensure the fair and free functioning of the single market and state subsidies were obviously one of the main threats to competition; DG II (Economic and Financial Affairs) was supporting trade liberalisation as a way to introduce competitiveness in the European economy; and finance ministers had an important role in designing both state aid and privatisation plans. There were also interest groups: though the steel sector was divided between private and state-owned industries, it was commonplace to say that the Union of European Steel Industries (EUROFER) had 'captured' EC steel policy.[20]

A DECISION-MAKING COLLAPSE

Struggles within the Commission

The first element in unleashing the crisis was the division within the European Commission. Negotiation of the association agreements was under the responsibility of the Directorate for Eastern Europe (DG I-E) of the Directorate General for External Relations (DG I), and specifically that of Commissioner Andriessen. However, the authority of this geographical unit was very limited: the positions it defended at the negotiating table were not only very closely scrutinised by the Council's Group of Eastern Europe and the COREPER (the Committee of Permanent Representatives of Member States), but also by other commissioners and directorates in the Commission and, more particularly, in DG I. The tight web of contacts between cabinets, directorates and units aimed at facilitating both vertical and horizontal co-ordination could do little to reconcile conflicting rationales.[21]

This was seen on 30 October 1991 when, three weeks before the association agreements were initialled, the COREPER met to discuss the steel package of the association agreements. There, the permanent representatives of five member states (Spain, France, Italy, Belgium and Portugal – all having large and subsidised steel sectors) demanded strongly that the Commission (represented by DG I-E) accept the inclusion in the agreements of a clause about VRAs. Under the combined pressure of these five representatives, DG I-E (Eastern Europe) bowed and issued a Commission declaration *envisaging* the introduction of 'voluntary restraint agreements' in the event of market disturbances. However, DG I-D (in charge of the international steel negotiations) convinced Commissioner Andriessen that this declaration would undermine the EC's negotiation position *vis-à-vis* the US in the Uruguay Round, where the EC wanted the US to suppress quantitative restrictions on European steel. Commissioner Andriessen forced DG I-E to withdraw the Commission's declaration and replace it with a generic reference to 'quantitative solutions consistent with the Community's international obligations', which obviously meant little in comparison with the previous declaration.[22]

The first consequences of the back-up ordered by Commissioner Andriessen were seen at the following COREPER meeting. First, the five countries whose victory had been suddenly invalidated demanded that Commissioner Andriessen respect the agreement reached between them and DG I-E. Second, politicisation forced those representatives (of Germany, Greece, Luxembourg and Ireland), who until then had remained silent to take sides in support of the inclusion of the VRAs in the agreements. The lack of co-ordination had a very clear result: Andriessen could only count now on the Dutch Presidency, the United Kingdom and Denmark (the most liberal countries when it came to steel trade and state aid), and had to find a way to appease nine member states.[23]

With the COREPER unable to find a solution to the issue, the question of the VRAs was sent up to the Council of General Affairs meeting on 4–5 November 1991. There, the Dutch Presidency and Commissioner Andriessen (External Relations) tried to dissolve the protectionist coalition by offering two bargaining chips. The first consisted of an offer of an 'early warning' system which would serve to anticipate the likely flows of eastern European steel and would allow borders to be closed before such imports hit markets and forced down prices. Second, the Commission committed itself to making clear to the future associates that if they did not strictly respect competition rules and fair-trade practices, it would not hesitate to use its armour of safeguard clauses. As the minutes of the Council meeting show, this was a crucial moment in the crisis.[24] After the Commission had made this offer, the silence which followed led everyone to believe that the issue had been settled. This meant that the offer was tempting. Yet, the Spanish junior minister for European affairs (Sectario de Estado) took the floor and said he refused the solution. He argued, first, that the Spanish steel industry was in an extremely difficult situation; second, that Spain itself had suffered VRAs when it joined the EC; and third, that safeguard clauses had long ago shown themselves to be ineffective in protecting EC industries.

Once temptation had been resisted, the Spanish junior minister was extremely tough: instead of being satisfied with an internal agreement within the EC, he wanted a formal, and thus binding, exchange of letters between the Commission and the future associates whereby the latter would 'take note', and thus accept, the possibility that the EC would reintroduce VRAs.

Decision by Subterfuge

What were the reasons impelling the Spanish junior minister to make such a demand? As seen, the division within DG I (External Relations) had helped to concentrate in one single decision (VRAs) a very complex and multi-faceted policy game. Besides, the importance of the steel dossier for the Spanish government was not fictitious. The state-owned steel sector had always been a major political headache for the Spanish socialist government in power between 1982 and 1996.

As early as 1984, the closure of the steel works of Altos Hornos del Mediterráneo (in Sagunto) had provoked the first crisis between the government and trade unions, especially with the ('brother') Unión General de Trabajadores. In 1986 the Treaty of Spanish accession to the European Community imposed very tough conditions on the Spanish steel sector: three years to enforce EC rules on state aid and competition and quantitative restrictions on Spanish exports to EC markets.[25]

By January 1989, when the single market in steel trade became a reality, the economic boom Spain had enjoyed had made it forget the much needed restructuring of state industry. When in 1991 recession again hit the Spanish industry, the balance was not very encouraging. Despite the loss of 30,000 workers (50 per cent of the 1980 workforce) and a capacity reduction of some seven million tonnes, the main industries (Altos Hornos de Vizcaya and ENSIDESA) desperately needed the injection of public money. Electoral reasons made the steel crisis a political priority. Both steel works constituted the heart of the socialist vote in the Cantabric Basin and the image of the Socialist Party was already torn by a massive general strike organised by the country's two main trade unions in 1989. By the end of 1991, the Spanish government was working on a new restructuring plan which would require the approval of Commissioner Leon Brittan and DG IV (Competition) would demand bigger production cuts and less aid. In return, the Spanish government wanted the EC to send a very clear signal to the future associates: the EC would not hesitate to re-introduce VRAs if eastern steel exports provoked market disturbances.[26]

As the foreign ministers in the Council of General Affairs had not been able to break the stalemate, the issue was sent back to the COREPER. At the meeting of 6 November 1991, both the Commission and the Spanish representative restated their positions. The Dutch representative, acting in his capacity as President of the Council of Ministers, tried to convince the Spanish representative to drop his demand for an exchange of letters but after a 'quite lively' (*sic*) exchange of views the Spanish representative put an end to the session by placing a formal reservation to the steel (ECSC) protocol of the association agreements.[27]

Here came the second element which would trigger the Spanish threat of veto. Politicisation had hardened the Spanish position, but no other representative had joined Spain in placing a formal reservation. In fact, various analyses highlighted the fact that the nine-member opposing coalition was not very solid and that it was only the stubbornness of Spain and the ambiguity of Germany that underpinned the conflict. The other permanent representatives were behaving rather opportunistically: they wanted the VRAs but were not willing to pay the political price. Behaviour at the COREPER was neither based on the interpretation of distinct national interests or on the existence of national instructions. Rather, there seemed to be ample margins for manoeuvre.[28]

Relying on this interpretation, the Dutch presidency decided to ignore the Spanish reservation and not to include in the agenda of the next Council of General Affairs (the last one before the closure of negotiations) the question of VRAs. Obviously, this subterfuge meant that the association agreements would not include VRAs but that member states could not be blamed for having approved their suppression. Thus, instead of assuming its responsibilities and change the directives to allow the Commission to suppress the VRAs from the agreements, the COREPER would hide behind the Commission. For its part, the Commission would justify the suppression of VRAs according to a wide web of technical and practical arguments: the existence of another mandate authorising the Commission to negotiate the suppression of VRAs, pre-existing agreements with the US in which the suppression of VRAs was envisaged, the evolution of the Uruguay Round and the benefits of the opening of the US steel market.

At first sight, the subterfuge had been a success. *Twice* before, the DG I-E (Eastern Europe) and Commissioner Andriessen had wanted to present to the COREPER their proposal for suppressing the VRAs. Yet, the informal channels of communication between the Commission and the Council had conveyed a clear message. The COREPER anticipated that a visible decision to suppress VRAs would have to face the combined opposition of the steel industry (EUROFER), trade unions, regional governments, and even industry ministers at a moment when it was evident that the international prestige of the Community could not face another protectionist crisis.

But with the subterfuge, even the Spanish vice-minister for European affairs could accept the suppression of VRAs. After all, the permanent representative had managed to obtain a declaration envisaging the possibility of 'quantitative solutions' in case of market disturbances. Also, there was a system of import licenses which would act as an 'early warning' to avert irreversible damage to European industries. Finally, the Commission had committed itself to communicate to the future associates the importance that the EC attached to a harmonious evolution of steel trade relations. These three elements configured the most desired result of the COREPER negotiation machinery: there were no winners or losers and there was no political visibility. Thus, the subterfuge had averted politicisation.

Politicisation

The prospect of a crisis would have been averted by this subterfuge had not it been for the ability of the Spanish industry minister to question the role played by the Spanish foreign and trade ministers in the negotiations, and to then take the dossier out of their hands and force the Brussels machinery to revise the agreements reached in the Council of General Affairs of 15 November. However, what was really decisive in shifting the balance of power within the Spanish cabinet was another co-ordination problem within DG I (External Relations).[29]

Once again, the negotiators of DG I-E (Eastern Europe) made a concession to the future associates without having consulted DG I-D (Multilateral Affairs). DG I-E agreed to raise from five years to ten the period during which the associates could invoke social or regional problems to continue subsidising their steel industries. Immediately, DG I-D, counting on the support of DG III (Industry), DG IV (Competition), industry ministers and the lobbying of EUROFER mobilised to convince

Commissioner Andriessen to force DG I-E to take back the concession.[30]

For the Spanish industry ministry, this concession was the straw that broke the camel's back and the definitive confirmation of the inability of the foreign and trade ministers to defend the interests of Spanish industry.[31] Yet, the fact that the industry junior minister was able to take control of the steel dossier over the head of the junior minister for European affairs was due to the different political weight they enjoyed within the Spanish cabinet. The former had significant political influence, good access to the prime minister and at the same time was one of the governing party's leading experts in industrial affairs. In contrast, the latter was a career diplomat who had previously served in Brussels as a permanent representative and had no political profile other than his sympathy with the Socialist Party. Meanwhile, the Spanish foreign affairs minister, the man who could have resisted the industry ministry, was absent from office due to a protracted illness.

The industry ministry's control over the dossier was felt immediately. In the Council of Industry of 18 November 1991, the Spanish industry junior minister protested about the way the steel package had been closed and warned that his government would not desist until it obtained the associates' acceptance that the EC could reintroduce VRAs in steel trade.[32]

The agreements were initialled by the Commission on 22 November 1991 without any explicit reference to VRAs. As they stood, the associates in eastern Europe would apply EC competition and state aid rules within three years in return for a progressive opening of EC markets to their steel. Within five years, the steel market would be completely liberalised and in ten years a full free-trade area (excluding agriculture) would exist between the parties. Besides, a good number of EC anti-dumping provisions ensured producers in western Europe that eastern producers would not flood European markets with artificially low-priced products. On the financial side, the Community would help the restructuring of the eastern European steel sector in return for capacity reduction. This was a balanced agreement: in return for increased market access -meaning the suppression of quantitative restrictions (especially VRAs) – East Europeans would reduce capacity and abide by EC legislation on state aid and competition.

Obviously, the agreements could have been improved. However, they were the result of a very delicate and exhausting equilibrium between many sectors, and it was illusory to believe that a reopening of the negotiations could be kept confined to the issue of steel trade.

The Permanent Traitor[33]

The Spanish industry ministry had decided to politicise the dossier. The first proof was the resort to the press, which immediately printed headlines highlighting the discrimination against Spanish industry in favour of

Eastern Europe and stressed the message that the Spanish government, despite the Commission having initialled the agreements on 22 November 1991, was not going to ratify the association agreements as they stood.[34] Then there was the threat of veto of 27 November, which immediately provoked a meeting between the Spanish permanent representative and President Delors' chef de cabinet.

However, this meeting, the ensuing moves by the Spanish permanent representative in Brussels and the reaction of the Spanish industry ministry would show that the threat of veto was being interpreted in very different ways. While the permanent representative saw the threat of a veto as a flashing light to demand the attention and flexibility of his fellow representatives at the COREPER, the threat was seen by Industry as a way to obtain by coercion what negotiations had not achieved.

Meeting with Delors' chef de cabinet, the Spanish permanent representative in Brussels downplayed the possibility of a real veto, insisted that the Spanish position was flexible and remarked that there were many possible solutions to the crisis if all showed the adequate willingness. He then conveyed to his counterparts at the COREPER the message that, above all, his government was seeking a correct political presentation of the issue of steel imports from Eastern Europe at a time of a delicate domestic situation in the steel sector. Also, there were moves around the cabinets of the Spanish Commissioners to improve the presentation of the case within the Commission. Finally, he manoeuvred to raise the sensitivity of both the Council and the Commission to the Spanish steel restructuring plan.[35]

The package of declarations obtained by the permanent representative as a result of these actions stood as follows. First, there was the commitment to set up an 'early warning' device to minimise floods of steel from Eastern Europe. Second, in the event of market disturbances, the Commission would take 'appropriate quantitative solutions, consistent with EC international obligations'. Third, the Commission guaranteed that the associates would observe 'strict discipline' on state aid and capacity reduction. Finally, after the signature of the agreements, the Commission would communicate to the associates the importance it attached to an 'orderly development' of steel exports from these countries to the Community.[36]

By any standard, the agreement was a good one: it reconciled all the parties' preoccupations; it did not leave winners or losers; it did not make it necessary to reopen the negotiations with the associate countries; it did not generate a protectionist image of the Community; it was consistent with the Uruguay Round; it had no elements to irritate the United States; and it ensured that the crisis in Spain would not be aggravated by a flood of steel imports. Obviously, the agreement was attractive enough to be sold to the Spanish press without much difficulty.

However, once again, the poor co-ordination mechanisms and the open distrust between the ministries of industry, trade and foreign affairs placed the decision-making system on the verge of collapse. To the surprise of EC foreign ministers, meeting on 16 December 1991 to sign the association agreements, the Spanish industry minister assumed the representation of Spain in the Council of General Affairs. Instead of limiting himself to a speech highlighting the sacrifices his country had incurred (and how he hoped to cash them in), he torpedoed the agreement that had been so carefully reached in the COREPER by the permanent representative of Spain and demanded that a clause explicitly envisaging the reintroduction of VRAs be included in the agreements.[37]

Whereas the Spanish permanent representative had managed, using his knowledge of the negotiation machinery in Brussels, to find a solution compatible with all the policy dimensions involved, the industry minister cared only about a single policy dimension and refused attempts to dilute the question of VRAs within a larger package.

To the industry minister, the package agreed at the COREPER was not worth the paper it was written on unless an explicit mention of VRAs was written into the agreements and thus visibly accepted by both the European Community and the future associates in an international treaty of a binding legal nature.

The Dutch Presidency did not show any interest in testing whether the Spanish industry minister was willing to veto the agreements, but instead showed a clear willingness to find a solution. Understanding that the problem was political, a solution was offered which would leave Spain in a good position. At the moment of signing the agreements, the Community would verbally and publicly inform the associates of the existence of an internal declaration on the importance that the Council and the Commission attached to the orderly development of trade in steel. This could have image consequences but no legal ones. But the Spanish minister refused. Then, the Dutch foreign affairs minister offered a public declaration by the EC on the existence of an internal declaration. As the Commission negotiated in the name of the member states, it was DG I-E (Eastern Europe) and Commissioner Andriessen (External Relations), not the Spanish representatives, who had to consult, first, with the negotiators of Poland, Hungary and Czechoslovakia, and later, at Spanish insistence, directly with the prime ministers of these three countries. When these made it clear that they would not sign any declaration accepting VRAs, the Spanish minister had to accept the solutions reached by the Spanish permanent representative the day before. In return for ruining the ceremony of signing the agreements, Spain only ensured that the EC verbally communicated at that moment (and not at a later more appropriate time) to the associates the importance they attached to the 'harmonious development of their countries' steel exports to the Community'.[38]

The balance of the crisis was very revealing. At the political level, the European Community had managed to project an extremely protectionist image on the very same day as it was signing an agreement for a very ambitious free-trade area. However, the particular balance of forces within the Spanish government had ensured that this result, obviously sub-optimal from a collective and foreign-policy point of view, was seen as politically satisfactory.

Thus was the crisis closed. Looking back, it was evident that the division within DG I had managed to isolate a single element (VRAs) within a very complex and multi-dimensional policy package. Isolation meant visibility, and visibility opened the way for politicisation. The COREPER, showing evident signs of a shared identity with respect to problem solving, identified a subterfuge with which to depoliticise the issue and dilute it again into the larger policy package. The system stalled because one element alien to this group – the Spanish industry ministry – was able to take control of the decision-making process in Spain. However, the subsequent events proved that control at home could mean little when compared with the resources at the disposal of the permanent representative in Brussels.

In the end, the intermeshing of functional areas was both the origin of as well as the solution to the crisis. A simple, yes/no decision about quantitative restrictions to steel imports from Eastern Europe was dissolved within an extended decision-making process about the European steel industry and, more particularly, about state aid for the steel industry. In the years that followed, steel imports from Eastern Europe and state aid were 'politics as usual', that is, a game of interests rather than 'national' interests. Thus, the crisis was defused when the focal point provoking it was diluted within a wide web of functional and temporal linkages of low political visibility.[39]

CONCLUSIONS

The goal of this article was to explore how decision-making crises could play the role of focal points from which to essay ways of theoretical convergence between the disciplines of comparative politics and international relations in relation to the study of the European Union's policy-making and polity-building processes.

Crises, the article has shown, arise from the structural ambivalence of the EU policy-making process. On the one hand, there is a *political* or policy-making game in which actors behave according to sectorial interests, align around functional areas, and in which policies are highly path-dependent. Hence, actors form coalitions which cut across national governments, the European Commission, the European Parliament and interest groups.[40]

If this game could be isolated, one could look at the resulting policy-making system from a comparative politics perspective, almost as 'any other political system'. In spite of the absence of true European political parties, media, or even a demos, issues of participation, interest-representation as well as ideological cleavages would be more important in explaining preferences and actor behaviour than territorial elements.

Yet, on the other hand, there is a *diplomatic* game between states in which the EU is predominantly a treaty-based intergovernmental organisation whereby member states seek to find and upgrade common interests. This game of territorial politics requires national governments to represent sovereign states, to behave *as if* they were unitary actors with distinctive and coherent national interests.

Problems arise when national governments are asked to aggregate contradictory preferences and behave as unitary actors, that is, as 'member states', over interconnected functional areas. Not only is it difficult to find a true, distinctive and unique national interest when the policy-making system fosters functional interests and ideological cleavages. What is more, there is also a wide set of 'European' interests (the single market, the EU's position in the world, etc.) to which national governments adhere and which they need to make compatible with 'domestic' interests.

The same is true of the Commission, where it is even more difficult to aggregate preferences and behave as a unitary actor. The Commission itself has to confront the existence of different, and even contradictory, European interests. At the same time, while there is enough evidence of the ability of interest groups to influence or even capture certain functional areas, national interests (territorial politics) do not seem to have much difficulty in penetrating the Commission.[41]

This complex exercise of aggregation of preferences and bargaining at multiple levels has been rightly described as a 'quagmire'.[42] As this article has shown, the absence in this quagmire of clear rules and lines of authority for resolving conflicting preferences makes the system especially ill-equipped to deal with multidimensional decisions. Also, it reveals an inherent tension between the path-dependency pattern of each functional policy area and the instability, proneness to crises and unpredictability governing multidimensional decision making.

More importantly, the effects of this structural ambivalence do not remain confined to the policy-making process. This ambivalence captures interests, preferences, actors, institutions, loyalties and identities, resulting in an extremely dynamic, fluid and elusive decision-making system. Behind this system in flux it is not difficult to see a polity-building process, be it called 'multi-level governance', 'beyond sovereignty' or, more simply, 'Europeanisation'. Nowhere is this more clearly seen than with the COREPER, theoretically the stronghold of national interests, but in fact something very different from a mere intergovernmental forum for negotiation, and a clear example of how institutions transform actors and become something more than arenas.[43] Thus, the interactions between actors and institutions do not only help to explain the policy-making system, but also its transformation, that is, the polity-building process.

NOTES

I thank Gabriel Saro, Vincent Wright, Nacho Molina, Andrew Richards and César Colino for their valuable suggestions and comments. The usual disclaimer applies.

1. S. Hix, 'The Study of the European Community: The Challenge to Comparative Politics', *West European Politics* 17/1 (Jan. 1994) pp.1–30; H. Kassim, 'Policy Networks, Networks and European Union Policy-Making: A Sceptical View', ibid. 17/4 (Oct. 1994) pp.15–27; J. Peterson, 'Policy Networks and European Union Policy-Making: A Reply to Kassim', ibid. 18/2 (April 1995) pp.389–407; A. Hurrell and A. Menon, 'Politics Like Any Other? Comparative Politics, International Relations and the Study of the EU', ibid. 19/2 (April 1996) pp.386–401; S. Hix, 'CP, IR and the EU – A Rejoinder to Hurrell and Menon', ibid. 19/4 (Oct. 1996) pp.802–4. See also S. Bulmer, 'The Governance of the European Union: A New Institutionalist Approach', *Journal of Public Policy* 13/4 (Dec. 1994) pp.351–80; J. Peterson, 'Decision-Making in the European Union: Towards a Framework for Analysis', *Journal of European Public Policy* 2/1 (March 1995) pp.69–94; J. Richardson, 'Policy-Making in the EU: Interests, Ideas and Garbage Cans of Primeval Soup', in idem (ed.) *European Union: Power and Policy-Making* (London: Routledge 1996) pp.3–23.
2. Peterson (note 1) criticises the new institutionalism for being 'long in jargon but short in explanation' (p.307) but he concludes his debate with Kassim (note 1) arguing that policy networks can best explain the informal processes dominating the policy-formulation stage and accepting that institutionalism could shed more light on the more formal policy-setting stage. Similarly, Hix (note 1) concedes international relations approaches the prerogative to explain the integration process but maintains that only comparative politics can explain the complexities of the European policy-making process. Similarly Richardson (note 1) concedes international relations to be the 'tip of the iceberg' represented by treaty bargaining and retains under comparative politics the other 9/10 of the day-to-day 'low politics' of European policy making.
3. On the limitations of international relations approaches, see J. Anderson, 'The State of the (European) Union: From the Single Market to Maastricht, From Singular Events to General Theories', *World Politics* 47/3 (April 1995) pp.445–65; T. Christiansen, 'European Integration between Political Science and International Relations Theory: The End of Sovereignty', *EUI/RSC Working Papers* 4 (1994); T. Risse-Kappen, 'Exploring the Nature of the Beast: International Relations Theory and Comparative Policy Analysis Meet the European Union', *Journal of Common Market Studies* 34/1 (March 1996) pp.53–80; S. Schmidt, 'Sterile Debates and Dubious Generalisations: European Integration Theory Tested by Telecommunications and Electricity', *Journal of Public Policy* 16/3 (1997) pp.233–71.
4. See T. Christiansen, 'Reconstructing European Space: From Territorial Politics to Multilevel Governance', in K.E. Joergensen (ed.) *Reflective Approaches to European Governance* (London: Macmillan 1997) pp.51–68; G. Fuchs, 'Policy-Making in a System of Multi-Level

Governance – the Commission of the European Communities and the Restructuring of the Telecommunications Sector', *Journal of European Public Policy* 1/2 (Autumn 1994) pp.178–94; E. Grande, 'The State and Interest Groups in a Framework of Multi-Level Decision-Making: The Case of the European Union', ibid. 3/3 (Sept. 1996) pp.318–38; M. Jachtenfuchs, 'Conceptualisms of European Governance', in K.E. Joergensen (ed.) *Reflective Approaches to European Governance* (London: Macmillan 1997) pp.39–50; B. Kohler-Koch, 'Catching Up with Change: The Transformation of Governance in the European Union', *Journal of European Public Policy* 3/3 (Sept. 1996) pp.359–80; and G. Marks, L. Hooghe, and K. Blank, 'European Integration from the 1980s: State-Centric v. Multi-level Governance', *Journal of Common Market Studies* 34/3 (Sept. 1996) pp.341–78.

5. As Hix (note 1) has stressed, both international relations and comparative politics share a debate between agent (rational choice) and structure (institutionalism). Bulmer (note 1) has also claimed that the new institutionalism and regime theory can help to bridge the gap between international relations and comparative politics. See also L. Cram, 'Integration Theory and the Study of the Policy Process', in Richardson, *European Union* (note 1) pp.40–60; S. Mazey and J. Richardson, 'Promiscuous Policymaking: The European Policy Style?', in C. Rhodes and S. Mazey (eds.) *The State of the European Union* Vol.3 (Boulder, CO: Lynne Rienner 1995) pp.337–59.
6. The idea that policies and day-to-day politics, more than intergovernmental treaty-bargaining, explain the European integration process is the central tenet of neo-functionalism. It is a paradox, and a sign of intellectual honesty, that neo-functionalism declared itself dead after having explained so much more than intergovernmentalism ever did. Intergovernmentalism has not hesitated to add the label of 'institutionalist' or 'liberal', thereby demonstrating its wide concern about preference-formation processes and domestic politics, but it still shares the neo-realist assumption of two-level games between a national and international sphere. See D. Wincott, 'Institutional Interaction and European Integration: Towards an Everyday Critique of Liberal Intergovernmentalism', *Journal of Common Market Studies* 33/4 (Dec. 1995) pp.597–609; and A. Moravcsik, 'Liberal Intergovernmentalism and Integration: A Rejoinder', ibid. pp.610–28.
7. This demand is especially justified taking into account the exceptionally rich contributions to explaining the European integration process which have originated in the opening up of the field to comparative politics. See A.M. Sbragia (ed.) *European Politics: Institutions and Policy-Making in the European Community* (Washington DC: Brookings 1992).
8. I follow here P. Hall and R.C. Taylor. 'Political Science and the Four New Institutionalisms', paper prepared for presentation at the Annual Meeting of the American Political Science Association (NY, Sept. 1994).
9. Note 5.
10. See Richardson (note 1); P. Haas (ed.) *Knowledge, Power, and International Policy Coordination* (Columbia: U. of South Carolina Press 1996), originally published in *International Organization* 46/1 (1992).
11. Hall and Taylor (note 8).
12. Decision-making crises can conform with the demand of Richardson (note 1) to design cases which can reveal the interaction of 'policy actor behaviour' and 'institutional relations' (p.26). Also, placing the decision, and not the level, at the core of the research can be crucial to determining whether decisions are atomised or path-dependent (Peterson, note 1, p.399). See also A. Héritier, 'Policy-Making by Subterfuge: Interest Accommodation, Innovation and Substitute Democratic Legitimation in Europe – Perspective from Different Policy Areas', *Journal of European Public Policy* 4/2 (June 1997) pp.171–89.
13. For an overview of EC relations with eastern Europe and the association agreements see J.I. Torreblanca, The European Community and Central Eastern Europe (1989–1993): Foreign Policy and Decision-Making (PhD, Madrid: Instituto Juan March 1997); B. Lippert and H. Schneider (eds.) *Monitoring Association and Beyond: The European Union and the Visegrad States* (Bonn: Europa Union Verlag 1995); U. Sedelmeier, 'The European Union's Association Policy Towards Central Eastern Europe: Political and Economic Rationales in

Conflict', *Sussex European Institute Working Papers* 7/1994.

14. *Interview* 2, Brussels, Nov. 1994; *Europolitique*, 22 Nov. 1991 p.V/7; and *Agence Europe*, 23 Nov. 1991, p.8.
15. European Commission, 'Letter from the Spanish Foreign Affairs Minister to the President of the Commission', 27 Nov. 1991, *DG I-L Archive*; *Interview* 10, Madrid, Sept. 1996; *Financial Times*, 17 Dec. 1991; *Agence Europe*, 16–17 Dec. 1991 p.8.
16. The Gulf War, Yugoslavia, the imminent collapse of the Soviet Union, and the crisis of the Albanian refugees had all throughout 1991 left in evidence an EC absorbed by the negotiations of the Maastricht Treaty with little capacity or interest, despite the evident challenges, to shape events in the wider Europe. Besides, the association agreements were already under fire. After the negotiations had started in Dec. 1990, all the problems had concentrated around the so-called sensitive sectors (steel and coal, textiles and agriculture). Agriculture had already been the subject of a crisis when the French government had blocked the negotiations of the association agreements as an electoral gesture to French farmers and as a message to the Commission about the agricultural package of the Uruguay Round. Now the problem revolved around steel trade. *Financial Times*, 9 Sept. 1991 ('More trade sought with Eastern Europe'); *Time*, 11 Sept.1991 ('The Mirror Cracks').
17. Technically, a VRA is defined as 'a bilateral agreement whereby an exporting country agrees to reduce or restrict exports without the importing country having to make use of quotas, tariffs, or other import controls'. In practice, the terms 'voluntary' and 'agreement' are only euphemisms, thereby explaining why these are called 'grey-area' measures in the WTO (GATT) jargon. J.M. Rosenberg, *Dictionary of International Trade* (NY: John Wiley 1994) pp.302–3
18. J. Rollo *The New Eastern Europe: Western Responses* (London: Pinter 1991); H. Kramer, 'EC Responses to the New Eastern Europe', *Journal of Common Market Studies* 31/2 (June 1993) pp.213–44.
19. See N. Bacon and P. Blyton, 'Re-Casting the Politics of Steel in Europe: The Impact on Trade Unions', *West European Politics* 19/4 (Oct. 1996) pp.770–86; G. Saro, 'Europeización o Privatización: Políticas Siderúrgicas CECA 1977–95', unpub. ms (Madrid: Institute Juan March 1997); A. Winters, 'Liberalisation of the European Steel Trade', in R. Faini and R. Portes (eds.) *European Union Trade with Eastern Europe* (London: CEPR 1995) pp.201–35.
20. *Interview* (Brussels), 6 and 15 Nov. 1994. Besides, given the social importance and electoral salience of the steel sector, there was the policy input of regional governments, trade unions, political parties and their representatives at local, regional, national or European level.
21. *Interview* (Brussels), 4, 6, 7, 8, 17 and 18 Nov. 1994.
22. European Commission, DG I-D, 'Steel Protocol with Poland, Hungary and Czechoslovakia', 21 Nov. 1991, *DG I-L Archive.*
23. European Commission, DG I-E, 'Acier: Accord d'association PECO', 4 Dec. 1991, *DG I-L Archive.*
24. European Commission, 1527 Council meeting, SI (91) 770 and SI (91) 772, *DG I-L Archive.*
25. Within the Spanish steel 'community' (including the Ministry of Industry), it was commonly believed that the Foreign Affairs and Trade Ministries had been unable to resist the pressure of European industries, thus resulting in an extremely asymmetrical agreement. See G. Saro (note 19); Ministerio de Industria, Comercio y Turismo *Diez años de política industrial* (Madrid: MICT 1993); Instituto Sindical de Estudios, 'La industria española: un problema estructural', in ISI (ed.) *Evolución Social en España* (Madrid: ISI 1994) pp.400–32; V. Oller and J. Conejos, 'Política industrial', in L. Gámir (ed.) *Política Económica de España* (Madrid: Alianza Universidad 1993) pp.249–68.
26. *El País,* 6 Nov. 1991 p.45.
27. European Commission, 1496 COREPER II meeting, SI (91) 782, *DG I-L Archive.*
28. *Agence Europe,* 8 Nov. 1991 p.8; *Europolitique*, 9 Nov. 1991, p.v/9. Germany was, for obvious reasons, the main promoter of the association agreements with Eastern Europe. However, its sectorial interests, especially with respect to steel and agriculture, forced it to be cautious when discussing trade liberalisation.

29. On the problems of European policy-making co-ordination in Spain, see F. Morata, 'Spain' in D. Rometsch and W. Wessels (eds.) *The European Union and the Member States: Towards Institutional Fusion?* (Manchester UP 1996) pp.134–54; E. Zapico, 'La adaptación de la Administración española a la Unión Europea: un proceso de evolución y aprendizaje permanente', *Gestión y Administración Pública* (Sept.–Dec. 1995) pp.47–65.
30. European Commission, DG IV, 'Accord d'association avec la Pologne', 21 Nov. 1991; DG I-D, 'Steel Protocol with Hungary, Poland and Czechoslovakia', 21 Nov. 1991; DG III, 'Accords d'association avec les PECO', dated 26 Nov. 1991. *DG I-L Archive.*
31. *Interview* (Madrid) 10 and 13 Sept. 1996.
32. *El País*, 19 Nov. 1991, p.55.
33. Germans often use this term to refer to the socialisation effects which the machinery of Brussels has over the permanent representatives. The term is a play on words: *Ständige Vertreter* means permanent representative but *Ständige Verräter* means permanent traitor. Mentioned in K.E. Joergensen, 'PoCo: The Diplomatic Republic of Europe', in idem (ed.) *Reflective Approaches to European Governance* (London: Macmillan 1997) pp.167–80. This view of permanent representatives having their own agendas was also shared by a former British minister, Alan Clark, who said of the British permanent representative in Brussels: 'Totally Europhile. Sole objective, as far as I could see, being to "expedite business", i.e. not make a fuss about anything, however monstrous. Or at least, you could make a fuss, but only a "show" fuss in order to get kudos from, soon after, surrendering in the interests of making progress.' Cited in F. Hayes-Renshaw and H. Wallace, *The Council of Ministers* (London: Macmillan 1997) p.82.
34. *El País*, 23 Nov. 1991, p.39.
35. European Commission, Cabinet du Président, 'Demarché espagnole', 29 Nov. 1991; Chiefs of Cabinet meeting of 5 Dec. 1991, SEC (91) 2327/3, 6 Dec. 1991; 1539 Council meeting, SI (91) 878, 3 Dec. 1991; 1501 COREPER II meeting, SI (91) 924, 13 Dec. 1991. *DG I-L Archive.*
36. Council, Group Eastern Europe, Doc. Seance 221 Rev 1, 11 Dec. 1991; Report from the COREPER to the Council, 10242/91 EST, 13 Dec. 1991.
37. European Commission, 1545 Council meeting, SI (91) 937, 17 Dec. 1991.
38. Council, Group Eastern Europe, Doc. Seance 291, 21 Jan. 1991, *DG I-L Archive*. See also *Agence Europe*, 16–17 Dec. 1991; *Financial Times*, 17 Dec. 1991; *Europolitique*, 18 Dec. 1991 p.v/2
39. This was seen later in 1992, when steel imports from Czechoslovakia registered a very important increase and many producers, especially the Spanish and French, claimed injury and called for the reintroduction of VRAs. Obviously, the preceding events led observers to expect that the situation would result in a new steel crisis. However, the issue was not politicised and the subsequent negotiations between the Commission, the member states and the Czechoslovak authorities developed on a rather technical and consensual basis with no mention at all of the reintroduction of VRAs. See Torreblanca (note 13) pp.455–8. In Dec.1993, the Council of Ministers authorised state aid to Eko Stahl and Freital in Germany, CSI and Sidenor in Spain, Ilva in Italy and Siderurgia Nacional in Portugal. Finally, in 1994, the Spanish government obtained the Commission's approval to build a modern steel plant in Sestao. See Bacon and Blyton (note 19) p.779.
40. The European Parliament has not been included in the analysis, but evidence stresses the difficult coexistence of a Committee structure based on policy areas with party cleavages and territorial politics. See F. Jacobs and R. Corbet, *The European Parliament* (Harlow: Longman 1990); M. Westlake, *A Modern Guide to the Parliament* (London: Pinter 1994).
41. See. G.B. Peters, 'Bureaucratic Politics and the Institutions of the European Community', in A. Sbragia (ed.) *European Politics: Institutions and Policy-Making in the European Community* (Washington DC: Brookings 1992) pp.75–122; ibid, 'Agenda-setting in the European Community', *Journal of European Public Policy* 1/1 (June 1994) pp.9–26; T.Christiansen, 'Tensions of European Governance: Politicized Bureaucracy and Multiple Accountability in the European Commission', ibid. 4/1 (March 1997) pp.73–90.

42. V. Wright, 'The National Co-ordination of European Policy-Making: Negotiating the Quagmire', in J.Richardson (ed.) *European Union: Power and Policy-Making* (London: Routledge 1996) pp.148–69.
43. F. Hayes-Renshaw and H. Wallace, 'Executive Power in the European Union: The Functions and Limits of the Council of Ministers', *Journal of European Public Policy* 2/4 (Dec. 1995) pp.559–82; M. Wind, 'Rediscovering Institutions: A Reflectivist Critique of Rational Institutionalism', in Joergensen (note 33) pp.15–37.

Social Capital and the Public–Private Divide in Greek Regions

CHRISTOS J. PARASKEVOPOULOS

This article argues that the concept of social capital, by facilitating collective action among the actors within institutional networks, constitutes a prerequisite for overcoming the public–private divide and achieving synergies at the regional and local levels. Thus, within the framework of European regional policy, it is considered to be the crucial factor for the processes of institutional learning and successful adaptation/Europeanisation of the subnational systems of governance. The case of Greece demonstrates that the combination of a centralised state structure and a weak civil society breeds the creation of hierarchical, clientelistic networks that undermine the process of crossing the public–private divide and inhibits the Europeanisation function of subnational governments.

SUBSIDIARITY, PARTNERSHIP AND SYNERGY IN EUROPEAN REGIONAL POLICY

The operationalisation of the principles of partnership and subsidiarity is considered to be the main component of European structural policy after the 1988 reforms of the Structural Funds, along with the geographical targeting of resources (Objectives 1, 2, 3, 4, 5a, 5b, 6), the change in emphasis from projects to programmes (Community Support Frameworks–CSFs), and the principles of additionality and proportionality. The operationalisation of the principles is seen as having far-reaching repercussions for the EU system of governance. First, although the formal incorporation of subsidiarity in the Treaty on European Union (TEU) (art.3B) poses it as a mainly procedural criterion for delineating competences between supranational institutions (EU Commission) and member-state governments, its substantive meaning – the need for policy to be made at the closest possible level to the citizen – plays a key role in promoting accountability and transparency in the policy-making process. Hence, it is seen as a recognition of the necessity for flexibility in the EU decision-making processes. Second, this flexibility

West European Politics, Vol.21, No.2 (April 1998), pp.154–177
PUBLISHED BY FRANK CASS, LONDON

implies the need for flexibility within member states: that is, the need for devolution of their administrative and economic structures. Third, the emphasis on partnership seeks to promote co-operation between supranational, national and regional élites and, at a second stage, to encourage the creation of synergistic networks between public, private and voluntary-community actors at the local level. Finally, the encouragement of synergies among the actors and the formulation of the system of intraregional interactions is closely linked to the outward-looking orientation of local governments, namely to their capacity to develop linkages and participate in transnational networks. In that sense the degree of partnerships and synergies creation at the regional and local levels has been adopted as a criterion for the degree of Europeanisation of local governments.[1]

Thus, partnership and subsidiarity as principles of regionalism have played an important role in the institutionalisation of subnational governments, which has substantiated their chance to develop direct linkages with the Commission and thus bypass the central governments in the policy-making process, challenging their traditional role as 'gatekeepers',[2] in S. Hoffmann's terms, between subnational and supranational levels of governance.

All these considerations constitute the theoretical and empirical underpinnings of the emerging system of 'multilevel governance' or ('co-operative regionalism')[3] in the European Union (EU), which implies that 'Europe of the regions' amounts to 'a regionalisation of Europe, as well as at the same time a Europeanisation of its regions'.[4]

Within this framework the states are seen as being 'outflanked'[5] on the one side by the transfer of authority to the EU supranational institutions and on the other by the emergence of powerful regional bodies. The main hypothesis behind the argument is that European states reflect neither the diverse cultures, languages and identities of Europeans nor the total of regional units of economic life. This point has been reinforced by recent research that sustains Marks' *Europe with the regions* thesis, showing that regional identity, enhanced subnational governments and conflicting national/regional interests are the factors underlying regional mobilisation at the European level rather than concerns to obtain funding and resources.[6]

The reformulation of European regional policy, however, is viewed not only as a means to promote democracy and administrative efficiency in the policy-making process, but it also should be linked to the economic, technological and political changes that have occurred since the early 1970s, involving the move from mass production towards the paradigm of 'flexible specialisation'. This process, which has been favoured by increased international competition, and the internationalisation, fragmentation and volatility of markets, is seen as a key factor in encouraging the re-emergence of the region as an integrated unit of production and as a key locus of socio-economic governance.[7] Thus, the emergence of regions is considered as a response to the increasing importance of quick adaptation to changing market demand and as a means for promoting viable small-scale production (economies of scope instead of economies of scale).

Nevertheless, the increasing intensity of the changing, globalising political economy does not necessarily imply a homogeneity of preferences in the framework of a global village, but rather stresses the existence of local specificities. Thus, the processes of globalisation and localisation coexist in the so-called 'global–local interplay'.[8] These seemingly contradictory movements are seen as having led to the 'hollowing out'[9] of the traditional nation-state. The response of most of the traditional European states, which overwhelmed by the globalisation of economic relationships, as well as of ecological crises and of the risks of financing the welfare state have adopted strategies of devolution and decentralisation, should be attributed to this trend.[10]

Furthermore, the processes of decentralisation and devolution may be interpreted as an adaptation to the increased importance of the local sphere in everyday life. The pressure throughout the world for larger political units capable of promoting economic development and raising standards of living has coincided with the search for identity which arises 'from the desire for smaller, more responsive to the individual citizen self-governing political units'.[11] In that sense, regionalisation and regionalism should be seen as interdependent and interrelated concepts, given that, while the former is interpreted as a process mainly from above, the latter constitutes a movement from below.[12]

Hence, within contemporary capitalism, the role of the nation-state as a reliable gatekeeper, balancing domestic demands and international pressures,[13] or as a viable locus of regional development strategies and guarantor of the interests of the less favoured regions, is questionable. On the other hand, it cannot be seen as a regulatory mechanism alternative to neo-liberalism in Europe, given that, at least after the completion of the internal market (SEA), its role has been replaced to a significant degree by the 'voluntarism of the market and civil society'.[14] Therefore, the key issue for today's regional policies, which has been the main target of the reform of the EU structural funds by enhancing partnership, is to develop certain capacities for collective action at the regional level that can counterbalance the global pressures and determine the outcome of the development process. Within this framework the debate on crossing the public–private divide and achieving collective action should take into account the changing role requirements of the state, civil society and the market in contemporary development strategies.

SOCIAL CAPITAL AND INSTITUTIONAL LEARNING IN OVERCOMING THE PUBLIC–PRIVATE DIVIDE

How and why dilemmas of collective action arise within contemporary economic and social structures, and the way in which they could be resolved, constitutes the crucial parameters upon which the creation of effective local synergies is dependent and, subsequently, the main issue for modern development strategies based on the bottom-up approach to regional development. The conceptualisation of the role of institutions and socio-cultural factors in resolving collective action problems and in determining thus the outcome of development policies should be seen as one of its key contributions.

Contemporary research in political science, economic history and economics is focused on the way in which rationality by individuals can be reconciled with rationality by society: that is the reason for the creation of dilemmas of collective action. 'Collective dilemmas arise when choices made by rational individuals lead to outcomes that no one prefers.'[15] Game theory has illustrated the essential property of collective dilemmas and the conditions under which rational self-interested individuals can arrive at a Pareto-inferior solution: that is, one that leaves both parties worse off than they would have been had they co-operated. It is generally accepted that co-operation is difficult to sustain when the game is not repeated, so the defector cannot be punished in successive rounds, when information on the other players is lacking and there are large numbers of players. When the prisoner's dilemma game is played only once, the dominant strategy for players is to defect. In an iterated prisoner's dilemma game, however, there is no dominant strategy. Axelrod's optimistic view about the ability of actors to devise co-operative solutions to problems without the intervention of a coercive power state is based on the assumption that the winning strategy under these conditions of repeated play is the strategy of 'tit-for-tat', that is one in which the player responds in kind to the action of other players.[16]

A renewed concern with institutions as a means for resolving collective dilemmas has emerged in a broad range of social sciences. New institutionalists and economic sociologists see in collective dilemmas reasons for the existence of institutions, that is, 'forms of hierarchy in which sanctions are employed to make self-interested choices consistent with the social good',[17] or 'the rules of the game in a society – the humanly devised constraints – that shape human interaction'.[18]

New institutionalists attempt to show, within the rational choice approach and neoclassical economic theory, 'both the conditions under which particular institutions arise and the effects of these institutions on the functioning of the system'.[19] Thus, they address the origins of efficient institutions that promote the making of contracts, the enforcement of property rights, the removal of production externalities and the provision of public goods, that is, mechanisms for reconciling the gap between individual and collective interests. New institutional economics, in particular, has emphasised the role played by formal institutions (i.e. hierarchical firms) in reducing transaction costs, in enabling agents thus to surmount problems of opportunism and in performing economic functions.[20] Given that both production externalities and public goods constitute prisoners' dilemmas, the new institutionalism's basic argument becomes clear: individuals facing collective dilemmas might prefer to live in a world in which the freedom to choose is constrained.

New institutionalism, however, leaves open a crucial problem: how and why are formal institutions provided? The problem seems to be similar to the solution of the third-party enforcement in the sense that the institutional solution itself constitutes a collective dilemma. The problem arises over whether to invest in moves that enhance the collective welfare. Even if the pay-offs were symmetric and all persons were made better off from the introduction of the institution, there would still be a failure of supply, since the institution would provide a collective good, and rational individuals would seek to secure its benefits for free. Therefore, the incentives to free-ride would undermine the incentives to organise a solution to the collective dilemma.

Hence, economic sociology's criticism of the undersocialised character of new institutional economics has focused on its attempt to explain social institutions from a functional neo-classical point of view. In particular, Granovetter's 'embeddedness argument' points to the role of personal relations and networks of relations in generating trust, in establishing expectations and in enforcing norms. Thus, the embeddedness approach focuses on: seeing economic action as social action; understanding networks as a function between markets and hierarchies; and tracking the processes of institution building.[21] In that sense, it points to the role of social and cultural contexts in affecting rational or purposive action and sees social structure, institutional and economic performance as interdependent and interactive systems. Granovetter's embeddedness thesis, Bates's criticism of new institutionalism and Coleman's theory of collective action are approaches engaged in the development of a new theoretical orientation, emphasising the role of social and cultural contexts in affecting rational or purposive action. Beyond the theoretical arguments there is evidence to suggest that the differentiation of social norms is highly correlated with varying levels of institutional and economic performance.[22] Social capital constitutes the conceptual foundation for this theoretical enterprise.

Social capital has emerged, recently, as a crucial conceptual tool for improving both political and economic performance by facilitating collective action among actors (persons or corporate actors), within political and economic institutional settings. It is also considered a necessary prerequisite for enhancing community action and enabling actors to be collectively involved in the provision of public goods at regional, local or sub-local levels. Coleman's definition of social capital as a set of socio-cultural resources inherent in a social organisation that constitute capital assets for the individual implies it refers 'to features of social organisation, such as trust, norms and networks that can improve the efficiency of society by facilitating co-ordinated action'.[23] Therefore, synergy and voluntary co-operation are easier in a community that has inherited a substantial stock of social capital, in which the pursuit of collective goods is not seen as a contradiction to the pursuit of maximizing individual wealth.

Trust constitutes the most important form of social capital. Sabel has underlined its crucial significance for modern economies and societies: 'trust, the mutual confidence that no party to an exchange will exploit the others' vulnerability, is today widely regarded as a precondition for competitive success'.[24] This presumption should be strictly linked to the volatility of modern economies, whose main features are: fragmented and volatile markets, rapid technological change and shorter product-life cycles. This is the main reason for the increasing attention many scholars have paid to the crucial role played by trust in the emergence of industrial districts and flexible regional economies since the 1970s. Given, however, that in modern economies and societies, what is required is the impersonal form of trust, a problem arises about how personal trust can become social trust.

Social trust can arise from two related forms of social capital: norms of reciprocity (balanced and generalised) and networks of civic engagement. Balanced reciprocity refers to a simultaneous exchange of equivalent values, while generalised reciprocity is based on a continuing relationship of exchange, which involves mutual expectations that a benefit granted now should be repaid in the future. Thus, norms are sustained by socialisation and by sanctions.

The shift in emphasis from economic to socio-cultural factors – what is known as 'institutional thickness' – as determinants of economic performance is seen as a great leap forward for development. Institutional thickness or density refers to the qualities of institutional infrastructure, namely, to 'the combination of factors including inter-institutional interaction and synergy, collective representation ... and shared cultural norms'.[25] In practical terms, thickness refers to the way in which institutions are networked and reveals network cohesion. Additionally, it constitutes an indicator of institutional learning. The concept of institutional learning is closely linked to the uncertainties and interdependence of contemporary economies and societies. It involves the dynamic processes of both institutional and policy adaptation to the rapidly changing conditions, through the involvement of institutional actors – both public and private – in 'joint learning by past successes and failures', facilitated by the presence of dialogue and communication procedures.

Therefore, institutional learning is the basis upon which the adaptation process relies. It implies that 'institutions must be adaptable, rather than adapted, to the changing economic and social conditions',[26] that is they must be able to change with changing conditions. Since learning and adaptation, however, very often necessitate changes, the involved organisations must be capable of adapting policy choices and structure: that is they must be flexible. Furthermore, the learning process usually requires some degree of specialisation from some of the participants. Because the network is considered the most appropriate institutional structure for this combination of flexibility and specialisation, the learning process requires the presence of learning institutional networks.

For the learning approach 'knowledge is the most fundamental resource in a modern economy and, accordingly, the most important process is learning', but 'learning is predominantly an interactive and, hence, a socially embedded process which cannot be understood without taking into consideration its institutional and cultural context'.[27] Moreover, learning and adaptation, as dynamic processes are about 'waking up and catching up',[28] so it is highly likely that may undermine the stability of relations between the transacting actors. Knowledge, on the other hand, is relational, and understanding cannot be disassociated from the relationships in which it is shared: hence the importance of trust, norms and conventions, as forms of social capital, which provide the glue that cements these relations and stabilises the system of inter-institutional and public–private interactions,[29] thus improving the functional performance of the network as a whole. These conventions, which emerge from rounds of action and interaction, and are sustained by sanctions and socialisation, make possible communication, interpretation and co-ordination among the public and private actors. Those forms of social capital (Storper's 'untraded interdependencies'[30]) facilitate the stability of intra-network relations by overcoming the public–private divide and hence the inbuilt capacity of institutional networks to learn and adapt to changing circumstances. Hence, social capital is seen as a prerequisite for institutional performance.

The most important institutional networks for development-sustaining activity based on the learning process are those centred on intraregional functional networks, because, by facilitating collective action among public and private actors, they constitute the appropriate regulatory framework for development strategies based on endogenous decision making.[31] So, where this type of network is in demand, as in most of the Objective 1 regions, the development strategies are driven by the central state administrative structures, that inhibit the bottom-up adaptation process.

BRINGING THE STATE BACK IN?

The crucial question which arises from the discussion so far is whether or not social capital can be created. A renewed concern with the role of the state in promoting collective action and building social capital through successful state/society synergies with specific reference to Third World countries has emerged recently.[32] The basic argument in the *problematique* of the interconnectedness between social capital and 'crossing the great divide' derives from the debate between the 'endowments' and the 'constructability' approaches to state/society synergies. The former emphasises the dependence of successful state/society synergies on a pre-existing strong civil society and presence of substantial stock of social capital and, therefore, points to a long-run process for success, while the latter stresses the possibility of short-run institution building through processes of synergistic relations.

According to the latter the joint involvement of state, market and civil society (voluntary) institutions in development projects, and the thus created synergistic relationships, are viewed as key factors for enhancing collective action and enabling actors to be involved in the production of public goods. The evidence of successful synergies with a key role attributed to the state comes from areas of the globe (i.e., Third World countries) where the presence of social capital is in demand. Moreover, this 'constructability', as regards social capital, effect of the state's involvement in synergistic relations with society, seems to be particularly relevant to success stories of development, such as those of the 'East-Asian miracle' countries. In analysing East-Asian countries the argument points to the complementary and mutually supportive relations between public and private actors that are substantiated with the development of dense networks that cross the two spheres and to the crucial role played by the presence of Weberian qualitative features in the structure of the public bureaucracy which add to its efficacy and facilitate the process of successful public–private synergies.[33]

The existing evidence from countries of southern Europe,[34] however, seems to point to the opposite direction: that the combination of a centralised state structure and a weak civil society creates conditions for hierarchical clientelistic or/and corporatist intergovernmental relations and networks that inhibit rather than encourage the long-standing process of successful synergies and social-capital building. Moreover, even though the role of the state in particular cases like those of East-Asian countries, or even in some traditionally rich in co-operative and coherent relations between public and private actors countries like Germany and the Nordic countries cannot be overlooked, the crucial question arises about to what extent these successful synergistic relations have been facilitated by pre-existing stocks of social capital and traditions of civicness and associational life. In that sense, the existing evidence on interregional (actually inter-*Länder*) differentiation in synergistic networks and subsequently successful or not adaptation in Germany – that is, Baden-Württemberg *vis-à-vis* North Rhine-Westphalia[35] – as well as, the strong associational tradition in the Nordic countries should be stressed.

In general, what the European experience seems to suggest is that issues, such as the structure and the degree of centralisation of the state and the strength of the civil society, constitute the crucial parameters that determine the administrative capacity of the state and shape the public–private relations. Thus the main features of the state structure in the degrees of bureaucratisation, centralisation and clientelism can account for the way in which local problems are regulated and the state/society relations are shaped. Top-down initiatives based on hierarchical (clientelistic) intergovernmental networks, or the processes of the neo-corporatist interest intermediation, cannot constitute a viable basis for the long-standing processes of social capital building and crossing the public–private divide. The implied and underlined question is whether the presence of a pre-existing strong civil society and social capital endowments are really prerequisites for successful state/society synergies.

Sabel's optimistic view, based on the notion of 'studied trust',[36] seems to be more relevant. Deriving from the model of 'learning to co-operate' – the outcome of a project for the revitalisation of Pennsylvania – it involves a shift in consensus from the view that individual actors know their interests and government's role is to remove the obstacles to realising them, to the view that only through the recognition of their mutual dependence can actors better define their distinct interests, and within this framework, the role of government is to encourage this process of recognising their collectivity and defining their particularity. Obviously, the concept of 'learning to co-operate' has relied on the bottom-up approach to development and proves the crucial role of the process of institutional learning in creating social capital and overcoming the public–private divide through successful co-operative relations between state and society. What

Sabel's optimism underlines is the cumulative character of social capital. Success in starting small-scale institutions enables individuals to build on the, thus created, social capital to solve larger problems with more complex institutional arrangements. Therefore, trust and other forms of social capital, such as norms and networks, constitute moral resources, that is resources 'whose supply increases through use and which become depleted if not used'.[37] Moreover, it points to the conditions under which public actors can make a positive contribution to sustaining synergistic relations.

Hence, from public policy's point of view, institutional learning implies the challenge to policy making, to establish and maintain the trajectory of norms and conventions which make possible certain capacities for collective action and co-ordination by facilitating the crossing of the public–private divide.

The key contribution of the learning approach is its attempt to go beyond new institutionalism and to capture the system of interactions between culture and structure, namely, the causal nexus between cultural norms, attitudes and the institutional structure (institutional networks) that make up the civic community. Effective institutional networks require civic engagement, that is the presence of social capital. This complex system of conventions, which has been overlooked by both neo-classical and left-wing economics, constitutes a necessary conceptual foundation for any regional development strategy today focusing on the creation of dynamic economies capable of adapting to the changing environment by 'investing' in capacities for collective action. Within this analytical framework, social capital and learning constitute the crucial conceptual tools for overcoming the public–private divide in European regional policy.

THE GREEK CASE: MAKING 'PATH DEPENDENCE' RELEVANT?

Two reasons make the example of Greece particularly relevant for an assessment of the impact of institutional learning and social capital on shaping the public–private relations and determining the outcome of the development strategies in the new Europe of the 1990s. First, though Greece has been a member of the EC since 1981 and a recipient of major funding programmes, its economy has not responded adequately to the flow of EC investment funds. Second, Greece is characterised by an over-centralised and weak national administrative structure and the lack of a viable system of subnational (regional) government.

Although the Europeanisation of regional policy with the introduction of the Integrated Mediterranean Programmes (IMPs) and the Community Support Frameworks (CSFs) in the 1980s can be seen as an external constraint to promote the reform of the administrative system, the performance of the Greek economy lags behind other peripheral states. Moreover, Greece's response towards the Europeanisation of regional policy in terms of the private sector's contribution to the Structural Fund payments and attracting foreign direct investments lags far behind that of the other peripheral member states.[38]

Even though a series of important institutional changes was introduced in 1986–87 by the implementation of the IMPs and the CSFs (the country was divided into 13 programme regions, with appointed regional councils headed by a government-appointed regional secretary), the planning role of the regional council and the region as a locus of politico-economic governance has not yet been established. In 1994 an elected second tier of local government – at prefecture level – was established, after a four-year delay (the election was to take place in October 1990, with the new councils scheduled to come into existence in January 1991). The new scheme of local governance consists of two tiers of elected governments – with unclearly allocated and overlapping responsibilities and a strong tradition in favour of the first tier as the oldest democratically-elected form of local government since the creation of the modern Greek state – and the regional secretariat being considered a substitute for the old prefecture, that is the central state representative at the local level. This determines to a significant extent the unbounded character of the system of local governance in Greece, since the dependence on the central state for key resources leaves little space for endogenous decision making.

The clientelistic political system, the lack of administrative transparency and the inadequate institutional infrastructure are the usual explanations for the relative divergence of Greek economy and society, all closely linked to an extremely weak civil society. The question of civicness constitutes a crucial as well as a neglected side of Greek socio-political structure.

Indeed, since the construction of the modern Greek state in the first half of the nineteenth century, its history has been dominated by a cross-cutting cultural schism – Diamandouros's *cultural dualism*[39] – between two powerful and conflicting cultural traditions, the Western on the one hand and the Byzantine-Ottoman on the other. The former is linked to the Western traditions of civicness, rule of law and constitutionalism, as they have been reformulated over time since their original Hellenic roots, and the latter to the precapitalist despotic tradition of strong state, clientelism and the Orthodox Church, that is a combination of the Byzantine and Ottoman heritages. Even the processes of liberation and building of the modern Greek state have been characterised by the conflict between the enlightened Greek diaspora of the West and the Orthodox Church.[40]

This cultural differentiation, a substantially Greek v. Hellenist antithesis, has had far-reaching repercussions for Greece's transition to modernity and its capacity for adapting to the changes occurring in the global or European environment. The predominance of Diamandouros' famous 'underdog culture' during the period of transition, and even during the later period after the Second World War and the Civil War, determined to a significant extent the 'qualities' of the contemporary Greek economy and society. The most distinctive features of this type of culture are: first and above all the preponderant role assigned to the state over civil society; second, the underestimation of the role of institutions; third, the central role of the family in combination with clientelistic practices; and finally, a conspirational interpretation of events, in particular towards the Western world, combined with an overestimation of the importance of Greece in international affairs. The rising subcultures of clientelism and populism, coupled with the quasi-capitalist character of the Greek economy which is characterised by the dominant role of the state, have led to interplay between an 'atrophic civil society' and a 'hypertrophic state'.[41] Deriving from this analysis and emphasising the weakness of civil society, there are similarities between Greece – as an exception from the other southern European countries – and Latin America, in particular, in the transition from authoritarianism.[42]

Although our analysis suggests the peculiar individualism of the Greek people has led to a country of free riders, in which civicness and social capital should be raised as the main issues, we have tried to identify a slight regional differentiation (definitely not the clear one identified by Putnam *et al.* in Italy) evolving from history and path-dependence analysis. Yet, there are pressures for change, either from above through the process of Europeanisation, or from below through changing attitudes, that is, postmodern reactions towards trade unionism, subject-oriented new social movements which subsequently cause instability and change in the political system, which, even after Andreas Papandreou's death, is still dominated by rivalry between modernisers and populists.

Evidence from the Aegean Islands

The stimulus for this research has derived from the politico-economic differentiation in the evolutionary and developmental path of the regions (NUTS 2) concerned, (Northern and Southern Aegean Islands). Beyond the well known repercussions of the multifragmentation of space (especially in the Southern Aegean), such as the fragmentation of cultural, political, and economic patterns among the islands (namely each island has its own specificities and milieu), there are important common features that differentiate the profile of each region. The most challenging facets of this differentiation refer to their prosperity and to their history.

The Southern Aegean Islands (SAI) region consists of two island complexes and prefectures, the Cyclades and the Dodecanese. Although there are significant intraregional (among the islands) differences in the rate of development, it is one of the most converging regions of the country – with three-year (1989–91) GDP average in PPS per inhabitant 52.2 compared with the Greek national average of 48.1 and a low 1993 unemployment rate of 3.6, when compared with the Greek national average of 7.8 – and also with a good ranking among European regions (NUTS 2).[43] Obviously, the economic and administrative centre of the region is shared among the most developed islands (the 'four motors' of development, i.e. Rhodes, Kos, Mykonos, Santorini).

Conversely, the Northern Aegean Islands (NAI) region, which consists of three big islands (Lesbos, Chios and Samos), each of which, along with some smaller islands, constitutes its own prefecture, lags behind within Greece – its three-year average in PPS per inhabitant is just 35.2 compared with the 48.1 average nationally, while its 1993 unemployment rate is one of the highest in Greece, 9.0 – as well as at the European level.[44]

The main qualitative difference in economic development between the SAI and the NAI regions is the adjustment of the economic structure of the former towards the development of the service (tertiary) sector of the economy, emphasising, in particular, tourism, whereas the latter has continued to rely on the traditional (for each island) productive sectors (agriculture with an emphasis on olive oil for Lesbos, shipping and maritime industry for Chios, and agriculture with some small-scale tourist development for Samos), demonstrating, in general, an incapacity for adapting to the changing environment. Even though the economic performance of the SAI region does not mean that the huge tourist industry has resolved the development problem of those islands – what remains to be seen is whether the tourist sector in these islands will be capable of adapting towards more flexible forms of leisure – the existing gap in the levels of development should be attributed to this difference in the adaptation process.

On the other hand, the Dodecanese, arguably the most prosperous of the two island complexes of the SAI, was incorporated into Greece only in 1947, being until then under Italian rule, and some of the islands in the Cyclades (Syros) have had strong traditions of trade and cultural relations with western Europe,[45] while the NAI followed the path of other Greek territories, being under Ottoman rule until the beginning of the twentieth century.

To identify the interactions between structure and culture at both the intraregional and interregional levels, the possible synergistic relations among public and private actors, as well as the interactions between the external shock caused by the implementation of the Structural Funds' programmes and the existing institutional infrastructure, we have carried out network analysis,[46] and tried to identify the presence of social capital. The network analysis is based on density/thickness, centrality and structural equivalence measurements for both the processes of general exchange and the implementation of the Structural Funds' programmes in the two regions. Density measurement refers to the degree of connectedness of the entire network, whereby zero indicates no connections between any actor and one means that all actors are linked to one another. Centrality measurements reveal actors' involvement in network relations and demonstrate the structure – horizontal or vertical – of the networks. Finally, structural equivalence reveals the network structure by categorising actors according to their common structural positions. The presence of social capital is usually identified either by mass survey data or by data on membership in voluntary-community organisations. Because of the lack of sufficient financial resources required for a mass survey, we have relied on data on memberships in voluntary organisations and on a qualitative analysis by fieldwork research.

TABLE 1
DENSITY MEASURES FOR GENERAL EXCHANGE AND POLICY NETWORKS

	Networks of General Exchange	Policy Networks
Dodecanese Prefecture	0.727	0.800
Cyclades Prefecture	0.545	0.636
Southern Aegean Islands	0.367	0.414
Lesbos Prefecture	0.418	0.564
Chios Prefecture	0.528	0.611
Samos Prefecture	0.595	0.667
Northern Aegean Islands	0.237	0.277

The first important outcome from the interregional comparison of both the density and centralisation measures is that not the regions but the prefectures should be the appropriate level of analysis. In the SAI region the density of the general exchange networks is just 0.367, while the situation is slightly better (0.414), at the policy network. In the NAI region the situation is even worse with the density measures ranging from 0.233 to 0.277 respectively. The general exchange and policy network centrality measures on the other hand are extremely high in both regions (83.55 per cent and 79.22 per cent in NAI and 70 per cent and 64.74 per cent for SAI respectively). What the low density rates and the high centrality measures indicate is that at the regional level, because, among other reasons, of the fragmentation of space, the networks are highly centralised around the

Regional Secretariat, while there are no intraregional networks but only ones within each prefecture. This fragmentation points initially to a highly unbounded local governance system, given its dependence on the central state for resources and decision making. What should be stressed about the interregional outlook is the different specific weight of the University of the Aegean between the two regions. Because of its location (its basic departments are located on the NA islands), it constitutes a more important actor for the NAI, rather than for the SAI.

TABLE 2
CENTRALITY MEASURES OF GENERAL EXCHANGE AND POLICY NETWORKS

	Networks of General Exchange %	Policy Networks %
Dodecanese Prefecture	33.33	24.44
Cyclades Prefecture	54.55	43.64
Southern Aegean Islands	70.00	64.74
Lesbos Prefecture	71.11	53.33
Chios Prefecture	60.71	50.00
Samos Prefecture	53.33	46.67
Northern Aegean Islands	83.55	79.22

The second important feature of the institutional infrastructure, which arises from the intraregional (at the prefectural level) comparisons, is the huge gap between, on the one hand, the Dodecanese prefecture and on the other, initially, all the other prefectures. What the structural equivalence of actors in the Dodecanese general exchange network reveals is that, beyond the block one public actors – Region's General Secretariat and Prefecture Council – which are completely connected to all other actors and can constitute the leadership of the network, there is a second block consisting of both public – Rhodes and Kos City Councils, Association of Municipalities – and private interest organisations – Chamber of Commerce (although in Greece, as in most continental European countries, the chambers are public bodies), Rhodes and Kos Hotel Owners' Associations and the Tourist Agents' Association. Even though they are not completely connected, with the exception of the two marginal actors of block three, namely the University and the Dodecanese Development Agency (DDA), they have a good rate of linkages within the network. The marginal character of the University and the DDA is because of the dislocation of the university departments among the Aegean Islands of the former, and the specific role of the latter as an organisation created primarily for the management of Structural Funds' programmes (Community Initiatives).

This thick (Table 1) and ideally centralised (Table 2) institutional infrastructure in the Dodecanese reflects its strong – for the Greek case – tradition of local governance, institution building and synergistic networks among public and private actors since its incorporation into the Greek state in the early 1950s. Since then the city councils in the Dodecanese have been proved particularly competent in comparison with their counterparts in other regions.[47] First, in financial resources the council tax that has been imposed (4 and 2 per cent on the value of imports and exports respectively) constitutes an important financial resource for all the councils of the prefecture and points to a comparatively bounded system of local governance. Second, the city councils, and especially the Rhodes and Kos councils have undertaken pioneering initiatives in creating infrastructure and providing social services. The Rhodes council has created the first municipal transport company in Greece (RODA) based on an initial Italian plan. Third, a horizontally structured mini-network, comprising the Hotel Owners Association, the Tourist Agents, the Chamber of Commerce and the Association of Municipalities and Communities, financed by a special council tax and focusing on tourist promotion, has been created around the Rhodes Organisation for Tourist Promotion. Finally, the Dodecanese Co-operative Bank, which has been created on a Chamber's initiative in co-operation with the Rhodes City Council, should be stressed. It constitutes a sort of rotating credit association and its branches' network includes the Rhodes and Kos islands.

The structural equivalence of actors in the policy network is based on linkages' identification and does not present the number of programmes' participation for each organisation. Structural equivalence reveals the following features of the policy network. First, with the exception of the University, almost all other actors are connected to each other. Second, because of the centralised administrative structure of the state (even in the implementation of the Community Initiatives and the Pilot Projects the state plays the key role), the public actors (Regional Secretariat, Prefecture Council, Cities' Councils) provide the leadership of the policy network. Third, the upgraded status of the Dodecanese Development Agency (DDA), which has been established by the Local Association of Municipalities and the Prefecture Council and focuses on the creation of networks around specific Community Initiatives (LEADER, INTERREG, VALOREN, etc.), indicates its successful involvement in the LEADER initiative. Fourth, the role of the Chamber, which constitutes the most historic and prominent private-interest organisation and simultaneously one of the key actors in the institutional structure of the prefecture, should be emphasised. It is the initiator of almost all the fora for information, dialogue and communication in the prefecture and has been involved in several programmes and Initiatives of European regional policy. Moreover, it has participated in important transregional networks. Finally, most of the other local actors have been involved either in implementing specific programmes of the CSF, or in monitoring the implementation process (monitoring committees).

The structural equivalence of the actors in both the general exchange and policy networks in Cyclades reveals a similar situation to that of the Dodecanese. Among the leading public actors (Regional Secretariat, Prefecture Council and Association of Municipalities), there is a group of public and private-interest organisations (Mykonos and Ermoupolis City Councils, Chamber, Hotel Owners' Association and Tourist Agents), which, although less connected within the network, contribute to its cohesive and horizontal character. This is not revealed in the density and centralisation measures (Tables 1 and 2) mainly because of the marginal presence of the University. One first explanation may be there is no university department located on any of the Cyclades islands. The upgraded status of the Cyclades Development Agency (established by an initiative of the Prefecture Council and the Association of Municipalities) and the Ermoupolis Development Agency (established by the Ermoupolis City Council) in the policy network points to their involvement in the LEADER and URBAN Community Initiatives respectively.

In general, the predominant feature of networks analysis in the SAI region is that, despite the centralised structure of the state and subsequently the crucial role of the Regional Secretariat, the implementation of European structural policy is a public rather than state driven process with a considerable presence of private-interest organisations and public–private synergistic networks. Thus, the relatively good institutional structure should be attributed to the pre-existing institutional capacity at the local level rather than to specific characteristics of the role of the state in the region.

The situation in the prefectures of NAI is completely different. The actors in the general exchange networks are loosely connected to each other, which reveals the lack of local initiatives and synergies, while it is significantly improved only in the policy networks. What the network analysis demonstrates is that because of the lack of institutional thickness, the main actor is the Regional Secretariat, whose relatively good administrative structure, in stability and continuity, provides some explanations for the comparatively effective response to the turbulence caused by the implementation of the IMP and CSF. The Chamber of Lesbos and the Mastic Producers' Association of Chios are the only relatively active private-interest organisations with some involvement in synergies, but strictly in the process of the implementation of Structural Funds' programmes. Indeed the former has been involved, along with the Association of Municipalities and the Farmers' Association, in the creation of the Lesbos Local Development Agency focused on the management of the LEADER Initiative, while the latter has been involved in the implementation of the Specific Aegean Islands Programme, which was an integral part of the first CSF (1989–93). Even though the LEADER I Initiative was focused on the reorientation of the agricultural sector in Lesbos (almost exclusively oriented towards the olive oil production), the achieved results were poor.

The institutional infrastructure in Lesbos and Chios illustrates the unboundedness of decision making, while, simultaneously, providing an explanation for the lack of adaptability of the productive system to changing external conditions. The upgraded role of the University in Lesbos (locus of two main departments) and Chios (locus of one important department) does not correspond to an education-services based model of development. In general, even though the debate on the need for adaptability of the productive system towards a combination of a flexible small-scale tourist development supported by the primary sector is just under way in these islands, and despite the plethora of development agencies involved, the real outcome of the implementation of the Community Initiatives in the NAI is poor.

Given the lack of interregional networks – with the exception of the Chambers of Commerce, which have developed a network for the entire Aegean as a response to an initiative of the Turkish Chambers across the Asia Minor coast – what the analysis thus far suggests, is there is a differentiation in institutional capacity first, between the Dodecanese and the other prefectures, and in a second phase between the SAI as a whole and the NAI region, which can to a significant extent explain the differentiation in adaptability.

Social Capital in the Aegean Islands

Even though in R. Inglehart's classification of European countries about mutual trust Greece appears to be above all parts of Italy,[48] research on social trust and civic engagement is completely overlooked in Greece. Thus, it has been difficult to identify clear-cut differences in the levels of social capital. The collection of the data in Table 3 has been facilitated to some extent by a research project on voluntary organisations which is being carried out in Greece.[49]

What the data for the two regions demonstrate – with a little doubt about the Chios/cultural indicator – is an almost clear differentiation in all the categories of voluntaristic participation between the SAI and NAI regions. Membership of professional associations and trade unions is not listed in the table, because it would create confusion given the high volume of membership, which does not necessarily mean voluntarism. In the NAI there is a huge number of members in agricultural associations (20,000) and a smaller participation in trade and other associations (12,000). Conversely, in the SAI there is a clear orientation towards trade and services (35,000), and a smaller number in agricultural associations (10,000).

TABLE 3
MEMBERSHIP IN VOLUNTARY ORGANISATIONS 1996
(PERCENTAGE OF POPULATION BY CATEGORY)

	Cultural	Athletic	Health Care	Environ-ment	Other	Total
Chios Prefecture	4.9	0.15	0.9	0.8	0.45	7.2
Lesbos Prefecture	1.1	0.18	–	0.15	0.1	1.53
Samos Prefecture	1.2	0.1	–	–	–	1.3
Northern Aegean Islands	2.15	0.15	0.25	0.3	0.17	3.02
Cyclades Prefecture	4.5	1.15	3.15	0.45	0.65	9.9
Dodecanese Prefecture	2.8	0.75	2.5	0.3	0.45	6.8
Southern Aegean Islands	3.4	0.9	2.8	0.35	0.5	7.95

Source: VOLMED Research Project (1996), author's research; elaborated by the author.

Looking at the qualitative features of the data the following points must be emphasised. First, the very important presence of health-care organisations in the Dodecanese and the Cyclades (Syros). In Syros an almost complete network for home-care services for disabled people has already been fully established. In the Dodecanese the Association of People with Special Needs with 2,000 members operates under city-council schemes, through which it has been involved in the implementation of several Structural Funds' programmes. During the period of the first CSF (1990–94) it had undertaken the implementation of the HORIZON initiative in the entire prefecture. Second, the important differences that evolve from cultural traditions among the islands should be emphasised: (a) most of the cultural organisations (Lyceums of Greek Women, theatre groups, etc.) in the SAI and, particularly, in the Dodecanese were established during the last quarter of the nineteenth century and demonstrate a preference towards Western cultural forms; (b) in some of the other Aegean islands, (i.e .Syros, Lesbos[50]), mostly because of the presence of a civil class and subsequently of a local leadership with strong Western cultural orientations during the nineteenth century, Western cultural forms were evident in the past, but they have gradually disappeared following the collapse of the civil class on these islands.

Thus, an interpretation of the existing differences in attitudes, mentality and orientation, which requires each region's qualitative features to be raised, should take into account each island's specificities. In that sense the first remarkable feature is Lesbos' collapse of the old civil class without it having been replaced. Hence, in Lesbos there is neither leadership nor networks. Chios, on the other hand, based on its ship-owner civil class demonstrates similar problems of a lack of leadership in all aspects of public life.

The second catalytic cultural factor that has been identified is the predominance of the Communist party of Greece (the Stalinist one[51]) in both the Lesbos and Samos prefectures. Lesbos and Samos have been considered to be the strongholds of this Communist Party almost since its foundation in the 1930s and definitely after the Civil War. The combination of the collapse of Asia Minor and the subsequent wave of refugees with the strong presence of the Communist Party, has created a specific victim's attitude and mentality and a particular type of conspirational approach to the events. The answer of one interviewee, to the question of 'what would best describe the region "honesty" or "corruption"?', was characteristic. He said: 'neither, only misery'.

CONCLUDING REMARKS

This article has argued that the concept of social capital, by facilitating collective action and subsequently the learning process within institutional networks, constitutes the basis for the creation of learning regional economies, capable of adapting to the rapidly changing European and global environment. In the planning and implementation processes of European structural policy, social capital constitutes the corner-stone of the bottom-up development strategies and of the regional mobilisation at the European level, by enhancing civic awareness and engagement, and by promoting synergistic effects among actors on a horizontal basis. This is illustrated by the EU Commission initiative to encourage partnership at all stages of the policy-making process, which constitutes a start-up for social capital formation at the regional level. In that sense the state–society or public–private great divide can be overcome at the regional and local levels.

Within the EU multilevel system of governance, which implies a shift from neo-corporatism – a predominant system of interest politics in specific nation-state structures (e.g., in Germany) – to the paradigm of 'competitive federalism',[52] social capital, being considered primarily a moral resource based public good, by promoting competition through co-operation, constitutes the conceptual foundation of the notion of collective competitiveness, which is the basis of learning economies. In that sense, it provides the ground for a real alternative to the neo-liberal predominance by overcoming individualism and making communitarianism relevant. Therefore, social capital, learning and the politico-economic performance of regions in Europe should be seen as interrelated and interdependent concepts.

In Greece the lack of social capital seems to be the main obstacle for achieving politico-economic performance, and adapting to the European environment. However, some kind of interregional differentiation has been identified among the Aegean islands, facilitating or inhibiting respectively the processes of economic and political adaptation of the regions.

Two important lessons should be drawn from the case of Greece. First, that the crucial issue for the less favoured regions in Europe is not the provision of financial support frameworks, but the mobilisation of civil society (networks of civic engagement) through the encouragement of partnership initiatives and networking, as a means to enable local and regional actors (citizens, institutions and corporate actors) to be actively involved in the provision of public goods that support the local productive system. This should be the main criterion for evaluating the success of the programmes financed by the Structural Funds. Second, the combination of a centralised state structure and a weak civil society creates conditions of poor institutional infrastructure at the regional and local levels, that breed hierarchical clientelistic relations between state and society and inhibit the horizontal synergies among public and private actors. In that sense norms and networks of civic engagement that sustain civicness and a strong civil society constitute a necessary prerequisite for effective partnerships between state, society and market organisations: for learning institutional networks that can lead to successful development strategies. Thus the concepts of social capital and institutional learning constitute revolutionary insights in the debate on overcoming the public–private divide.

NOTES

An earlier version of this article was presented as a paper to the 25th ECPR Workshop on 'Social Capital and Socio-Economic Performance', Bern, Switzerland, 27 Feb. to 4 March 1997.

1. Peter John, 'What is the European function?', *Local Government Policy Making* 20/5 (1994) pp.11–13; John Benington and Janet Harvey, 'Spheres or Tiers? The Significance of Transnational Local Authority Networks', in idem. pp.21–30; Mike Goldsmith, 'The Europeanisation of Local Government', *Urban Studies* 30/4 and 5 (1993) pp.683–99; and M. Geddes, 'Local Partnership and Social Capital', paper presented to the 25th ECPR Workshop on Social Capital and Politico-Economic Performance, University of Bern, Switzerland, 27 Feb. to 4 March 1997.
2. See Stanley Hoffmann, 'Obstinate or obsolete? The Fate of the Nation-State and the Case of Western Europe', *Daedalus* 95 (1996) pp.862–915.
3. For an overview, see G. Marks, 'Structural Policy and Multilevel Governance in the EC', in Alan W. Cafruny and Glenda G. Rosenthal (eds.) *The State of the European Community: The Maastricht Debates and Beyond*, Vol.2 (London: Longman 1993); A. Scott, J. Peterson and D. Millar, 'Subsidiarity: A "Europe of the Regions" v. the British Constitution?', *Journal of Common Market Studies* 32/1 (1994) pp.47–67.
4. See Wolfgang Streeck and P.C. Schmitter, 'From National Corporatism to Transnational

Pluralism: Organised Interests in the Single European Market', *Politics and Society* 19/2 (1991) pp.133–64.

5. G. Marks, 'Structural Policy in the European Community' in A. Sbragia (ed.) *Euro-politics, Institutions and Policy-Making in the 'New' European Community* (Washington DC: Brookings 1992).
6. Gary Marks, Nielsen Francois, Ray Leonard and Jane Salk, 'Competencies, Cracks and Conflicts: Regional Mobilisation in the European Union', in Gary Marks, Fritz W. Scharpf, Philippe Schmitter and Wolfgang Streeck (eds.) *Governance in the European Union* (London: Sage 1996) pp.40–63 .
7. For an overview on the link between flexible specialisation and the emergence of regions, see M. Piore and C. Sabel, *The Second Industrial Divide* (NY: Basic Books 1984); Charles Sabel, 'Flexible Specialisation and the Re-emergence of Regional Economies', in Ash Amin (ed.) *Post-Fordism: A Reader* (Oxford: Blackwell 1994a) pp.101–56; P. Hirst and J. Zeitlin, 'Flexible Specialisation versus Post-Fordism: Theory, Evidence, and Policy Implications', in M. Storper and A. J. Scott (eds.) *Pathways to Industrialisation and Regional Development*, (London: Routledge 1992) pp.70–115.
8. M. Dunford and G. Kafkalas, 'The Global-Local Interplay, Corporate Geographies and Spatial Development Strategies in Europe', in ibid. (eds.) *Cities and Regions in the New Europe: The Global–Local Interplay and Spatial Development Strategies* (London: Belhaven Press 1992).
9. Bob Jessop, 'Post-Fordism and the State', in Amin (note 7) pp.251–79.
10. G. Smith has distinguished between two main types of decentralisation in Europe: one deriving from cultural differentiation (Belgium, Spain) and the 'deliberately conceived' one (Italy, Germany), that is interpreted as a response to functional needs. See G. Smith, 'The Crisis of the West European State', in D.M. Cameron (ed.) *Regionalism and Supranationalism: Challenges and Alternatives to the Nation-State in Canada and Europe* (Montreal: Inst. for Research on Public Policy 1981). On decentralisation in Europe see, R. Leonardi, 'The Regional Reform in Italy: From Centralised to Regionalised State', in idem *The Regions and the European Community: The Regional Response to the Single Market in the Underdeveloped Areas* (London: Frank Cass 1993); and idem and S. Garmise, 'Sub-National Elites and the European Community', in ibid.
11. Roland Watts, 'Federalism, Regionalism, and Political Integration', in Cameron (note 10) pp.3–19.
12. Giddens's conceptualisation of regionalisation as a process concerning time and space and of 'regions' as "contexts of interactions", combining thus structure and actors within the framework of structuration theory, is extremely relevant to this point. See A. Giddens, *The Constitution of Society* (Cambridge: Polity Press 1984) pp.110–32.
13. On the role of the state according to the intergovernmentalist approach to regional integration, see A. Moravcsik, 'Preferences and power in the European Community: a liberal intergovernmentalist approach', *Journal of Common Market Studies* 31/4 (1993) pp.473–524; on consociationalism see Paul Taylor, 'The European Community and the State: Assumptions, Theories and Propositions', *Review of International Studies* 17 (1991) pp.109–25; idem, *International Organisation in the Modern World: The Regional and the Global Process*, Sec.2 (London: Pinter 1993); D.N. Chryssochoou, 'European Union and the Dynamics of Confederal Consociation: Problems and Prospects for a Democratic Future', *Journal of European Integration* 18/2 and 3 (1995).
14. Streeck and Schmitter (note 4).
15. Robert Bates, 'Contra Contractarianism: Some Reflections on the New Institutionalism', *Politics and Society* 16/2 and 3 (1988) pp.387–401.
16. The 'Folk Theorem', one version of this strategy, holds that 'always defect' is not a unique equilibrium in the repeat-play prisoner's dilemma. See R. Axelrod, *The Evolution of Co-operation* (NY: Basic Books 1984).
17. Bates (note 15).
18. Douglass North, *Institutions, Institutional Change and Economic Performance* (Cambridge: CUP 1990) p.3.
19. Adrienne Windhoff-Heritier's notion of institution as 'restriction and opportunity' shows that

new institutionalism is not inconsistent with the rational choice approach. See her 'Institutions, Interests, and Political Choice', in Roland M. Czada and Adrienne Windhoff-Heritier (eds.) *Political Choice: Institutions, Rules, and the Limits of Rationality* (Frankfurt: Campus Verlag and Westview Press 1991) p.41; on new institutionalism and collective action problems, see James S. Coleman, 'Social Capital in the Creation of Human Capital', *American Journal of Sociology* 94 (1988) Supplement, pp.95–120.

20. On new institutional economics' approach to collective action, see O.E Williamson, *Markets and Hierarchies: Analysis and Antitrust Implications* (NY: Free Press 1975); and Oliver E. Williamson, 'Hierarchies, Markets and Power in the Economy: An Economic Perspective', *Industrial and Corporate Change* 4/1 (1995) pp.21–49.
21. Mark Granovetter, 'Economic Action and Social Structure: The Problem of Embeddedness', *American Journal of Sociology* 91/3 (1985) pp.481–510.
22. See Robert Putnam, with R. Leonardi and R. Nanetti, *Making Democracy Work: Civic Traditions in Modern Italy* (Princeton UP 1993); Robert D. Putnam, 'Tuning In, Tuning Out: The Strange Disappearance of Social Capital in America', *Political Science and Politics* 28/4 (1995) pp.664–83; and Paul Whiteley, 'Economic Growth and Social Capital', paper presented to the ECPR Workshop on Social Capital (note 1).
23. Putnam *et al.*, ibid. p.167; on other definitions of Social Capital, see James S. Coleman, *Foundations of Social Theory* (Cambridge, MA: Harvard UP 1990) Chs.8, 12, pp.300–2.
24. Charles Sabel, 'Studied Trust: Building New Forms of Co-operation in a Volatile Economy', in R. Swedberg (ed.) *Explorations in Economic Sociology* (NY: Russell Sage Fdn 1993) pp.104–44; on the role of trust and other forms of social capital in modern economies, see also Mark Granovetter, 'The Nature of Economic Relationships', in ibid.
25. Ash Amin and N.Thrift, 'Living in the Global', in idem. (eds.) *Globalisation, Institutions, and Regional Development in Europe* (Oxford: OUP 1994) pp.14–16.
26. Shari O. Garmise, 'Institutional Networks and Industrial Restructuring: Local Initiatives toward the Textile Industry in Nottingham and Prato', Unpublished PhD Thesis, LSE 1995.
27. Bengt A. Lundvall, *National Systems of Innovation: Towards a Theory of Innovation and Interactive Learning* (London: Pinter 1992) p.1.
28. Charles Sabel, 'Learning by Monitoring: The Institutions of Economic Development', in N.J. Smelser and Richard Swedberg (eds.) *The Handbook of Economic Sociology* (Princeton UP 1994).
29. On the importance of 'joint learning' and stability within institutional networks for governance, see B. Kohler-Koch, 'Catching up with Change: The Transformation of Governance in the European Union', *Journal of European Public Policy* 3/3 (1996) pp.359–80.
30. For the role of social capital in facilitating the learning process, see Michael Storper, 'The Resurgence of Regional Economies, Ten Years Later: The Region as a Nexus of Untraded Interdependencies', *European Urban and Regional Studies* 2/3 (1995) pp.191–221.
31. Garmise (note 26).
32. On the state-driven process of synergies and collective action, see Peter Evans, 'Introduction: Development Strategies across the Public-Private Divide', *World Development* 24/6 (1996) pp.1033–7; and 'Government Action, Social Capital and Development: Reviewing the Evidence on Synergy', ibid. pp.1119–32; Jonathan Fox, 'How Does Civil Society Thicken? The Political Construction of Social Capital in Rural Mexico', ibid. pp.1089–103; Patrick Heller, 'Social Capital as a Product of Class Mobilisation and State Intervention: Industrial Workers in Kerala, India', ibid. pp.1055–71; Elinor Ostrom, 'Crossing the Great Divide: Coproduction, Synergy and Development', ibid. pp.1073–87.
33. On the evidence from the East Asian countries, see Peter Evans, 'Government Action, Social Capital and Development: Reviewing the Evidence on Synergy', *World Development* in ibid. pp.1119–32.
34. See, in particular, Jürgen Grote, 'Policy Networks in the South of the South', paper presented at the 25th ECPR Joint Sessions of Workshops (note 1); and Putnam *et al.* (note 22).
35. On the importance of adaptability in networks, see Gernot Grabher, (1993), 'The Weakness of Strong Ties: The Lock-In of Regional Development in the Ruhr Area', in idem (ed.), *The Embedded Firm: On the Socioeconomics of Industrial Networks* (London: Routledge 1993) pp.255–77.

36. *Studied trust* refers to a 'kind of consensus and the associated forms of economic transactions' that theoretically result from *'associative'* or *'co-operative'* or *'autopoietic'* – that is self-creating – *'reflexive'* systems. These are systems in which 'the logic governing the development of each of the elements is constantly reshaped by the development of all the others: the parts reflect the whole and vice versa' (Sabel, note 24) pp.125–30). Sabel's optimistic view on the creation of trust is based on the hypothesis that 'trust is a constitutive – hence in principle extensive – feature of social life, ibid. p.140.
37. Diego Gambetta, 'Can We Trust Trust?' in idem (ed.) *Trust: Making and Breaking Co-operative Relations* (Oxford: Blackwell 1988).
38. See CEC, *Competitiveness and Cohesion: Trends in the Regions*, Fifth Periodic Report on the Social and Economic Situation and Development of the Regions in the Community, Brussels (1994) pp.83–94.
39. On 'cultural dualism' and the weakness of civil society in Greece, see Nikiforos Diamandouros, *Cultural Dualism and Political Change in Postauthoritarian Greece*, Estudio/Working Paper 50 (Madrid: Juan March Institute 1994); Nicos Mouzelis, 'Greece in the Twenty-first Century: Institutions and Political Culture', in Dimitri Constas and Theofanis G. Stavrou (eds.) *Greece Prepares for the Twenty-first Century* (Washington DC: Johns Hopkins UP 1995); and *Politics in the Semi-Periphery: Early Parliamentarism and Late Industrialisation in the Balkans and Latin America* (London: Macmillan 1986); Dimitris Charalambis and Nicolas Demertzis, 'Politics and Citizenship in Greece: Cultural and Structural Facets', *Journal of Modern Greek Studies* 11 (1993).
40. See Richard Clogg, *A Short History of Modern Greece* (Cambridge: CUP 1979).
41. For an in-depth analysis of the interactions between clientelism and populism, and the state/society relations in Greece, see Mouzelis (note 39); C. Tsoukalas, 'Free Riders in Wonderland; or, Of Greeks in Greece', in Constas and Stavrou (note 39); and J. Campbell, *Honour, Family and Patronage: A Study of Institutions and Moral Values in a Greek Mountain Community* (London: OUP 1964).
42. See Philippe Schmitter, 'An Introduction to Southern European Transitions from Authoritarian Rule: Italy, Greece, Portugal, Spain, and Turkey', in Guillermo O'Donnell, Philippe C. Schmitter, and Laurence Whitehead (eds.) *Transitions from Authoritarian Rule: Southern Europe* (London: Johns Hopkins UP 1986).
43. CEC (note 38).
44. Ibid.
45. V. Kardasis, *Syros: Crossroads of Eastern Mediterranean (1832–1857)* (Athens: Cultural Fdn of the National Bank of Greece 1987).
46. The network analysis is based on extensive fieldwork involving around 70 semi-structured in-depth interviews with representatives of the most prominent institutional actors in the regions concerned, and the *UCINET IV* Version 1.00, has been used (S.P. Borgatti, M.G. Everett and L.C. Freeman, Columbia: Analytic Technologies 1992).
47. Getimis, P. 'Development Issues and Local Regulation: The Case of the Dodecanese Prefecture' (in Greek) in K. Psychopedis and P. Getimis (eds.) *Regulation of Local Problems* (Athens: Fdn for Med. Studies 1982).
48. R. Inglehart, 'The Renaissance of Political Culture', *American Political Science Review* 82/4 (1988) pp.1203–30.
49. The 'VOLMED' research project is financed by the EU Commission (DG V) and focuses on registering the voluntary organisations in the Mediterranean countries. The research for Greece has been undertaken by the Panteion Univ. of Social Sciences (Dept. of Social Statistics); co-ordinator: Associate Prof. Ms Stasinopoulou.
50. Evridike Siphnaeou , *Lesbos: Economic and Social History (1840–1912)* (Athens: Trochalia 1996).
51. In Greece, since 1968, there have been two communist parties: one reformist and Euro-communist that has more or less followed the trajectory of the Italian PCI and currently participates in the Coalition of the Left, and the hard-core more powerful party, which was well-disposed towards the former Soviet Union.
52. Streeck and Schmitter (note 4) p.159.

Swapping the Reins of the Emerald Tiger: The Irish General Election of June 1997

BRENDAN O'DUFFY

The defeat in the June 1997 election of the coalition government supports the 'prospective' version of the theory of economic-issue voting, and represents a hiatus in the trend towards realignment away from the catch-all centrism of the 'Civil War' parties. With the Irish economy enjoying an unprecedented growth rate of more than six per cent per annum, unemployment falling, and with public accounts set to meet the criteria for entry into the European Monetary Union (EMU) by the 1999 deadline, the governing coalition was not so much rejected as un-packed by the fickle Irish electorate. Both of the centrist, catch-all, 'Civil War' parties gained seats at the expense of parties with more distinct left (Labour, Democratic Left) and right (Progressive Democrat) cleavage bases. While this does not necessarily signal a return to 'Civil War' politics (shaped by the historical party positions concerning the partition which created Northern Ireland), it does suggest that with a booming economy and a smattering of sleaze spread across the political spectrum, the 'national question', remains a distinct cleavage in Irish politics.

The Rainbow coalition, comprising the centre-right, Christian-democratic Fine Gael, Labour and the Democratic Left (formerly the Workers Party), formed a government in December 1995 following the fall of the Fianna Fáil-Labour coalition formed after the election of November 1992.[1] Like the fall of the Fianna Fáil-Progressive Democrat coalition government which led to the November 1992 election, the Fianna Fáil-Labour coalition imploded because of a scandal which split the coalition partners. In November 1994, the Labour leader Dick Spring, and his colleagues resigned from the government over the conduct of Albert Reynolds, Fianna Fáil's leader, in the handling of the extradition of an accused paedophile priest to face charges in Northern Ireland. The second successive fall of a coalition government due to scandal goes some way towards explaining the low turnout in 1997 (67 per cent, compared to 77 per cent in 1981), as well as the success of independent candidates running on

* Queen Mary and Westfield College, London

West European Politics, Vol.21, No.2 (April 1998), pp.178–186
PUBLISHED BY FRANK CASS, LONDON

anti-system, single-issue platforms such as water rates and television signal deflectors. As we shall see, the resilience of the 'establishment' parties despite the plethora of scandals and sleaze is partly a result of the increasing disproportionality of the electoral system in turning votes to seats, rather than a rejection of radical (right or left) politics. Therefore, the 1997 election may signal only a hiatus in the realignment of the Irish party system.[2]

PARTY PERFORMANCES

Fine Gael

The senior partner in the governing coalition improved its vote and seat share more than any other party, increasing its first-preference vote share by 3.5 per cent, gaining 11 seats (see Table 1). The party was rewarded by the electorate for its stewardship of the economy, with a RTÉ/Lansdowne post-election poll showing a solid majority of voters (57 per cent) satisfied with the coalition government's handling of the economy, and an equally high 'satisfaction rating' on leaving government. The party leader and Taoiseach John Bruton demonstrated conviction in office and communicated an empathetic, if paternalistic benevolence towards Ireland's persistent underclass. In the campaign Bruton outshone both his coalition partner Dick Spring and his Fianna Fáil rival, Bertie Ahern, in debate, while promoting a political message which attempted to absorb much of the 'social-democratic' rhetoric, if not the policies of both Labour and the Democratic Left.

The Fine Gael leader was less convincing in his stewardship of the British-Irish peace talks over Northern Ireland, an issue which was deemed to be 'important' or 'very important' by a majority of respondents to an *Irish Times*/MRBI poll (May 1997). Bruton was widely criticised for failing to put sufficient pressure on the British government during the first peace process which ended with the IRA bombing of the Canary Wharf in London in February 1996. The coalition government was held partly responsible for allowing the British government to run the process into the ground by insisting on the decommissioning of IRA weapons before Sinn Féin's (the IRA's political wing) entry into the talks process. Bruton's condemnatory and moralistic response to the IRA's return to violence may have been principled, but it was not balanced by hard-nosed diplomacy with the British government. In addition, Dick Spring, the Labour leader and Deputy Prime Minister (Tanaiste) with responsibility for Northern Ireland was also accused of allowing the British government to raise the decommissioning issue to that of a precondition for Sinn Féin entry into the talks. As a result

TABLE 1

FIRST-PREFERENCE VOTE-SHARES, SEAT SHARES AND DEVIATION FROM PROPORTIONALITY, 1997

Party	First vote %	preference (Δ 92-97)	Seats in Dáil Éireann	(%)	Deviation from proportionality
Fianna Fáil	39.3	(+0.22)	77	(46.4%)	+7.1
Fine Gael	27.9	(+3.47)	54	(32.5%)	+4.6
Labour	10.4	(-8.91)	17	(10.2%)	-0.2
Progressive Democrats	4.7	(0.00)	4	(2.4%)	-2.3
Democratic Left	2.5	(-0.29)	4	(2.4%)	-0.1
Green Alliance	2.8	(+1.36)	2	(1.2%)	-1.6
Sinn Féin	2.5	(+0.96)	1	(0.6%)	-1.9
Workers Party	0.4	(-0.23)	0	(0.0%)	-0.4
Other/Independents	9.4	(+3.42)	7	(4.2%)	-5.2
			166	(99.9%)	

Gallagher Least-squares index of proportionality = 7.42; more than double the value of 3.56 for the 1992 election.
Effective number of parties in votes ($1/\sum v_i^2$) = 3.9.
Effective number of parties in seats ($1/\sum s_i^2$) = 3.0. Note that the calculations of both votes and seats treats Other/Independents as a single party.[3]

Sources: *The Irish Times* and author's calculations.

TABLE 2

SEATS HELD BY PARTIES IN DÁIL ÉIREANN 1987–97

Party	1987	1989	1992	1997	Net Gain 1987–97	Net gain 1992–97
Fianna Fáil	81	77	68	77	-4	+9
Fine Gael	51	55	45	54	+3	+9
Labour	12	15	33	17	+5	-16
Progressive Democrats	14	6	10	4	-10	-6
Workers Party*	4	7	0	0	-4	0
Democratic Left			4	4	+4	0
Green Alliance	0	1	1	2	+2	+1
Sinn Féin	0	0	0	1	+1	+1
Other/Independents	4	5	5	7	+3	+2

Notes: * Democratic Left was formed in 1987 by former members of the Workers Party.

Sources: O'Leary, 1993 and *The Irish Times*

of their mis-handling of the peace process, public opinion viewed the prospective Fianna Fáil-Progressive Democrat alliance as likely to 'best handle the Northern Ireland problem' by a margin of 45 per cent to 30 per cent over the Fine Gael–Labour–Democratic Left coalition.

Labour

By far the most significant trend of the 1997 election was the fall in support for Labour, which lost nearly half of the 33 seats it won in the 1992 election, including the seats of one government minister and two ministers of state. Labour's first-preference vote share dropped by 8.9 per cent, accounting for almost the entire swing in the electorate. Labour's collapse was attributed to three factors. First, middle-class contentment with the economic boom, combined with lower unemployment withered the appeal of Labour radicalism. Second, Labour's decision in 1992 to form a coalition with Fianna Fáil in 1992 alienated a significant proportion of the new supporters who looked to Labour to lead a break from the scandal-tainted, patronage politics of the two Civil War parties. Labour had captured the moral high-ground in the run up to the 1992 election, suggesting it would be content to retain its principles in opposition rather than form a coalition with either Fianna Fáil or Fine Gael. The party's decision, after six weeks of negotiation, to enter a coalition with Fianna Fáil was greeted with some scepticism, despite the obvious concessions made by Fianna Fáil to adopt Labour's agenda on 'clean government' and the promotion of 'moral liberalism' through constitutional referendums to support the legalisation of divorce, homosexuality and access to information on abortion, and the right to travel abroad to receive an abortion. Once in government, Labour was criticised for office-seeking and abuse of power following well-publicised appointments of family members of Labour ministers, and the use of state cars in the exaggerated 'Mercs and perks' scandals. The media's focus on Labour's enjoyment of the trappings of office applied blatant double standards. But, like the media backlash against the British Conservative government from 1992, Labour's assumption of the moral high ground before taking office set standards which would be difficult for any governing party to maintain, and set themselves up for charges of hypocrisy.

Third, Labour's very success in promoting significant constitutional reforms on questions of moral liberalism appears to have exhausted that particular agenda as the remaining conflict over the legality of abortion *in Ireland,* is too divisive to be absorbed by any prospective governing party. While Labour may have been rewarded for forcing Fianna Fáil to shift its morally conservative agenda, that coalition did not last long enough to reap any rewards for Labour on that front. When Labour went into coalition with Fine Gael and the Democratic Left at the end of 1994, its agenda on moral questions was effectively shared with and absorbed by Fine Gael. Finally, Labour's failure to manage votes and transfers was attributed to its failure to develop party machinery in local constituencies, making it more difficult to hold on to the floating voters which supported the party in 1992, especially in Dublin where the party had made great inroads. Instead, Fine Gael benefited disproportionately from the transfer arrangements among the governing coalition partners.

Democratic Left

The smallest of the partners in the rainbow coalition retained its four seats while suffering a marginal decline in its share of the first preference votes (Table 1). While the Democratic Left will be happy not to have suffered the same loss of electoral support as Labour, it will be disappointed not to have picked up more first-preference votes from the other social-democratic party, a development which would have been expected if Labour's fall was a result of disaffection among ideologically committed socialists.

Fianna Fáil

After Labour's significant decline, the second most important trend in the 1997 election was Fianna Fáil's successful use of vote management to maximise its seat-share despite a small increase in its share of first-preference votes (Table 1). The electoral alliance with the Progressive Democrats clearly worked in Fianna Fáil's favour, and together with better strategic planning (the party contested 11 fewer seats than in 1992) and the vote-getting of the legendary party machine, ensured an unprecedented seats-vote ratio. Pre-election opinion polls indicated that electorate was confident that a Fianna Fáil-Progressive Democrat coalition would be best placed to handle the residual issues generated by the economic boom (taxation and crime) as well as the Northern Ireland negotiations (discussed above), both because of Fine Gael-Labour mismanagement, as well as the fact that Fianna Fáil is a historical 'cousin' of Sinn Féin, and, therefore, more likely to promote successfully a renewed IRA ceasefire and Sinn Féin entry into the negotiations (both of which occurred in the summer of 1997). Overall, the election did not signal a reversal of the significant decline suffered by Fianna Fáil since 1981 (see Figure 1), suggesting that Fianna Fáil will be forced to continue to govern in coalition rather than alone for the foreseeable future.

Progressive Democrats

While the Progressive Democrats held their first-preference vote share, they lost half of the eight seats won in 1992. The party of fiscal conservatism, and small government had high expectations going into the election and appears to have been overly confident that the economic boom would

FIGURE 1
FIRST-PREFERENCE VOTES OF THE TWO LARGEST PARTIES SINCE 1923

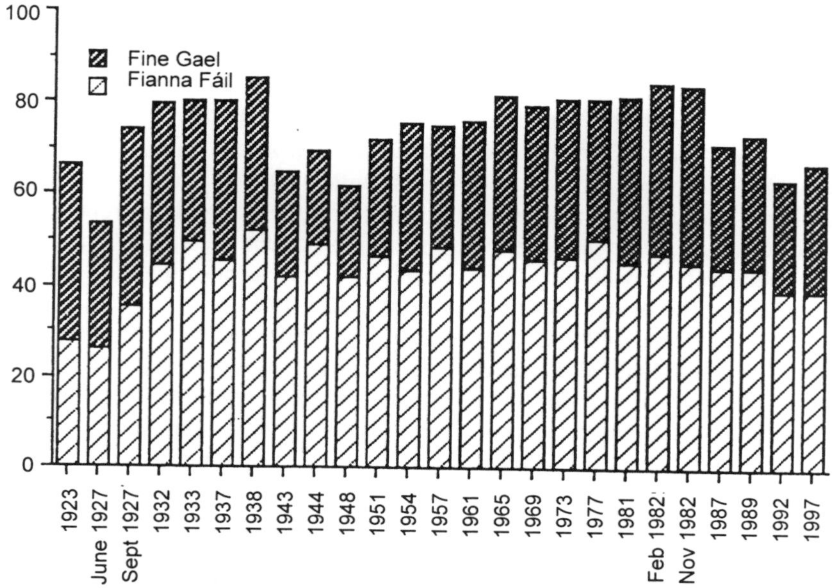

Sources: Nealon's Guide to the 27th Dail & Seanad Election '92 and *The Irish Times*

reward right-wing rhetoric. The party's most controversial proposal was to cut the size of the public-sector workforce by 25,000 jobs. With a persistently high unemployment rate (between 11 and 12 per cent depending on estimates) the prosposed swingeing job cuts struck the wrong chord with the electorate, a chord which was made even more dissonant with the party leader, Mary Harney's, suggestion that single mothers should be 'encouraged' through the benefits system, to live with their parents. Partly as a result of insensitivity to Ireland's persistent under-class, the party's vote-transfer alliance heavily favoured the prospective coalition partner, Fianna Fáil.

'Significant Others': Green(s) Reds and Independents

The single most significant seat won in the election was that of Sinn Féin's Caoimhghín Ó Caoláin who topped the poll in the border constituency of Cavan-Monaghan. Even this single seat represents a significant breakthrough for Sinn Féin's 'peace strategy' because it supports the arguments of Sinn Féin leaders like Gerry Adams and Martin McGuinness who are trying to guide the 'republican movement', including the IRA, into constitutional politics on an all-Ireland basis.

As the first post-war seat won by Sinn Féin in the Irish Republic since they began contesting elections in 1986, it may represent a breakthrough by the 'green nationalist' republican party, which nearly doubled its small first-preference vote share to 2.6 per cent. While the party did not win any seats in Dublin, it did eat into the first-preferences of both of its erstwhile republican cousins Democratic Left and the Workers Party, and polled strongly in North Kerry, suggesting that with sustained peace in Northern Ireland, Sinn Féin stands a realistic chance of consolidating a 'republican left' cleavage, especially given Sinn Féin's recent electoral success in Northern Ireland, where its unprecedented 16.5 per cent of the vote elected two MPs at the British General Election of May 1997.

The (environmental) Green Alliance also improved its first-preference vote share and doubled its share of seats from one to two with a particularly notable victory in Dublin South East after multiple recounts. However, its expected breakthrough did not materialise, and what success it enjoyed appears to be a result of the anti-Labour backlash rather than a pro-Green shift.

As a group, independent candidates achieved the second largest swing (+3.42 per cent of first-preference votes, see Table 1). Notable successes included the Socialist, Joe Higgins', campaign against the imposition of water-rates and Thomas Gildea's campaign upholding the rights of television signal pirateers against a state-sanctioned television company. The civil-war contestation of state legitimacy, like Finland, leaves fertile ground for anti-establishment ('agin the state') politics, which is also facilitated by the STV electoral system's facilitation of high-profile, candidate-centred campaigns. But the majority of independents elected were erstwhile members of the two Civil War parties, including three former Fianna Fáil members and most notably, the ex-Fine Gael minister, Michael Lowry, from Tipperary who topped the poll in his constituency, despite having been forced to resign over sleaze allegations.

THE FORMATION OF THE FIANNA FÁIL–PROGRESSIVE DEMOCRAT COALITION

Despite Fine Gael's strong result, the decline of its coalition partners Labour and the Democratic Left meant that a Fianna Fáil-Progressive Democrat coalition had the only realistic possibility of winning the investiture vote needed to form a government. But the two parties combined total of 81 seats was two short of the 83 required to form a bare majority government in the 166-seat Dáil (where the Ceann Comhairle or Chair chosen from the elected

TDs does not vote). Fianna Fáil's leader, Bertie Ahern had promised not to enter a coalition with Sinn Féin (because of the latter's support for the IRA, which had not yet called its second ceasefire) and as the negotiations with the independents began, he also asserted that he would not buy the votes of any independents with the type of lavish deals that had been used in the past.

Over the next two weeks independents were courted while the leaders of the Fianna Fáil and Progressive Democrats merged their campaign proposals into a programme of government which emphasised the promotion of a lasting settlement in Northern Ireland, sustained economic based along with limited state spending to maintain the Maastricht criteria for entry into the EMU in 1999. The only 'boom dividend' promised was in the form of a reduction in the top rate of income tax from 48 to 42 per cent, and a gradual reduction of the standard rate from 26 to 20 per cent over five years.

The allocation of ministerial portfolios was consistent with the seat shares of the two coalition partners. The Progressive Democrats secured only one senior ministerial position, party leader, Mary Harney, was nominated as Tánaiste, but the post was stripped of its most important role as Foreign Minister (including Northern Ireland). Instead, Harney was given the Enterprise, Employment and Trade Ministry. Given its poor electoral performance and the coalition government's narrow majority, it is likely that the Progressive Democrats will attempt to 'punch above its weight', placing breaks on public spending (particularly public-sector pay) which could be difficult for Fianna Fáil to resist as long as the economic boom continues. Nevertheless, the Fianna Fáil leanings of the majority of the seven independents, combined with the quiet shelving of Fianna Fáil's commitment to introduce a referendum on the divisive issue of abortion, suggests that the coalition government will be more stable than its bare majority would indicate.

CONCLUSION

Despite the gains in seats made by the two centrist, Civil War parties of Fianna Fáil and Fine Gael, the 1997 election does not necessarily indicate an end to the realignment and Europeanisation of Irish politics (see Figure 1). Fianna Fáil's seat gains were products of vote management and the optimisation of the electoral system, rather than a significant increase in its first-preference vote share. And while it is true that Fine Gael's share of votes and seats represents a successful appropriation of social-democratic issues, the losses suffered by Labour do not indicate a reduction in radical-left politics as much as a punishment for Labour's compromises over the issue of entering coalition with Fianna Fáil, and Labour's failure to redistribute economic prosperity to local-constituency level while in government with Fine Gael. Both of these errors are reversible through a shift towards pragmatism regarding potential coalition partners, as well as through the development of party machinery at constituency level. In terms of Europeanisation, it is clear that commitment to the EMU is shared by the three largest parties, with the Progressive Democrats being more cautious, but by no means anti-European. The measurements of deviation from proportionality and the effective number of parties support the view that realignment is ongoing. The doubling of the disproportionality between 1992 and 1997 in terms of the seats-to-votes ratio reveals the extent to which the Civil War parties benefited from vote management rather than a change in the first preferences of voters. Further, the Gallagher Least-Squares measure of effective number of parties reveals that the Irish party system still approximates a four-party system in terms of first-preference votes. The lessons of coalition strategy, vote management and party machinery will be learned by Labour, while the economic boom which has facilitated a pooling of votes for the centrist parties will be subject to the vagaries of the EMU project.

Finally, the first priority listed in the Fianna Fáil-Progressive Democrat programme for government was Northern Ireland, suggesting that at least within the current bubble of economic prosperity, the national question (concerning negotiations over the future of Northern Ireland) remains a significant, if usually latent, cleavage in Irish politics. In turn, the Irish electorate's judgement as to the likelihood of a Fianna Fáil-led government successfully negotiating a stable regulation of the conflict represents a 'realist' nationalist position *vis-à-vis* Britain, and in my view, an approach more likely to succeed in securing a stable regulation of that conflict. By contrast, Fine Gael's strong performance suggests that there remains a solid minority which accepts the partition of Ireland. In other words, the Civil War split is alive and well, if not as prominent as before.

NOTES

1. Brendan O'Leary, 'Affairs, Partner-Swapping, and Spring Tides: The Irish General Election of November 1992', *West European Politics* 16/3 (July 1993) pp.401–12.
2. Peter Mair, *The Changing Irish Party System* (London: Pinter 1997); O'Leary (note 1); Brendan O'Leary and John Peterson 'Further Europeanisation and Realignment. The Irish General Election, June 1989', *West European Politics* 13/1 (Jan. 1989) pp.124–36; Brendan O'Leary, 'Towards Europeanisation and Realignment? The Irish General Election, February 1987', *West European Politics* 10/3 (July 1987) pp.455–65.
3. Arend Lijphart, *Electoral Systems and Party Systems: A Study of Twenty-Seven Democracies, 1945–1990* (Oxford: OUP 1994) pp.60–1.

The Politics of Embarrassment: Norway's 1997 Election

JOHN MADELEY*

If a country's economic success can normally be expected to redound to the support and re-election of an incumbent government, then Norway is not normal. Of course its abnormality has been reflected in several areas where its status as a statistical, as much as a geographical and political, outlier has long been appreciated. Over the four years since the 1993 election, growth had been strong (in 1996–67 running at some 3.5 per cent); the growth in employment had helped to halve the 1993 unemployment rate and bring it down to under four per cent; inflation at a rate of 2.5 per cent lay behind an average increase of three per cent in wages, while interest rates continued to fall; and the principal medium-term economic difficulty was how the vast flow of wealth from the North Sea could be deployed in a manner which did not undermine the rest of the economy. Unusually for an OECD economy, Norway was faced with a positive *embarras de richesse.* As the world's second largest oil exporter after Saudi Arabia, it had by 1995 paid off all its foreign debt and was exercised over what it could responsibly do with a budget surplus running at $9 billion a year.

In order to insulate the economy from the destabilising effects which would result from spending more than a relatively modest extra amount at home, the Labour government had set up an Oil Fund. Its original remit was to invest the large surplus flows in foreign government bonds with a view (a) to providing for the day some decades hence when the reserves will finally be depleted and (b) to finance large, otherwise-unfunded pension claims, which are foreseen from about 2020. This cautious fix of the country's overhanging 'crisis of affluence' as it might be called, with its opportunity costs in terms of deferred social spending, was, however, constructively rejected at the 1997 election and Labour accordingly was dismissed from office.

The reasons for Labour's dismissal after presiding over Norwegian affairs for 10 of the previous 11 years concern more than its record in nurturing the country's embarrassingly rude economic health. They lie

*Department of Government, LSE

West European Politics, Vol.21, No.2 (April 1998), pp.187–194
PUBLISHED BY FRANK CASS, LONDON

rather in three other areas: the inherent weaknesses of the party's claim on government office, based as it was as much as anything on the inability of the non-socialist parties to provide a coherent alternative; the mistakes and misfortunes of the Labour government over the year since its leadership changed, not least during the election campaign; and the extraordinary volatility of an electorate once famous for its stability, but now seemingly as febrile as any in Europe, East or West, North or South. The benchline for the steady-state politics with which the current flux can be contrasted lasted for 16 years from 1945 when Labour governed on the basis of an absolute majority in Norway's parliament, the *Storting*. The party was the beneficiary of the slight but important bias in the then-current version of the list PR system in favour of the largest parties.[1] In 1961, however, with the election of two representatives of a break-away left-socialist party, the era of Labour majorities in the Storting came to an end, seemingly (in retrospect) for all time. When at the next election (1965) the non-socialists formed a majority coalition, for the first time since the 1920s, the system seemed likely to change from one of single-party (Labour) domination to one of stable alternation between equally matched alternatives of right and left. And so it might have, had the world-wide turbulence of the 1970s not supervened and confounded the emergent pattern by introducing on the one hand, a new polarisation between (relative) extremes of left and right and on the other, a deep and bitter source of division among the established non-socialist parties over the issue of relations with Europe which cross-cut the left–right dimension.

For all that it lost its Storting majority in 1961, Labour has been able to sustain in office single-party minority governments during 25 of the last 36 years. At no time has it invited the left-socialists to join it even during those periods (1961–65, 1973–81 and 1993–97) when an accommodation might have provided the basis for a majority coalition of the left. Nor has it looked for stable support arrangements with the centrist parties (as has been the case in Denmark) or with the Conservative Party (as has occurred in Finland recently). Instead, like its Swedish counterpart, it has preferred to remain alone in office and proceed 'slalom-like' on an issue-by-issue basis, veering from left to right in search of policy majorities. It has been able to do this so successfully because of the chronic divisions which, in particular, the issue of relations with Europe has given rise to among the non-socialist parties, thereby subverting the feasibility of a stable alternative to Labour. While the anti-EU left-socialists have contributed to undermining Labour's own internal cohesion on the issue, this has been as nothing compared to the flat party opposition between the solidly anti-EU (former Agrarian) Centre Party (CP) and the solidly pro-EU Conservatives, with the Christian People's Party (CPP) hovering awkwardly in between. Under former prime minister, Gro Harlem Brundtland, the Labour leadership could claim some credit for adroit handling of the issue — including, more often than not, avoidance — but it might principally be seen as an element of luck without which the partyty's claim on government would have been considerably weaker over the last 30 years.

The European issue first emerged to wreck non-socialist co-operation around 1970, bringing the four-party majority Borten government down in 1971. Twenty years later when the question of EC/EU membership again surfaced it also featured as the principal issue over which the Syse non-socialist coalition foundered in 1990 after only one year. For the 20 years in between, ways were sought on all sides to neutralise the issue or provide some alternative fix; the negotiation of the European Economic Area treaty between the EU and EFTA, completed in 1992, represented Labour's last attempt to finesse the difficulty. It was seen to have failed when, released from the constraints of Cold War bloc politics, Europe's neutrals opted either to negotiate for entry into the EU (Sweden, Finland and Austria) or to repudiate the treaty altogether (Switzerland).

In late 1992 Norway also therefore entered negotiations for accession to the EU and these were still ongoing at the 1993 election when Prime Minister Brundtland attempted to defuse the issue by promising to honour the outcome of a referendum to be held once the negotiations had been completed. Despite her and others' efforts, the issue none the less dominated the election and gave an enormous boost to the Centre Party under its leader, Anne Enger Lahnstein – Norway's 'No-Queen' as she came to be called. In the subsequent referendum campaign a very similar coalition of forces as had won the day in 1972 – centrists in the periphery and radicals at the centre – delivered an almost identical verdict; on 28 November 1994 a majority of 52.2 per cent voted 'no'. Mrs Brundtland continued in government for a further two years and then, having been Labour's prime minister on and off since 1981, handed over the reins to the party's parliamentary party leader, Thorbjørn Jagland, in October 1996.

Dr Brundtland – known universally as Gro – had by the time of her retirement from office grown to become almost the mother of the nation even though she had only ever enjoyed office as the leader of a minority Labour governmentnt.[2] It is not surprising, therefore, that her successor had difficulty filling the space her retirement left, but Jagland's premiership was in addition dogged from the start by bad luck and/or bad judgement. Within three weeks his planning minister who had announced bold perspectives on the re-building of 'Norway's House' was forced to resign over allegations about his tax affairs; about a month later another minister had to resign after a security scandal involving covert surveillance of the leader of the Socialist Left Party was exposed and, finally, the new justice minister (a former bestselling crime novelist) resigned for reasons of ill health after a further three months. Despite the country's vigorous economic health and the government's almost austere fiscal orthodoxy, election year opened with a whiff of something rotten (or stale at least) in the state of Norway. The principal beneficiary of the government's unpopularity until the middle of 1997 was a resurgent Progress Party (PP) which registered support of over 20 per cent in the opinion polls.

The campaign itself opened ominously with the PP's leader, Carl I. Hagen, attacking special rights granted to the indigenous Samis in the far north of the country. The party also continued to underline its xenophobia under cover of its opposition to multiculturalism and a stress on law-and-order issues, particularly as these affected the status of immigrants and political refugees.[3] In a switch of tactics however it supplemented these messages with demands that more money be spent on the welfare of Norwegians for example through health care, pensions and education, the extra expenditure to be funded out of oil revenues in preference to locking them up in the Oil Fund. The left-socialist and centrist parties also committed themselves to a range of extra spending pledges and Labour found itself on the defensive against this new wave of fiscal populism. It directed its principal fire at the PP, however; a tactical choice which had the useful quality of deflecting attention from the fact that the principal challenge to its hold on government came from the combination of the centrist parties (the Centre Party (CP), the Christian People's Party (CPP) and the revived Liberal Party (LP)). A sub-plot of the campaign meantime concerned the increasingly bitter opposition between the CP and the Conservatives over European-related issues as well as those of economic management, with each arguing that only an alignment which excluded the other offered the electorate a sound alternative to Labour.

In early August Labour had announced that it would regard the election as an effective national vote of confidence, resigning office if it were to receive less than the 36.9 per cent of the vote which it had received at the previous election. The strategy (a repeat of that employed successfully in 1993) seemed at first to work remarkably well, galvanising the Labour party organisation and mobilising its marginal voters. Indeed, three days before the vote it looked as though it had paid off, with the polls indicating that up to 40 per cent of the electorate intended to support the government. On the day of the election, however, when the final reckoning showed only 35.0 per cent had actually voted Labour, the government was hoist by its own petard while the main target of its invective, the PP, had posted striking gains across the country.

Analysis of the full election result indicated very significant shifts in the electorate since the previous election. Seemingly, the EU-related distortions of 1993 had been 'corrected', the CP coincidentally losing the same quota of 21 seats it had gained four years earlier. Attempts to put Norway's accession agreement on Schengen at the centre of the debate alongside other CP core issues' had manifestly failed and Anne Enger Lahnstein's erratic style as party leader had been subjected to brutal scrutiny.[4] The Conservative Party also emerged as a big loser registering the lowest vote of its entire history (i.e. since 1884). The biggest winner was the PP which more than doubled its vote to become the second largest party after Labour, overtaking both the the Conservatives and the CP and taking seats in all 20 constituencies for the first time.

The PP's electoral success was almost matched by the other major winner, the CPP, which achieved its highest level of support ever; in this it was doubtless helped by the fact that its leader, Kjell Magne Bondevik, was the centrist alternative's prime ministerial candidate. Despite being patronised as 'an amiable non-entity' by the *Economist*, he used the experience gained over 24 years in parliament (he is 50 years old and, unusually for his party, an ordained member of the clergy) successfully to project himself as a more popular potential government leader than the lacklustre Jagland. While his party glossed its concerns with the issues of abortion and drug (including alcohol) control in the less specific demand that Christian values be reaffirmed, these were also linked with such 'warm' issues as improving care for the elderly, increasing the basic state pension and providing cash benefits for mothers who opted to forego employment and stay at home in order to provide child care. The centrist alternative thus competed vigorously in a virtual auction of overbidding which pitted itself against both the PP to its right and Socialist Left to its left; and with the relative abeyance of 'high-politics' issues much of the campaign had come to revolve around which party would promise to raise student grants by the greatest percentage, or build more housing, or expand kindergarten capacity, or (as in the case of the otherwise cautious Conservatives as well as the PP) who would cut taxation most. Jagland complained indeed that the centrist parties had virtually attempted to buy the election with reckless promises which would be all the more difficult to fund because of their commitment at the same time to cut back on the tempo of oil and gas production. While these (and similar noises on the part of the Conservatives) were appreciated by the markets and the business press, the electoral dividends were shared by the PP, the CPP — and, to a lesser extent, by the Liberals who surmounted the four per cent threshold and increased their representation from one to six.

As Table 1 shows the overall result entailed a moderate shift to the right with both the left and centre blocs of parties both losing out. The most significant single figure was of course that for the Labour percentage share

TABLE 1
ELECTIONS TO THE STORTING, 13 SEPTEMBER 1997
(BY PARTIES AND BLOCS)

	1989 Vote	1993 Vote	1997 Vote	1997 Seats
Labour	34.3	36.9	35.0	65 (–2)
Socialist Left	10.1	7.9	6.0	9 (–4)
Red Election Alliance	0.5	1.1	1.7	0 (–1)
Left Bloc	*44.9*	*45.9*	*42.7*	*74 (–7)*
Xn. People's (CPP)	8.5	7.9	13.7	25 (+12)
Centre (CP)	6.5	16.8	7.9	11 (–21)
Liberal (LP)	3.2	3.6	4.5	6 (+5)
Centrist Bloc	*18.2*	*28.3*	*25.1*	*42 (–4)*
Conservative	22.2	17.0	14.3	23 (–5)
Progress (PP)	13.0	6.3	15.3	25 (+15)
Right Bloc	*35.2*	*25.8*	*31.2*	*48 (+10)*
Others	1.7	2.6	1.6	1 (+1)*
TURNOUT	(82.3)	(76.0)	(77.1)	(T=165 seats)

Note: In 1993 the sole representative under Others had been the first successful candidate ever for the Red Election Alliance, a Marxist-Leninist party which took only 1.1 per cent of the national vote, but broke through in Oslo. In 1997 this candidate lost but Steinar bastesen, a spokesman for Norway's whalers, was elected in the province of Nordland on the Coastal Party ticket. For a report on the 1993 election, see *West European Politics* 17/2 (April 1994) pp.197–203.

of the vote; when it became clear that it showed a decline from 1993 Jagland announced that the government would resign as soon as it had presented its draft budget in mid-October – this, despite the fact that on its own it had received almost ten per cent more votes and 23 more seats than the centrist alternative. During the intervening month Bondevik first assured himself that the Conservatives would not follow through on the threat made during the campaign to oppose a non-socialist government from which they were excluded at its inception. He then convened the parties of the Centre alternative for negotiations on such a government's precise shape and programme. Among the problems were the fact that, with their weakened electoral base, the prospects for achieving many of their distinctive objectives, such as opposition to Norway's membership of the Schengen group of countries or the cancellation of plans for gas-fired power stations, seemed dim indeed; after all, on both issues a simple combination of Labour and the Conservatives who shared a common view on these issues (as well as on relative fiscal conservatism) would be sufficient to bring defeat.

The prospective difficulties seemed to be somewhat alleviated, or at least postponable, by the fact that on the one hand the Amsterdam treaty of June 1997 had unilaterally moved Schengen into the EU first pillar and some renegotiation was, therefore, unavoidable anyhow, while on the other the upcoming world conference on global warming at Kyoto in December 1997 could be expected to put the question of gas-fired stations in a new light. Other potential problems could perhaps be handled by use of the same 'slalom' tactic that Labour had used to such effect over the previous decade and more; thus, on a slight softening of policy on refugees and asylum seekers, support could be reliably expected from Labour itself, while on the provision of cash benefits to stay-at-home mothers, the Conservatives were already committed. On certain popular spending issues such as the increase in the basic pension the centrist parties calculated that they could afford to dare Labour and/or the Conservatives to oppose them.

The prospects for the Bondevik government, unlike the economy for the forseeable future, are distinctly uncertain. Its parliamentary base is weaker than that of any government since the 1920s including the only other government led by a CPP premier: that of 1972 to 1973, also brought to office by the resignation of a Labour government which had dared the electorate to go against its wishes (at that time by voting against membership of the EC). Its only real bankable asset is the one Labour had previously been able to rely on: that it was in office *faute de mieux* – for the lack of a better alternative. In the absence of the constitutional possibility of dissolving parliament and calling new elections, this lack is a great boon for as long as a Bondevik government can show itself preferable – or, at least, preferred – to Labour. With the CP locked in and so precluded from providing the tactical support for Labour which had been critical in 1990 when the Syse government fell and with the CP still bitterly opposed to Labour's stance on Europe, the latter's return seems unlikely unless and until some descent into parliamentary chaos gives birth to a Labour-Conservative *rapprochement*. Such an apocalyptic outcome seems unlikely, although it is clear that the balance between the Storting and such a weakly based government is likely to tilt in favour of the former. The latter will presumably have to preside over policy outcomes decided by parliamentary majorities not of its own making or liking; its willingness to do this will probably be most tested most severely on matters of relations with Europe where Labour and the right (including the PP) are most often of a single mind.[5]

NOTES

1. In fact, the highest popular vote the party ever received was 48.3 per cent in 1957 and its average over the four elections from 1945 to 1957 was 45.4 per cent.

2. Brundtland's electoral record had not been a particularly impressive one; although she was prime minister three times, she never came into government by winning an election but was twice ejected on losing one (1981, 1989). Only in 1993 did she actually manage to hold on through an election.
3. In one political advertisement it stated, above pictures of the Ayatollah Khomeini, stone-throwing Palestinians and Muslims at prayer: 'We wish all those who don't want to fit into Norwegian society *a really good voyage home!'*
4. After 1993, as leader of the then second-largest party, she had pledged to work across the normal political divides in an attempt to fashion Norway as the Different Country' (*Annerledeslandet*), dedicated to the maintenance of a system of values which promoted welfare, social solidarity, environmentalism and sustainable development in defiance of world market forces. On many points she was seen to have taken her party to the left of Labour in quixotic pursuit of what many had come to see as a chimera.
5. It might be noted in this connection that the predicament is not a new one for the CPP: in the early 1980s it finally recognised that there was no Storting – or government – majority for its restrictive line on abortion, but none the less opted to join the Willoch government. If the CPP can allow one of its core issues to be sidelined in this way, it might be supple enough to last longer at the helm than most commentators allow.

Book Reviews

Citizens and the State. Edited by HANS-DIETER KLINGEMANN and DIETER FUCHS. Oxford: Oxford University Press, 1995. Pp.xxi + 474, 35 figures, 93 tables, biblio., index. £35. ISBN 0-19-827955-8

Beliefs in Government. Edited by MAX KAASE and KENNETH NEWTON. Oxford: Oxford University Press, 1995. Pp.xvii + 217, 4 figures, 21 tables, biblio., index. £25. ISBN 0-19-827956-6

BIG stands for Beliefs in Government, and this is a big project indeed. It had a long gestation going back to a proposal by Jean Blondel in 1986 which was subsequently sponsored by the European Science Foundation, but it was well worth waiting for. The study is, in all likelihood, the most exhaustive analysis of mass political beliefs and attitudes in western Europe over the last one or two decades in the up to 17 countries for which information was available. The goal is to understand the nature and extent of shifts in mass opinion about the proper role and scope of government and to disentangle national idiosyncrasies from general patterns. BIG did not conduct surveys itself. It re-analysed masses of comparative and country specific data, in some instances going back as far as 1952. This by itself is no small feat since it required making national studies compatible, thus putting lesser known national studies into a long-term and comparative perspective.

This first review of three covers the first and last volumes of a set of five. The Klingemann/Fuchs first volume assembles 13 contributors, most of them well known figures in European survey research, to deal with: political participation, voting turnout, party identification and party membership, membership of intermediary organisations, trust in organisations, support for democratic values and practices, and trust in politicians. Has the relationship between citizens and the state undergone a fundamental change in the last decades? Several influential studies have claimed it has. Ten hypotheses on participation, political attachment and system support are singled out to form the backdrop of the empirical analysis. It is not possible to discuss individual articles, but it should be emphasised that all, without exception, are well argued.

Overall, the evidence shows that despite major social, cultural and economic changes, the citizens of western Europe continue to support their democracies. The electorate has not become hostile to the mechanisms or the agents of representative democracy even though they are more quick to react now, if dissatisfied, and more ready to use non-institutional forms of political action. Identification with parties has declined, even though here, as in other areas, variation between countries is significant. Satisfaction with the functioning of democracy and popular support for the political regime is substantially lower in east-central Europe, but Gábor Tóka argues that this is not permanent. Another exception consistently displaying low levels of satisfaction with the way democracy works is Italy. Considering the recent turmoil in Italian politics, this finding clearly indicates the warning-sign quality of political science data, to be ignored at one's peril.

In their concluding chapter, Fuchs and Klingemann point out that change in the relationship between citizens and the state is properly seen as adaptation. The high degree of citizen satisfaction with their democracy persisted because of the greater responsiveness of major political actors and because of the openness of the democratic system with regard to the extension of citizen's participatory repertoire. I fully concur with their argument that greater willingness to criticise parties and governments should not be confused with a crisis of democracy itself, although this is what established political parties understandably want to make us believe. Yet I doubt that the existence of citizens' groups and new social movements alone is sufficient evidence of the flexibility of representative democracy. Adaptation must be a continual process. It seems to me that not all important actors are fit to meet the new participation demands of citizens. One example is the German constitutional commission established to evaluate changes in the Basic Law after unification. The governing parties refused to consider any institutional reforms to inject even small doses of direct democracy into the German constitutional framework. This is not to say that Max Kaase's old warning about the non-intended consequences of direct democracy are unfounded. If the preference of the active and inactive parts of the population differ substantially, political equality may suffer. All the greater, then, is democracy's need for innovative experimentation in citizen participation. Political scientists have been wanting in this respect.

The final volume, which includes a history of the research project and the original proposal, adds to that discussion. Max Kaase and Ken Newton provide a succinct summary of the project. Empirical evidence does not support any legitimacy crisis theory. A further finding, of particular importance for European integration, regards public opinion towards public services and the welfare state. Traditional attitudes toward social and economic equality and towards the social responsibility of the state prevail extremely consistently across all western European nations. True, individualism has grown, but the flaw in the middle-class backlash theory seems to be the assumption that individualism would automatically translate into opposition to taxes and the welfare state.

After having persuasively refuted doom and gloom theories, it is surprising that the concluding chapters in both volumes end on somewhat dismal notes, taking the fall of communism as their point of departure. The expectation is that citizens in western democracies will scrutinise their political systems even more critically after the demise of the arch-enemy and that they will direct their attention more strongly than before to the economic performance of their states. While it may seem self-evident that the comparison with communism did put western democracies in a relatively comfortable position, this proposition is actually untested. Not only are there still powerful countries around with bad human rights records, the proposition also runs counter to the adaptive capacity of western societies for which the volumes found so ample evidence. Skilful citizens, it seems, can be well aware of the limits of the democratic process.

STEFAN IMMERFALL
Universität Passau, Germany

Public Opinion and Internationalized Governance. Edited by OSCAR NIEDERMAYER and RICHARD SINNOTT. Oxford, Oxford University Press, 1995. Pp.xx + 487, 64 figures, 95 tables, biblio., index. £40. ISBN 0-19-827958-2

The Impact of Values. Edited by JAN W. VAN DETH and ELINOR SCARBROUGH. Oxford, Oxford University Press, 1995. Pp.xix + 588, 33 figures, 94 tables, biblio., index, £40. ISBN 0-19-827957-4

This second review of three covers volumes two and four of the Beliefs in Government study. These volumes are to be welcomed for the range and diversity of the issues treated in them, and for the close attention in each to a specific theme, though approached from different perspectives. The Niedermayer and Sinnott volume is concerned with public opinion and European integration, whereas that of van Deth and Scarbrough focuses on the materialist-postmaterialist debate. Neither volume is narrow because of the specificity of focus, indeed, there is much to commend the controlled focus for this allows individual contributors to bring their particular approach to bear on the issue. Of the wealth of material covered, this review addresses only a limited number.

Van Deth and Scarbrough isolate three areas for consideration: (1) left-right materialism; (2) materialism–post-materialism; and (3) the religious–secular cleavage. The influence of Lipset and Rokkan's classic study of social cleavage and voter alignment is clear here as is that of Inglehart and the postmaterialists. The background is established by the editors' opening chapters on how values might be studied, and this is supplemented by van Deth's discussion of the economic, political and social development of post-war Europe. Implicit here and elsewhere is the view that the affluence, growth and stability of post-war western Europe provided the basis for long-term value change.

There has been considerable change in religious values over this period. In three chapters, Dobbelaere and Jagodzinski outline the dramatic changes in religious identity, belief and behaviour. Regular church-going has declined almost everywhere (Ireland and Italy are partial exceptions). According to this view, Europe has become increasingly secularised, the moral authority of the churches has been weakened, and social groups traditionally associated with church-going (such as women) no longer do so. In political terms, the divisions between clerical and anti-clerical have largely disappeared.

In an impressive chapter, Scarbrough assesses the significance of materialist-postmaterialist orientations. She notes that about half of the European electorate have mixed orientations in respect of this dimension. While the war years and immediate post-war period did contribute to the expansion of postmaterialist sensibilities, she adds intriguingly that 'postmaterialism is not much more widespread among post-war cohorts than it would have been had there been no post-war years of "unprecedented" peace and prosperity.' One would have welcomed some further discussion of this. What it does highlight, though, is that the relationship between economic change and values may be much weaker than some deterministic models suggest. This analysis also suggests that the emergence of postmaterialism may be more complex, fragmented and less pervasive than Inglehart claims.

Adherents of new values and politics are not dominant in Europe. Though postmaterialists are highly educated, only about one sixth of the highly educated are, in fact, postmaterialists. Much the same can be said about feminists and greens. Surprisingly small numbers of individuals in Europe are actually feminists or greens, though quite large percentages are supportive of the policies advocated by both these movements. Lundmark argues that feminism is a distinct political culture and she provides a model by which this can be assessed. She claims that patriarchal attitudes remain dominant, though an alternative reading is also possible. What the data do show is that there is little room for radical feminism on the political spectrum, but considerable space for reformist strategies. Even more than feminism, green values can be seen to have quite limited appeal. While public opinion is quite concerned about the environment and wants governments to be more active, 50 per cent of those interviewed in Germany and Britain would not be willing to pay more tax to achieve this objective.

Of the other chapters in this useful volume, that on 'Party Choice' by Oddbjørn Knutsen is of particular interest. Knutsen reviews the three dimensions and assesses the impact of values on them. He confirms the traditional saliency of religion over class in most European states since 1945. However, what was a dominant cleavage is now much reduced in significance. Those who attend church regularly still vote for the centre or the right, but the percentage of those who actually attend regularly continues to decline. The most salient orientation for party identity remains the distinction between left and right materialists. Conservative, Christian democratic and liberal parties tend to be materialist in their politics and support base, and indeed this may provide the basis for the continuation of parties which traditionally have been dependent on a religious and female vote. Socialist parties tend to have a more postmaterialist electorate, but socialist voters are generally closer to the materialism of the centre-right than to the new politics of the Greens or New Left parties. This helps to explain the pressure that social democratic parties have been under: they are squeezed from the left and the right. Only in Germany is materialism-postmaterialism the most important feature of the cleavage patterns associated with party choice.

Van Deth and Scarbrough provide a useful perspective on value change in the final chapter, highlighting several findings. Thus, Western Europe is becoming less religious, more left-materialist and rather more postmaterialist. Associated with this change is a move towards ethical pluralism which is a consequence of generational change. However, there are no easy conclusions to be drawn from this. Instead, the editors suggest that politics have become highly differentiated, and that even notions of postmaterialism are extremely complex. One fascinating conclusion is that 'the nation state has not been rejected' and its authority has not been endangered. The dominant feature seems to be change within stable structures rather than radical transformation.

The Niedermayer and Sinnott volume examines the continuing efficacy of the nation state in several chapters, and the issue is implicit in others. Sinnott makes a brave, if ultimately unsuccessful, attempt to convince the reader that integration theory has paid attention to public opinion. However, it is a useful review of the literature and introduces themes to be considered in individual chapters. Bosch and Newton report that support for the EC (now EU) is not generally based on economic calculation (despite a widespread view that this is the case), nor do respondents make a connection between their own economic well-being and the EC. It may be that the EC was irrelevant to the European public, and this is confirmed by other data: Europeans generally look to the state, not to the EU, for economic benefits, and praise and blame national governments. European elections are often surrogate national elections. The data in this book suggests that until very recently the EC had little meaning for most Europeans, except at the most general level. Support was not deeply rooted, though broadly speaking, elites and opinion-makers have been more favourable to further integration than mass opinion. While this finding should not surprise, there are some interesting data on the way different political ideologies align in respect of integration. There continues to be strong support for membership among most ideological platforms, though there are national differences. Support is weakest among greens, communists, socialists and nationalists. it is strongest among liberals, the religious (Christian Democrats) and conservatives. Support for continuing membership remains especially weak among British and Danish respondents. Mean support for unification is much weaker, never moving above 50 per cent, with only liberals showing a consistent pattern of support for it.

Two chapters directly address the question of the nation state. There is a difficulty with the way this research is organised which, unfortunately, cannot be discussed in detail here. Martinotti and Stefanizzi provide a ratio between satisfaction with democracy (i.e. national government) and evaluation of EC membership. The authors then devise a fairly complex model to evaluate this outcome, providing four types of orientation for the period 1975–93. According to this, those with a positive view of national government and EC membership have been on the increase, while other alternatives have been stable or in decline (p.177). The relationship is quite suspect, however, as these are two distinct issues. The evaluation of the national political system is more complex and subtle than any assessment of the EC which, as is shown in other chapters, is much more diffuse and weak. The authors do recognise some of the difficulties associated with this approach (p.188) but do not come to terms with the conceptual or methodological problems involved.

In an important chapter, Duchesne and Frognier report on the weakness of European identity for the majority of Europeans. The nation, the town or the region remain far more important for all but a minority of Europeans. Indeed, while being European and Irish or German may not be incompatible for some Europeans, it still seems that the vast majority focus their loyalties on the nation state. The authors are surely correct when they conclude that though Europe produces positive responses, they are not those associated with a 'real community of belonging of the kind experienced in nation states'. The assessment provided by Sinnott in his chapter, 'Policy, Subsidiarity and Legitimacy', also confirms the continuing relevance of the nation state in the lives of most Europeans. The evidence from other chapters shows that Europeans in east and west welcome co-operation and are not in principle opposed to membership in the EU, or to their states acting in consort for common ends. However, what it does highlight is that if further integration is to take place, and if these changes involve significant change in the institutions normally associated with the nation state, such as currency, foreign or defence policy, then those advocating change will have to persuade mass opinion that this is in their interest. Recent Eurobarometer polls indicate that this has yet to be achieved.

One of the surprising weaknesses in these books is the failure to discuss what is probably the most important single value in Europe today, and that is national identity or nationalism. Nationalism has been the most influential ideology in the world over the past 200 years and there is little evidence that European integration has replaced it as the key form of association or identity. To discuss European values or European integration without a discussion of the nature of nationalism and its continuing significance is a large oversight. Perhaps the respective editors do not consider it important enough?

BRIAN GIRVIN
University of Glasgow

The Scope of Government. Edited by OLE BORRE and ELINOR SCARBROUGH. Oxford: Oxford University Press, 1995. Pp.xviii + 437, 24 figures, 108 tables, biblio., index. £40. ISBN 0-19-827954-X

This last review of three is devoted to the middle, or third, of the five volumes which comprise the Beliefs in Government programme, or BIG. Appropiately, its focus is on public attitudes to big government which, as per the collection's title, is defined in terms of scope, and this in two dimensions: range and degree. Range refers to the whole gamut of policy goals and areas for which government is responsible. Degree refers to the intensity of government activity within a policy goal or area.

With its focus on public attitudes to big government, the 1970s conservative hypothesis of 'government overload' was, perhaps, the most obvious theoretical construct to take as a reference point for discussion in this volume. Also considered is the 'marginal utility hypothesis' according to which public opinion in more highly-developed economies will be less supportive of government intervention than in less developed ones because the effectiveness of government intervention declines as economies mature. Here, it might have been helpful if a broader context than the European one could have been considered. However, whilst the introductory chapter outlining the growth of government might rather easily have included data on less economically-developed contexts, the corresponding data on public attitudes would have been almost impossible to find.

Ole Borre acknowledges in the first of the concluding chapters that it is difficult to place much significance on differences of socio-economic maturity within Europe given the lack of data even in this information-rich environment which results in just three countries, Germany, Britain and Italy, being compared in Chapter 12. But perhaps the point is a more general one, that the west European countries are, in any case, essentially similar. Certainly, it is not at all clear that Italy is 'less advanced' than Britain in socio-economic terms, whether one refers to production statistics or quality of life indices, even if many administrative institutions (and cultural attitudes regarding them) can much more readily be thus described. Finally, if extensive comparison is difficult, a more historical account of the growth of government might have brought with it some reflection on pre-World War II concerns about the rising size of the public sector which proved equally unfounded in their forecast of dire economic consequences.

More generally, analytical caution is a striking feature of the contributions by both the editors and authors throughout this collection. There is a general recognition that the data available do not reach back far enough to provide a 'backdrop' (p.367) or base-line against which to measure presumed change in the 1970s and 1980s. Often, too, it is frustrating that they do not reach as far forward as they might, or at least as one would like, given the new wave of electoral defreezing in the 1990s which now affects the right, and especially the Christian democratic parties, as much as the social democratic left. For example, while it is not clear that using the 1990 data for Austria (instead of only up to 1985, p.115) would have allowed the identification of a 'contractionist' attitude to government, it would be nice to know if the dramatic change in the Austrian party system which began in the late 1980s was at least paralleled, if not pre-figured, by changing attitudes to the size and scope of government. Yet perhaps the key to the FPÖ (and green) attack on Austria's neo-corporatist government concerns not the 'scope' of government in terms of policy range and intensity of action, so much as the 'reach' of policy into the population at large. That is to say, there might be a third dimension of scope which is the distinction, or perceived distinction, between those whom corporatist and consociational systems include, the so-called protected or guaranteed, and those which such systems exclude. But here we are hypothesising about the quality of welfare state and democratic inclusiveness, an issue which the current interest in citizenship studies takes very seriously.

In finding against the government overload thesis, the contributors to this volume find that the 'new politics' agenda increased the range dimension of expected government intervention, whilst socio-economic demands have not decreased. The only decline in expectations of government action comes in the external security, or defence, sector, and this is a result of détente (for the data refers to the period before 1990) rather than government action. The evidence, then reveals, no 'declining revolution of expectations' resulting from government action in the 1980s. One wonders if later and more extensive survey data might reveal such an outcome? Certainly, the contributors frequently suggest that there may be something of a see-saw interaction between government actions and public attitudes – and one would arguably expect just this from political systems which promote medium-term, interactive learning processes between elites and the public. Thus, with governments of the centre-right in power in much of Europe in the 1980s, public attitudes may well have become more defensive of the welfare state than they had been in the later 1970s when the welfare state was seen as undermining economic growth – on which welfare state provision itself depended.

Finally, on the theme of cause and effect and government-public interaction, several chapters signal the relative autonomy of the political in policy making and the importance of party and/or more general left-right political cues as well as of national political cultures or traditions in explaining public attitudes. Attention is thus thrown to the other volumes in the series, discussed above. In conclusion, it should be said that this volume is, like the others in the series, extremely well crafted, both within individual chapters and as a whole. The components of the series are thus easy to read, even if the set presents a daunting task, and the whole provides a useful reference work thanks to the wealth of comparative data provided. It is difficult to imagine, however, that many individual scholars will be minded to buy the set given its overall price.

MARK DONOVAN
University of Wales, Cardiff

A New Handbook of Political Science. Edited by R. E. GOODIN and H.-D. KLINGEMANN. Oxford: Oxford University Press, 1996. Pp.xvii+845, index. £60. ISBN 0-19-828015-7.

There is no way of synthesising what political science is today. There are several ways of presenting a collective portrait of the discipline, its research areas, its methods, its achievements. Goodin and Klingemann have chosen a sort of virtuous mix: the history of the discipline, the analysis of political institutions and political behaviour, comparative politics, international relations, political theory, public policy and administration, political economy, political methodology. In some selected cases, an overall attempt is made to compare the old with the new, and these are usually the most instructive chapters: by Guy Peters (Political Institutions); Warren E. Miller (Political Behaviour); David E. Apter (Comparative Politics); Robert O. Keohane (International Relations); Brian Barry (Political Theory); Guy Peters and Vincent Wright (Public Policy and Administration); A. B. Atkinson (Political Economy); and Hayward R. Alker (Political Methodology).

This new *Handbook* contains a multifaceted, though perhaps, at times, somewhat complacent, assessment of the discipline, its problems, its developments, its achievements. Goodin and Klingemann are convinced that the discipline is fully professionalised and substantially mature. Obviously, this evaluation cannot rule out that many practitioners often are not especially innovative and seem to be rather self-referential. Among the various efforts to reconstruct the history of the discipline I have been especially impressed by Gabriel Almond's *tour de force* in tracing the roots of political science and disentangling its many threads through time. However, from Almond's contribution and from all the chapters in the section on 'Political Theory' I have been unable to understand and evaluate how contemporary political scientists can use the wealth of knowledge of classical theorists and how they are really trying to do so. Still, Brian Barry offers a powerful interpretation of the continuing importance of liberalism 'liberally' interpreted and a strong attack on rational choice theory. Incidentally, rational choice theory is variously criticised and extolled (for instance by Grofman) throughout the *Handbook.*

I have also found very useful, balanced, and illuminating the chapters by Bo Rothstein and Barry R. Weingast on the controversy between neo-institutionalism and rational choice theory. This section could have been expanded analysing not so much the old, though in some cases revered, institutionalism, but also the contributions of the new institutionalism, apparently the only remaining competing theory capable of offering an alternative to rational choice. It might have also been better integrated with the section on Political Economy.

Finally, I am somewhat dissatisfied with the lack of integration between the studies of political modernisation and development and those on democratisation. Laurence Whitehead does not do justice to some not so old theorisations produced in the studies on political development and does not convey to the readers the wealth of data, of interpretations, even of quasi theories formulated by the students of democratisation. Finally, I would have read with pleasure a chapter, or two, concerning the relationship between 'pure' and applied political science (not just in terms of public policies).

In the new *Handbook* there are no chapters explicitly devoted to classic subjects: parties, parliaments, governments. One could make a case in favour of a more conservative approach that would include these important subjects. After all, much of the work of contemporary political scientists is still focused on parties, parliaments, and governments. More recently, an additional focus has been provided by the analysis of groups: neo-corporatism. Not just a passing fashion, the analysis of groups, old and new, could have made for a splendid chapter since many excellent scholars have worked in this area.

It is not inappropriate to conclude with a few words on the editors' own introduction concerning the discipline as such. They identify two major trends: differentiation and integration. The differentiation of political science into many subdisciplines is easy to argue and to document. By contrast, the process of integration does not appear to me to be in any sense under way and the choice of the persons of the 'integrators', who are all excellent scholars, does not appear convincing. Indeed, it may be a good idea to ask some scholars, perhaps even, though not only, those who have admirably contributed to this *Handbook*, to identify and review the best and/or the most influential books of the past three decades. There may be less consensus, and more diversity, than Goodin and Klingemann suggest.

All this said, though a very different product from the eight-volume *Handbook of Political Science* edited by Greenstein and Polsby more than 20 years ago, the one-volume edited by Goodin and Klingemann will serve scholars and students alike in a more than satisfactory manner. It is much more than a reference book. It contains thoughtful analyses and ideas and guidelines for future research and for future theorisation. An accomplishment that is to be envied and commended.

GIANFRANCO PASQUINO
Hopkins Bologna Center
University of Bologna

Comparing Electoral Systems, by DAVID M. FARRELL. London: Prentice-Hall, 1996. Pp.xi + 191, 35 tables, 13 figures, index. £13.99 (paper). ISBN 0-13-434077-9.

The book compares five types of electoral systems: first-past-the-post, majoritarian (second ballot and the alternative vote), list PR, the single transferable vote (STV), and the 'two-vote system' PR. One chapter is devoted to each type. Farrell describes how the system operates and examines its e#ffects on the political system. Particular attention is paid to the UK though the analysis is widely comparative. The concluding chapter reviews the debate about the consequences of electoral systems.

The book is aimed at an undergraduate and lay audience. The presentation is clear, precise and concrete. This is a very good overview of the different types of electoral systems, their concrete mechanics, their consequences on political life, and the debate about the virtues and vices of the various options. Farrell uses a simple and clear typology: plurality, majority and PR, the latter being subdivided into three variants: list PR, STV, and what is called the 'two-vote system'. He shows that plurality and majority are two distinct systems with quite distinct logics. The book also neatly points out the similarities and the differences between list PR and STV.

I find more questionable the concept of the 'two-vote system of PR'. While the term may seem to fit the German case, which is used as the main example, it just does not work for cases like Japan and Russia, where plurality and PR are simply superposed. Is it not more appropriate to call these cases mixed systems? Similarly, Farrell does not take into account those mixed systems, like the Italian Senate, where there is only one vote that counts for both the PR and the plurality elections.

In the conclusion, Farrell comes down in favour of PR, more specifically STV. In his view, the main criticism addressed to PR – that it promotes instability – is not supported by the facts. But it is not clear at all that the instability argument is the most compelling reason against PR. In my view, the most important objection against PR concerns accountability. Farrell points out that coalitions are sometimes formed before an election and can sometimes be predicted beforehand even if they have not been announced. Yet, coalitions are also sometimes produced after the election on the basis of backroom deals among the parties. The bottom line is that PR does not yield as much accountability as the plurality system, and that there is a real trade-off between representativeness and accountability.

Whatever their normative preferences, students and the lay public will greatly benefit from reading this book. It manages to be simple and clear while covering a lot of ground in a systematically comparative fashion. I would argue that the potential drawbacks of PR are somewhat underestimated, but the review of the debate is balanced and fair.

ANDRÉ BLAIS
Université de Montréal

Principles of Electoral Reform. By MICHAEL DUMMETT. Oxford: Oxford University Press, 1997. Pp.xi + 193, author and subject indexes, biblio. £35 (cloth); £12.99 (paper) ISBN 0-19-829247-3 and -829246-5

Once electoral systems have been formulated and utilised, they are very seldom changed. For better or for worse, electoral systems create vested interests and political rents. Those parties that find themselves on the losing side do not have enough seats and power to impose change. In many cases they may even oppose any change for fear of losing more and of finding themselves in a worse situation than the one existing. On the other hand, parties on the winning side have no need and no incentive to reform those electoral systems that have served them well. They may even be restrained in their unlikely inclination to draft a reform by the fear of miscalculating its effects. Therefore, most electoral systems, though imperfect from several points of view, continue as they are, and continue being duly criticised. This well-known situation has fortunately not discouraged, or perhaps has on the contrary encouraged, Michael Dummett from writing a pugnacious book aimed at identifying the best principles to be observed when planning a decent electoral system.

Dummett's analysis begins by asking two sets of major questions. First, which candidate will best represent a given constituency and what system will bring about the election of that candidate? Second, what should be the best distribution of seats in a given parliament and what electoral system will bring about such a distribution? Unfortunately, it is impossible to summarise in any meaningful way the subtleties and the details of Dummett's stringent reasoning. The author leads the reader through the difficult path of electoral reform step by step in a very convincing manner. His conclusions are simple and important. First, he explains why the best electoral system is the one capable of preventing, or at least reducing to the minimum, the use of tactical voting. Then tactical voters prevail 'an advantage' is given 'to the well-informed irrelevant to the workings of democracy. More precisely, even when tactical voters do not win they succeed in distorting the outcome as compared with the 'true' preferences of the majority of the voters. Second, the most representative candidate for single-member constituencies is likely to be chosen in the best way by using a combination of the Condorcet and the Borda principles. The Condorcet winner is the one who is preferred by a majority to each other candidate taken separately. The Borda winner is the one who obtains the highest number of votes 'in all his contests with other candidates, regardless of which of them he won and which he lost'.

While Dummett suggests a more complex criterion combining the pure Borda count, the Condorcet criterion supplemented directly by the Borda count, and the Condorcet criterion supplemented first by the Copeland number criterion, based on the voters' real preferences, and then by the Borda count, he is very critical of the Single Transferable Vote system. STV 'is founded on no clear principle, and its operation is haphazard; very small variations in the votes cast can produce overwhelming changes in the final outcomes. It has all the disadvantages of AV [Alternative Vote], and, since more candidates are involved, it has them in a higher degree.' Finally, as to the best composition of parliament, Dummett seems to be unable to go beyond the classical dilemma between parliament elected by the Winner Take All system, 'recommended on the grounds that it promotes strong and stable government', and a parliament elected through Proportional Representation that 'usually results in coalition governments'. His most precise suggestion is that, in order to obtain a satisfactory proportional outcome, the number of seats allocated to each party should be proportional to their weighted Borda score – that is the sum of all the points any party receives from all the ballot papers when the parties are allotted those points in an upward ranking.

Dummett has produced a powerful and cogent analysis of how electoral systems ought to be drafted in order to elect to best candidate and to create the most proportionally-representative parliament. While I believe that his solutions are all too complex ever to be accepted by policy-makers, my opinion should be taken as a compliment for the author of a truly intelligent book.

GIANFRANCO PASQUINO
Hopkins Bologna Center, University of Bologna

Political Parties and Party Systems. By ALAN WARE. Oxford: Oxford University Press, 1996. Pp.xix + 435. £45 (cloth); £14.99 (paper). ISBN 0-19-878-076-1 and 076-1

Taking into account the very wide coverage of *Political Parties and Party Systems,* Alan Ware has been remarkably successful in bringing together in one volume all the major aspects of contemporary party and party system theory, and combining that with a wealth of reference to individual parties and systems. Besides this incidental illustration, five countries are singled out for detailed treatment – France, Germany, Britain, Japan and the United States.

In order to hold a book of this wide scope together, Ware adopts a strictly systematic approach, otherwise it might have become unmanageable. Thus the book is divided into three main sections: 'Parties', 'Party Systems', and 'Moving Towards Government', that is, voting behaviour, elections and government formation. Within each section, Ware examines several topics. For example, the 'Party Systems' section has chapters on: the classification of party systems; why party systems differ; stability and change; and one on non-liberal-democratic regimes. As a conclusion to most chapters in the book, aspects of the five selected countries are examined in turn to illustrate relevant features of the preceding theory.

Ware has the happy knack of making party theory appear simple – or at last digestible – without over-simplification. Sartori's scheme of party system classification, for instance, is actually made to seem quite approachable. Moreover, place is found for fairly recent developments, such as the Katz and Mair formulation of the 'cartel party' as a new party type.

With all these virtues, it may come amiss to express any reservations at all. Nevertheless, some may feel that the 'potted' five-country interspersions throughout the book are intrusive and could have been dispensed with. Others may think that the ambit is rather too wide for most university courses and that an intra-area concentration makes for better comparability, an objection that gains in force considering Ware's decision to include non-liberal democratic systems.

Of course, European area party specialists have quite enough to satisfy them especially now with east-central Europe firmly in the liberal democratic fold. Why concern ourselves – they may ask – with the different world of Latin America or the one-off cases of the United States and Japan? It is one more example of the never-ending dispute as to how the study of comparative politics is best advanced. Regardless of that debate, however, on its own terms *Political Parties and Party Systems* has to be counted as an important addition to the available literature, a lucid and reliable textbook that will be widely used.

GORDON SMITH
London School of Economics

Party System Change. Approaches and Interpretations. By PETER MAIR. Oxford: Clarendon Press, 1997. Pp.xi + 244, 154 tables, 4 figures, biblio.,subject and author indexes. £35). (cloth). ISBN 0-19-829235-X.

For the analysts of parties and party systems, the major empirical and theoretical problem remains the following: 'have party systems really remained frozen' as stated in a most frequently quoted generalization by Lipset and Roickan published in 1967? It is a challenging empirical and theoretical problem because in order to provide a correct and persuasive answer any scholar is obliged to tackle a multiplicity of tasks related not only to individual parties and to party systems change. This book by Peter Mair aims at providing a set of convincing answers, and further questions. In so doing, the author offers several contributions. First of all, he successfully criticises the widespread opinion that political parties are declining. On the contrary, he shows that contemporary political parties are adapting to different circumstances and different tasks. Their strength resides in their organisational flexibility; their successful adaptation is a function of the stability of party systems, and/or vice versa. Second, he indicates that the ability of parties to change may prolong the freezing of party systems, that is the known pattern of continuity of party interactions.

To be more precise, political parties are still capable of structuring their electorates and of controlling and exploiting their cleavages. Third, 'there has been no Europe-wide trend towards electoral instability'. Even the Italian case, which is undergoing a complex transition, is characterised by a comparatively and relatively low level of electoral instability. This indicates the ability of the parties to structure the vote. Fourth, it is, understandably, central and east European party systems that show high levels of electoral volatility. Not only do their party systems appear not to be frozen, but also their individual parties are by no means stabilised. Moreover, the pool of voters unattached to any individual party and still available for electoral competition is large indeed. Mair concludes that 'the combination of a weak cleavage structure, an uncertain and volatile institutional environment, and a very open and unpredictable structure of competition cannot enhance the prospect of rapid consolidation.' Nevertheless, seen from this perspective, some, central and eastern European political systems have already performed better than expected. Finally, though controversially, 'party systems are increasingly characterised by a gradual broadening of coalition alternatives, creating the impression of a growing promiscuity in the process of coalition formation.'

Building on several previously published essays of his, Mair has produced a precious little book. I particularly admire his ability to construct his argument with reference to the existing theories and to buttress it resorting to the available data. Moreover, he cleverly suggests different lines of interpretation and areas where new research is needed. However, I take issue with three aspects of his analysis. First, I do not believe that the existence of a new party model, the cartel party, is convincingly formulated, justified, and adequately tested with reference to the available evidence. In any case, mass parties, catch-all parties, and electoral professional parties seem still capable of surviving and thriving – not to speak of Berlusconi's political movement Forza Italia, yet to be classified, capable of winning a national election at a stroke. In all likelihood, there is no such thing as a cartel party. However, there may be tendencies on the part of some, perhaps several, parties to appropriate resources from the state. Are these tendencies irresistible or temporary?

My second objection concerns the role of party members. Mair claims that 'many parties are attempting to give their members more say rather than less, and ... they are empowering rather than marginalizing them' (p.148). I do not believe the available evidence, scantily quoted by the author, will prove his point. On the contrary, party democracy still remains a very rare commodity. Moreover, if the cartel party were to prevail as an organisational alternative, not only the entirety of the members but, even more, the internal opposition will be further deprived of democratic instruments. Finally, Mair believes that more attention should be addressed to the analysis of party organisations. I agree, but his analysis of the party on the ground is only suggestive of one organisational aspect to be taken into account. The author knows a lot about party membership and party paid staffs. More material ought to be gathered concerning party finances, though only when detailed analyses of the concrete workings of basic party units are available will we be in a position to say anything meaningful about party organisation and party democracy. Notwithstanding my small objections and my minor criticisms, there is a lot to be learned and to be utilised in Mair's analysis. The book is to be commended both for what it says and for what it suggests.

GIANFRANCO PASQUINO
Hopkins Bologna Center
University of Bologna

Parties and their Members: Organising for Victory in Britain and Germany. by SUSAN E. SCARROW. Oxford: Oxford University Press, 1996. Pp.vii + 277, 12 tables, 9 figures, biblio., index. £37.50 ISBN 0-19827918-3

This very worthy volume makes an excellent contribution to the literature on party organisation and membership in Europe, a subject in which there has been a considerable revival of interest in recent years. However, whereas previous publications have concentrated on explaining the problem of membership decline in terms of what Scarrow refers to as 'supply-side' factors – for instance, the impact of social and educational change in weakening the inclination of citizens to join parties – she prefers to focus on the demand side of the membership equation. Thus, Scarrow trawls through the evidence set out in party publications and strategy documents through the years in order to gauge whether it really supports the frequently repeated contention that major parties no longer require large numbers of active members. Her unequivocal finding is that it does not. A careful examination of material drawn from the archives of the major parties in Britain and Germany since 1945 confirms that leaders and strategists have consistently valued members for at least three reasons, including the labour and financial resources they represent, as well as the legitimising and 'outreach' benefits they bring with them as the parties' 'ambassadors in the community'.

Those coming afresh to the study of political parties will find that, among other things, Scarrow provides an admirably clear introduction to some of the main themes of the literature on party organisation. More valuable for established scholars is her interesting three-dimensional view of party change in which she argues that the cases she studies (the British Conservatives excepted) have generally followed a similar trajectory of development in becoming more 'inclusive' (chiefly by lowering the costs of membership) and reducing the role of the party bureaucracy in 'mediating' the leader-member relationship. However, I find the discussion of Scarrow's third dimension ('centralisation') misleading in one sense. While she is quite correct to highlight the ways in which leaders have obliged local party elites to cede powers over candidate-selection to grassroots members in these parties, does this really constitute 'decentralisation'? Although it undeniably rebalances power *within* local party organisations, in itself it does nothing to affect the balance of power *between* national party leaderships and local parties. Indeed, many critics would argue that modern parties like New Labour have found a variety of ways in which to ensure the growing centralisation of power.

Nevertheless this is a good book which provides a valuable corrective to the party decline literature, not least in so far as it cautions us not to be seduced by the myth of a golden age of activist members. Moreover, strategists in the one case in Scarrow's study which has, until recently, had least incentive to change organisationally – the British Conservative Party – might find some interesting food for thought in its pages.

PAUL WEBB
Brunel University
Uxbridge, England

Problems of Democratic Transition and Consolidation. Southern Europe, South America and Post-Communist Europe. By JUAN J. LINZ and ALFRED STEPAN. Baltimore and London: The Johns Hopkins University Press, 1996. Pp.xx + 479. £45.50 (cloth); £15.50 (paper). ISBN 0-8018-5157-2 and 5158-0.

The study of the processes of transition from non-democratic regimes to consolidated democracies constitutes one of the most exciting research areas of contemporary political science. The number of countries experiencing a democratic transition and struggling to consolidate their democratic regimes is growing. Several good case studies and comparative analyses have been produced in recent years. Building on the existing literature and drawing from their previous contributions and their impressive knowledge, Juan Linz and Alfred Stepan provide the first comparative treatment of a large variety of cases. *Problems of Democratic Consolidation* is not just a comprehensive overview of south European, Latin American and east and central European transition and democratisation problems and processes. It is also an attempt to provide an overall theory of these processes. Henceforth, I will highlight the major contributions made by the authors.

First, Linz and Stepan redefine what they consider the five major arenas of a modern consolidated democracy: civil society, characterised by freedom of association and communication; political society, characterised by free and inclusive electoral contests; the rule of law as expressed in constitutionalism; a usable state apparatus working according to rational-legal bureaucratic norms; a politically and socially regulated market, that is the existence of what they call an 'economic society'. Then, in a powerful chapter they argue the importance of democratically defining the citizenship of a state and, if necessary, of creating multinational states in order to construct a democratic regime. If the problem of stateness is not solved, it will be impossible to inaugurate any stable and viable democratic regime. I agree. My only surprise is that, notwithstanding the massive number of highly informative footnotes, neither here nor when analysing pacts do Linz and Stepan quote the seminal article by Dankwart Rustow 'Transitions to Democracy' (*Comparative Politics*, April 1970).

Third, they provide a useful redefinition of non-democratic regimes, by far more manageable than the one originally presented by Linz in 1975, distinguishing authoritarian, totalitarian, post-totalitarian, and sultanistic regimes with reference to pluralism, ideology, mobilisation, and leadership. Moreover, they differentiate among post-totalitarian regimes on the basis of several variations in their components and consequently identify early post-totalitarian, frozen post-totalitarian, and mature, that is ready for a transition, post-totalitarian regimes. Finally, they stress that in any analysis of democratic transitions from military governments it is indispensable to analyse the nature of the previous military government, whether hierarchical, that is supported by the military institution as such, or non-hierarchical, when the officers in the government have subverted the internal military hierarchy.

Equipped with these powerful analytical tools, the authors analyse and compare three southern European cases: Spain, Portugal, and Greece; four Latin American cases: Uruguay, Brazil, Argentina, and Chile; several east and central European cases: Poland, Bulgaria, Romania, the former USSR, the Baltic States. All the case studies are extremely interesting and highly illuminating. Unfortunately, I cannot summarise the numerous substantive and comparative conclusions drawn by the authors. However, I feel it is fair to stress three fundamental points. First, Linz and Stepan believe that there will be no democratic consolidation unless the issue of stateness is pre-solved in a democratic way through an inclusionary strategy aimed at granting to, and protecting, the political and social rights of all the minorities. Second, Linz and Stepan state very clearly that democratic consolidation will be achieved in a more effective way when political reforms anticipate social and economic reforms. Only when the rules of the game are agreed upon, and solidly established and state-wide elections have produced legitimate democratic authorities, will it be possible to launch and sustain significant social and economic reforms. Third, their institutional and constitutional preferences go to parliamentary models and to proportional representation. Repeatedly, they criticise the Latin American presidential models and even the semi-presidential models utilised, for instance, in Poland and Bulgaria. I remain unconvinced. Incidentally, in what amounts to a real constitutional obsession they describe incorrectly the French case of cohabitation (p.279) and almost completely neglect the Portuguese case. Moreover, they never precisely define what model of parliamentarism they would consider suitable and applicable, and do not explicitly say if some institutional models are preferable during the transition, but 'discardable' and replaceable in a consolidated democracy.

Finally, they indicate and document that democracy is a political regime that may receive favourable evaluations by its citizens even in times of economic difficulty and duress. Not only may democracy appear as 'the only game in town', it will also be considered preferable to other already played, already seen, games. This does not imply that all those political actors who accept and welcome democracy are obliged to fundamentally reject the previous regime. Indeed, Linz and Stepan make a powerful case in favour of those citizens who convert themselves to a democratic experience without completely abjuring their political and social past. They also make an even more powerful case for the resilience of democratic regimes in providing incentives and constraints for all actors, obliging them, for instance, the former communists in east and central Europe, to behave according to the rules of the game.

In conclusion, *Problems of Democratic Conclusion* is a splendid book by two accomplished scholars who tackle in a brilliant way the most important political issue of our time: the crafting and nurturing of democratic regimes.

GIANFRANCO PASQUINO
Hopkins Bologna Center
University of Bologna

The Politics of Democratic Consolidation (Vol.1 of Southern Europe in Comparative Perspective). Edited by RICHARD GUNTHER, P. NIKIFOROS DIAMANDOUROS, and HANS-JÜRGEN PUHLE. Baltimore and London: Johns Hopkins University Press 1995. Pp.xxxiii + 493, index. NP (cloth); £15 (paper). ISBN 0-8018-4981-0 and 4982-9.

Southern Europe Since 1945. Tradition and Modernity in Portugal, Spain, Italy Greece and Turkey. By GIULİO SAPELLI. Harlow: Longman, 1995. Pp.x + 251, 4 figures, 17 tables, index. £35 (cloth); £12 (paper). ISBN 0-582-07064-3 and -070651.

In recent times the number of studies on Southern Europe has increased considerably. This area of study had been neglected for some decades, because the authoritarian regimes in Portugal, Spain, Greece and Turkey had led to a decline of research interest in these countries. Research on these three countries was a challenge to any political scientist who wanted to get accurate information. Even today, most of the research on Portugal, Spain and Greece is primary research. Lack of information made it difficult for political scientists to undertake more accurate comparative analysis. The case of southern Europe confirms that political science is closely intertwined with democracy. It is a science that fosters transparency and democratic accountability. Equally a democratic society needs accurate and reliable information.

These two 1995 titles are two highly sophisticated responses to this lack of data on southern European politics and society. Although both books deal with southern Europe as an area of study, their approaches differ considerably. Sapelli is interested in studying the transformation of southern European societies from a traditional to a modern society. The nature of southern European politics is seen in the context of social and economic change which is reviewed from 1945. The book comprises both comparative analysis as well as thick description of specific phenomenon in particular societies. One of Sapelli's main theses is that the southern European countries were not able to establish a market society based on universalistic principles. The legal-rational approach inherent in most modern political systems did not permeate thoroughly the culture of southern European societies. Clientelism, patrimonialism and patronage seem to undermine the complete inculcation of market values. This has had consequences for the political realm. Politics follows the logic of patrimonialism. Sapelli speaks of a neo-*caciquism* which establishes electoral machines (e.g. Italy before *tangentopoli* or Greece in the 1980s) which perpetuate oligarchic forms of power and undermine the democratisation of society. The book is a difficult, fascinating introduction to southern European society and politics. It tries to analyse adequately the *mixtum compositum* of cultural forms of modernity and traditionalism that coexist in all five countries studied by Sapelli. The book is an excellent piece of research which makes one think of southern Europe as one of many Europes comprising this continent.

Quite a different approach is adopted by Gunther, Diamandouros and Puhle in the first of five volumes which will cover different aspects of democratic consolidation in southern Europe. It is the product of research by a large scientific community based throughout Western Europe and financed by the American Social Sciences Research Council (SSRC) and the German Volkswagen Foundation. The project can be regarded unofficially as a follow-up to the excellent work of Guillermo O'Donnell, Philippe Schmitter and Lawrence Whitehead which culminated in the publication of the three-volume *Transitions from Authoritarian Rule* (1986). This 1995 project seeks to study democratisation processes beyond democratic consolidation. Therefore, the directors of the project were not content with studying merely the political field. On the contrary, the greatest achievement of this research has been the capacity to study different dimensions of democratisation such as the economy, the state and the crucial aspect of culture (including the study of clientelism and patronage). This first volume can be regarded as an introduction to the politics of southern Europe over the past two decades, examined in the context of democratic consolidation. Different aspects are analysed in comparison with South America and Eastern Europe. Thus, Felipe Aguero compares the role of the military in southern Europe and Latin America and concludes that in Southern Europe the civilian elites were able to redirect the role of the military in the new democratic societies.

The chapter by Geoffrey Pridham highlights the importance of taking the international dimension into account when analysing democratic transition and consolidation. He further develops his concepts of 'negative' and 'positive' consolidation to characterise different forms of democratic political actors and different political dimensions. His controversial notion of 'deconsolidation' made the debates of the SSRC subcommittee on southern Europe quite vivid. Sidney Tarrow's chapter comparing the period between 1918 and 1922 in Italy and the Spanish transition makes us aware that mass mobilisation has to be taken into consideration when analysing regime change. This has to be read together with Edward Malefakis's chapter on the history of southern Europe which delineates the main developments on the political history of the countries concerned.

A chapter by Leonardo Morlino and Juan Ramon Montero on legitimacy and democracy and one by Gianfranco Pasquino on executive-legislative relations makes us aware of the fact that democracy is still in the making in these countries. This is confirmed by Leonardo Morlino's chapter on political parties. This excellent chapter is probably the most thorough contribution on political parties and the party system in southern Europe, including data on inter- and intra-block volatility since the mid-1970s to 1994. Further, it provides the reader with an analysis of the mid-1990s Italian party system. This is preceded by a chapter by Philippe C. Schmitter on interest groups. Like Morlino's chapter it is extremely useful because it makes data on the interest groups in Portugal, Spain, Italy, Greece and Turkey available to a wider public. The book also includes an introduction and conclusion by the editors which give cohesion to the whole. The thorough editorial work of Richard Gunther makes this work the most authoritative and complete on the politics of southern Europe carried out to date. We eagerly await future volumes on the series. Giulio Sapelli also intends to write a further volume on the anthropology of southern Europe. This new research activism indicates that southern Europe will be an interesting area of study for many years to come.

JOSÉ MAGONE
University of Hull

Regimes, Politics and Markets: Democratisation and Economic Change in Southern and Eastern Europe. By JOSÉ MARIA MARAVALL. Oxford: Oxford University Press, 1997. Pp.xi+269, 3 appendices, index. £30. ISBN 0-19-828083-1.

Few are better qualified than Maravall to write on the relationships between democratisation and economic change. As a member of the Spanish Socialist Party (PSOE), he militated for and wrote on the transition from the Franco regime and then served as Minister of Education, to return then to academe. This book reflects his experience, and also his conviction, that democracies are better at managing modern economies than dictatorships, and that the social democratic agenda which focuses on social and fiscal policies is preferable to more conservative policies which aim, verbally at least, for macro-economic equilibrium.

His first chapter mounts a sound case against the functionalist argument that economic growth is a cause of democratisation and makes the telling point that dictatorships have limited capacity to confront economic crises. He develops this theme in the second chapter with reference to Portugal, Spain and Greece in the early 1970s, and the Communist Party-states of central-eastern Europe in the 1980s. His third chapter on the political economy of democratisation concludes that the new democracies in central-eastern Europe 'offer no support for the thesis that markets can only be established by authoritarian regimes, or that the most viable sequences are those in which economic reforms come before political reforms' (p.125). Chapter 4 elaborates on his theme of the specific features of social democratic economic policies in southern Europe during the 1980s, and his last chapter on economic policy and political culture sounds a warning against democrats allowing disaffection towards politics to grow.

Curiously,the arguments built carefully in this significant contribution to the literature on democratisation and economic policy deal vigorously with the claims made for dictatorships over democracies, but then become less sure footed as the the world economy becomes more integrated. His theme that 'the social democratic identity was typically expressed in different combinations of competitiveness and redistribution' (p.199) can hardly be reassuring to social democrats, as liberal democrats or moderate conservative parties would hardly disclaim such identities for themselves. It is almost as if Maravall concludes that the source of disillusion is the politics of TINA (there is no alternative). His book is a *cri de coeur* in academic guise.

JONATHAN STORY
INSTEAD
Fontainebleau

German Politics: 1945–1995. By PETER PULZER. Oxford: Oxford University Press, 1995. Pp. xv + 195, 2 tables, 1 figure, index. £25 (cloth); £8.99 (paper) ISBN 0-19-878110-5 and 878111-3.

The New Germany: Social, Political and Cultural Challenges of Unification. Edited by DEREK LEWIS and JOHN R.P. McKENZIE. Exeter: University of Exeter Press, 1995. Pp. ix + 365, 6 maps, 5 tables, biblio., index. £30 (cloth); £12.95 (paper) ISBN 0-85989-494-0 and 442-8.

Developments in German Politics 2. Edited by GORDON SMITH, WILLIAM E. PATERSON and STEPHEN PADGETT. London: Macmillan, 1996. Pp. xix + 348, 2 maps, 4 figures, 23 tables, biblio., index. c.£40/$59.95 (cloth); £14.50 (paper) ISBN 0-333-65902-3 and 65903-1.

German politics has changed substantially over the past few years. Fortunately, texts that set out to examine these changes are also more available than ever before. The three texts under review here can all be considered books about German politics; however, their approaches are quite different from each other and their themes are distinct. Each of these books makes a valuable and well-organized contribution to our knowledge of German politics. *German Politics*, by Peter Pulzer, is a short book that provides a succinct exploration of the events that have taken place in Germany since World War II. Pulzer's politically-focused historical examination is this book's strength. The second text, *The New Germany*, has a particular emphasis on the social ramifications of reunification, looking at how eastern Germany has had to transform itself. *Developments in German Politics 2* is the most detailed work of the three. Here, contributors specialising in several fields present expert analyses of nearly every aspect of contemporary German politics.

Peter Pulzer is one of the most respected authorities in the field of German politics. As Gladstone Professor of Government and Public Administration at Oxford and Fellow of All Souls College, Pulzer is well-known on both sides of the Atlantic and his *German Politics: 1945–1995* is perhaps the finest example of a concise work in English contributing to the study of modern German politics to have been released in recent years. The book begins with an analysis of the state of affairs between eastern and western Germans based on a short review of their separate post-war histories. As Pulzer explains, this text is 'aimed at all those who want to understand how Germans got from there to here'. Thus, the majority of Pulzer's book is dedicated to an historical analysis of Germany since 1945. Chapter 2 covers what most texts on Germany do not: it is a short, but superb, examination of what occurred in Germany just after the Second World War. This chapter is well-suited for students to learn about the formation of the two Germanys and sets the stage (with excellent retrospective analysis) of the nation's division. Chapters 3, 4,6 and 7 review the history of the Federal Republic's political growth and change. Here students can study the first rise and fall of the Christian Democratic Union, the rise and fall of the Social Democrats, and the rise of Helmut Kohl. Finally, Pulzer brings the reader up-to-date with the last chapter and his conclusion. Within the conclusion, scholars of Germany will find an interesting analysis of how the office of the Chancellor is forever changing. By themselves, each of these chapters provides a useful resume for scholars and students alike who are interested in the specific time periods that the chapters cover. Collectively, these chapters contribute to our understanding of what made Germany today.

The New Germany is a text with a different focus. Rather than concentrating on politics, this text is more culturally centred. Few of the authors in this work come out of political or economic fields. Rather, most of the writers have their roots in the humanities. Both editors, Derek Lewis and John R. P. McKenzie, are Lecturers in German at Exeter. This work devotes particular attention to Germans in the new, once eastern, federal states. Throughout the text, one major theme stands out: Germans in the former GDR are having difficulty adapting to the new governmental system. The feelings of alienation that have developed are highlighted in this work. According to the authors, these feelings have found expression largely in literature and the arts. Lewis and McKenzie assert that this book will be 'useful for students of German politics who desire to deepen their knowledge of German institutions and culture'. Indeed, the strength of this book is its concentration on the cultural differences that are evident between eastern and western Germans. With that said, this book was written for a particular audience. Lewis and McKenzie state that 'students following an arts-based German or European Studies degree course and requiring background information about contemporary Germany will find it especially useful'. Thus, many of the chapters are written by those who highlight the experiences of non-politicians (artists, ordinary citizens, journalists, etc.). For example, Chapter 1 is based on the case study of a family living in the east German town of Rostock. In fact, the entire first section of this book focuses on how the 'revolution' of 1989–90 affected the citizens in the former GDR. Part II analyses the political and economic issues relating to reunification with a definite social slant. Part III shows the affect that reunification has had on the media and the arts. The 'Western takeover' of the eastern media is one of the key subjects covered.

Developments in German Politics 2 constitutes one of the definitive sources for scholars and students wishing to keep up-to-date on political developments in Germany. This edition is an update to the previous *Developments in German Politics* by the same editors. Although some of the authors have changed over the years, this series began many years ago as *Developments in West German Politics* and has consistently been at the cutting edge in its analysis of current political affairs in Germany. Each section of this book is well-organised and tackles just about every conceivable topic in German politics. Section I examines the institutional and political system; section two examines German foreign policy; Section III examines the economy and social policy; and Section IV is dedicated to covering a wide-range of current topics. For students interested in expanding their knowledge in any of the topics discussed within this text, there is an excellent guide for further reading broken down by chapter. The 1992 edition of *Developments* dealt with reunification and its immediate aftermath. This text, however, has a more analytical framework. The theme of this book revolves around what the editors call the 'second phase' of reunification. With more materials to examine, the contributors are better able to investigate how the process is developing and to dig deeper into German political, social and economic issues. Indeed, what sets this text above the rest is its superior critique of the modern German political process often only available in journals and German publications.

In conclusion, each of the texts under review offer scholars and students something different. Pulzer masterfully guides the reader through 50 years of western German politics. Lewis and McKenzie present a unique glimpse into the hearts and minds of former East Germans struggling to adjust in a new Germany. Finally, Smith, Paterson and Padgett provide an update to the successful series on German political development by bringing together respected scholars to examine German politics in detail.

RICHARD R. MOELLER
The University of Nevada Las Vegas